RUSSIAN ORGANIZED CRIME

Russian Organized Crime:
The New Threat?

Edited by

Phil Williams

FRANK CASS
LONDON • PORTLAND, OR

First published in 1997 in Great Britain by
FRANK CASS PUBLISHERS
Newbury House, 900 Eastern Avenue,
London IG2 7HH

and in the United States of America by
FRANK CASS PUBLISHERS
c/o ISBS
5804 N.E. Hassalo Street
Portland, Oregon 97213-3644

Website: www.frankcass.com

Copyright © 2000 Frank Cass Publishers
Reprinted 2000

Library of Congress Cataloging-in-Publication Data

Russian organized crime: the new threat? / edited by Phil Williams.
    p.   cm.
Includes bibliographical references.
ISBN 0-7146-4763-2. – ISBN 0-7146-4312-2 (pbk.)
1. Organized crime – Russia (Federation). 2. Political corruption –
Russia (Federation) 3. Russia (Federation) – Social
conditions – 1991– 4. Organized crime – New York Metropolitan Area.
5. Russian American criminals – New York Metropolitan Area.
I. Williams, Phil, 1948–
HV6453.R8R87   1997
364.1'06'0947 – dc21   96-30098
                                                        CIP

British Library Cataloguing in Publication Data

A catalogue record of this book is available from the British Library.

ISBN 0-7146-4763-2 (cloth)
ISBN 0-7146-4312-2 (paper)

This group of studies first appeared in a Special Issue on
'Russian Organized Crime' in *Transnational Organized Crime*
(ISSN 1357-7387), Vol.2, Nos.2/3, Summer/Autumn 1996, published by Frank Cass.

Printed in Great Britain by
Antony Rowe Ltd., Chippenham, Wiltshire

Contents

Introduction:
How Serious a Threat is
Russian Organized Crime?

PHIL WILLIAMS

During the 1990s transnational criminal organizations of all kinds have received increased scrutiny from law enforcement agencies, intelligence analysts, and academic researchers. While there are many differences of both interpretation and assessment regarding a whole range of issues, divisions are particularly acute in the area of Russian organized crime. Assessments of the seriousness of the challenge from Russian organized crime diverge remarkably. At one end of the spectrum are those who consider Russian organized crime a dangerous successor to the threat posed to Western values and Western societies by the Soviet Union. Adherents of this view provide what is, in effect, a worst case estimate of the Russian organized crime threat. At the other end of the spectrum are those who not only believe that the threat from Russian organized crime is greatly exaggerated in many Russian and Western commentaries, but also argue that, in present circumstances, organized crime has certain positive functions in Russian society and the economy. Members of this group, providing what is in essence a best case analysis, contend that Russian organized crime has attained considerable prominence only because of the particular set of economic and political conditions that currently exist throughout the Commonwealth of Independent States. The corollary is that as these conditions change then organized crime is likely to diminish in importance.

In some respects these contrasting assessments can be understood as the new variant of the Cold War debate between hawks and doves. As in this previous debate, however, neither the worst case nor the best case assessment is wholly compelling. Many proponents of the worst case assessment tend to be more concerned with highlighting and publicizing what they see as a new threat to Western security rather than with a systematic analysis of the phenomenon of organized crime in Russia; while those at the other end of the spectrum depreciate the seriousness of the challenge posed by Russian organized crime either to transition processes in Russia or to other states. The problem with the worst case assessment is partly one of exaggeration – a tendency to draw facile conclusions from partial evidence – but even more one of over-simplification. Not only do the members of this group tend to seize on particular aspects of the problem and give them a salience that is unwarranted, but they describe the issue in terms such as 'crimefest' and 'kleptocracy' that have maximum emotional impact but minimum analytical utility or rigor.

On the other side, those who believe that the problem has been greatly exaggerated are generally much more analytical in their approach. Partly in an effort to redress the balance in a debate that, at the popular level at least, tends to be dominated by the worst case assessment, the best case advocates downplay the adverse consequences of Russian organized crime. The argument here, however, is that both approaches have serious shortcomings. The worst case thinkers are too mesmerized by the threat from Russian organized crime to assess it critically; while the best case analysts are too enamored of the free market economy to accept its limitations. Moreover, there is a central irony in this debate: the worst case assessment may be more accurate but not for the reasons that its proponents suggest; the best case perspective is less compelling but, because of its more analytical approach, highlights the need to go beyond rhetorical slogans and engage in a systematic and rigorous analysis. This introduction to what is an eclectic and extremely useful set of articles aims to provide such an analysis. Although it arrives at conclusions that are close to the worst case assessment – these conclusions are related in part to weaknesses in the arguments provided by those at the other end of the spectrum. While accepting the best case assessment that organized crime has certain benefits in contemporary Russia, the analysis here suggests that these are outweighed by the costs and negative consequences. It also suggests that these adverse consequences are likely to be more far more enduring than the best case assessment acknowledges. This is a conclusion that is shared by several – although by no means all – the contributors to this collection of essays.

The next part of the analysis attempts to crystallize the key elements in the position enunciated by the worst case and best case advocates. The third section elucidates the complexities and the limitations of Russian organized crime. It presents the major features of Russian organized crime with particular emphasis on its scope or dimensions and its importance in the Russian economy. In essence, it attempts to offer a dispassionate analysis that neither simplifies nor downplays the threat posed by Russian criminal organizations. The final section of the paper uses the empirical analysis to offer a critique of both the worst case and the best case positions, while also assessing the challenge Russian organized crime poses to the transition process in the Former Soviet Union and to other societies in which Russian criminal organizations have also become active. This section also offers a brief prognosis for the future. It identifies contrasting models of the ways in which organized crime might evolve, drawing on the experience of other countries such as the United States and Italy and taking into account the strengths and weaknesses of those who argue that Russian organized crime is or is not a major threat.

The Contrasting Assessments

The Worst Case Assessment

The worst case assessment of Russian organized crime can be seen as the direct heir to the conservative assessment of the Soviet Union threat during the Cold War. For those who still cling to the belief that the Soviet collapse was a ruse, Russian organized crime is an enormously convenient if very natural target. There are several features of Russian organized crime that are emphasized in the worst case approach:

1. Its highly predatory nature As Claire Sterling has noted: 'Russia is so chaotic and broke that few people can stay honest and survive. Yet if not all lawbreakers are mafiosi, the mafia swims among them like a great predatory shark, recruiting some, exacting payoffs from others, frightening away rivals. Insatiable and seemingly invulnerable, it swallows factories, co-ops, private enterprises, real estate, raw materials, currency and gold: one-quarter of Russia's economy in 1991, between one-third and one-half by 1992'.[1]

2. The highly structured nature of the challenge. Although there are few observers who, when pressed, would deny that there are important divisions within Russian organized crime, there is nevertheless a tendency among certain commentators to treat it as a highly cohesive force that is largely dominated by past KGB operatives, as well as some current members of the security services, who have transferred their skills to personal profit while retaining their malevolence to the West and its institutions. In addition, considerable importance is given to the role of the 'thieves professing the code' who are generally portrayed as the Russian equivalent of Mafia 'godfathers'. The thieves are seen as the organizers of the criminal world and as the leaders who develop the overall strategy that gives direction and form to criminal activities.

3. An emphasis on the excellence of Russian organized crime. Russian criminal organizations are seen as surpassing Colombian drug cartels, Chinese Triads, or the various branches of the Italian Mafia. They are

portrayed as more ruthless, more skillful, and more successful than organizations that are better known and more deeply entrenched. As well as the KGB influence this is attributed to the experience of the criminal organizations in circumventing a totalitarian political system. As Claire Sterling, once again, observed, 'The Russian mafia is a union of racketeers without equal. Unlike the mafia in Sicily, which it admires and copies as a standard of excellence, it has no home seat or central command. There are no ancestral memories or common bloodlines. Nevertheless, its proliferating clans are invading every sphere of life, usurping political power, taking over state enterprises and fleecing natural resources. They are engaged in extortion, theft, forgery, armed assault, contract killing, swindling, drug running, arms smuggling, prostitution, gambling, loan sharking, embezzling, money laundering and black marketing – all on a monumental and increasingly international scale'.[2]

4. Another component of the worst case analysis is the emphasis placed on the linkage between Russian organized crime and nuclear material trafficking. It is sometimes implied and sometimes stated unequivocally that the Russian mafia is trafficking in nuclear materials, and that Russian organized crime may well have developed an alliance with pariah states or terrorist organizations. This tends to be particularly powerful in the public debate as it combines elements of the familiar Cold War paradigm relating to the nuclear danger with the new 'red Mafia'.

5. Another element in this assessment of Russian organized crime emphasizes the close links between Russian organized crime and criminal organizations from other nations, especially the Italian Mafia and the Colombian drug trafficking organizations. Claire Sterling has suggested that these links are developing into a 'pax mafiosa', a series of criminal conglomerates that are threatening global security and stability.[3] Support for this assessment is provided by a succession of what are described as summit meetings between the leaders of national organized crime groups, including most notably one in Prague in October 1992.[4]

6. The worst case assessment also emphasizes the political consequences of Russian organized crime. Not only is it argued that Russian organized crime could derail the process of democratization and create such a backlash that ultra-nationalists or communists who want to reimpose some kind of authoritarian rule are likely to come to power, but it is even suggested that the Russian state itself could fall under the domination of

organized crime. The fact that the number of criminal organizations in Russia has increased from 3,000 in the early 1990s to over 8,000 at the end of 1995 is seen as indicative of the growing power of Russian organized crime and the severity of the threat it poses to the Russian state and the democratization process. Indeed, in some variants of the worst case analysis the struggle has already been lost and Russia has already become a criminal superpower.

While not all those who adhere to the worst case analysis would necessarily accept every detail of this picture as presented above, there is certainly a consensus on the seriousness of the threat both domestically and, increasingly, internationally. At the other end of the spectrum are those who, in effect, deny that Russian organized crime poses a real threat to national or international security. In this view – promulgated by some economists and some criminologists – organized crime in Russia is far from the negative phenomenon portrayed in the worst case assessment.

The Best Case Assessment

In some respects, the best case assessment of Russian organized crime is more difficult to crystallize than the worst case analysis. Part of the reason for this is that those who have made such an assessment do it in a more analytical way than many of their more pessimistic counterparts. Nevertheless, it is still possible to discern several major themes that are central to the best case analysis:

1. A consistent theme of the best case analysis is that Russian organized crime currently fulfills certain positive functions in Russian economic and social life. In particular, it is argued, organized crime has become a substitute for government, particularly in the matter of contract enforcement. Jim Leitzel, for example, a specialist on Russian economic reform, has argued that the main problem in Russia is that the reform process is incomplete, with the continued absence of contract law, continued government monopolies, and continued ambivalence to private economic activity. The first of these is particularly important: 'If the state is unable to enforce private contracts business people must look elsewhere. Organized crime can provide the contractual security that business people need to enter into deals in the first place'.[5] In a similar vein, one Russian analysis noted that 'Russia's criminal world ... has become the only force that can give stability, that is capable of stamping out debts, of guaranteeing the banks repayment of loans and of considering property disputes efficiently and fairly. The criminal world has essentially taken on the state functions of legislative and judicial

authority'.[6] In other words, organized crime offers the protection and contract enforcement that are not provided by the state but that are crucial to the functioning of a market economy. The implication of this is that rather than organized crime infiltrating business, business will often seek out organized crime to fulfill the needed functions of contract enforcement. Indeed, 'in the last year or two, serious criminal groups have not "cornered" anyone, that is, they do not forcibly thrust their protection on anyone; they have more than enough requests of this kind. For many businessmen in Russia, it is not the choice of a bank or a partner that is more important, but the correct choice of a "roof"'.[7]

This argument is given credence by those who emphasize that something similar occurred in Sicily. Diego Gambetta, in particular, has argued that the Sicilian Mafia grew up in response to a weak state, and the concomitant absence of a legitimate body to enforce business contracts and property rights.[8] With an economy permeated by a basic lack of trust, protection becomes essential. The Mafia provides this protection. This is a process, it is argued, that is fundamentally different from extortion in which businessmen pay simply to avoid being beaten up, robbed or killed by those who are selling the protection. In other words, organized crime is providing a necessary function that is crucial to the functioning of a market economy where there is a lack of regulation and enforcement. Moreover, it does so in response to requests for assistance. Protection is something that businessmen voluntarily choose rather than something they have forced upon them. In short, the introduction of private property and private business in Russia has led to a demand for protection which the state has been unable to meet – and that organized crime is meeting instead.

2. The second component of the best case analysis is that organized crime simply represents the ultimate form of capitalism, a form that is unregulated by either law or morality, and therefore is particularly efficient at capital accumulation. In this view, criminal organizations are among the most progressive forces in the former Soviet Union since they are among the strongest supporters – and are certainly one of the main beneficiaries – of the privatization process. Furthermore, as the profits from organized crime and drug trafficking are reinvested in the legitimate economy, they will provide a considerable boost to the development of the market economy. In other words, every transition is a rough one and what we are seeing is the Russian equivalent of the nineteenth century robber barons who played such an important role in the industrialization of the United States. At a time when the market

remains imperfect and there is a lack of clarity about what kind of behavior is permitted and what is prohibited, entrepreneurial activity, to be effective, has to be ruthless. In these circumstances, it is hardly surprising that entrepreneurship and criminal activity are closely linked.

3. The third component of the best case assessment is that the situation is likely to improve since organized crime is a transient phenomenon that is the product of particular conditions. As the conditions change, organized crime will become weaker rather than stronger. This argument has again been articulated most effectively by Leitzel, who argues that although organized crime fulfills several positive and necessary functions in the economies of states in transition, its 'sphere of influence' is likely to dwindle to 'normal' Western levels as reform proceeds.' As the state gradually fills the role currently occupied by organized crime then the opportunities available to criminal organizations will diminish. Similarly, as the reform process is completed, government monopolies disappear, and private economic activity becomes the norm so, the argument goes, organized crime will find fewer avenues for advancement. And as the opportunities for organized crime contract, so will its power. The concomitant is that criminal organizations will gradually be assimilated into the legitimate economy and its leaders become respectable legitimate businessmen, the source of whose wealth is less important than the wealth itself. The power of the market is such that the prevalence of organized crime will diminish as the market becomes free.

Neither of these highly discrepant views is without merit. The big problem with the worst case assessment is that it engages in threat inflation through over-simplification. The problem with the best case assessment is that the focus primarily on the economic aspects of organized crime ignores the potential for its consolidation, the development of symbiotic links with political and economic elites, and the capacity of organized crime to perpetuate the conditions that initially gave rise to it and allow it to flourish. The best case is too sanguine, with an over-emphasis on the positive contribution of Russian organized crime and insufficient attention to the deleterious nature of much organized criminal activity throughout the CIS. Accordingly the next section of the paper examines the current state of organized crime in Russia, providing an overview of the organizations and their criminal activities. It begins, however, with a brief analysis of the reasons why organized crime has emerged so strikingly in Russia, and, indeed, in other states of the former Soviet Union.

Net Assessment

In order to assess the prospects for future changes in the role and impact of Russian organized crime, it is necessary to examine the rise of organized crime and explain why it has become so central in the Russian economy and society. A major component of the explanation is that the weakness of the Russian state provided unprecedented opportunities for organized crime and corruption. This is a theme that is developed much more fully in the article by Patricia Rawlinson. In an incisive and compelling analysis, Rawlinson contends that the role and impact of organized crime in a society is determined in large part by the strength of the legitimate structures. She traces the rise of Russian organized crime through several distinct phases, and shows how the passive assimilation of the Soviet regime gave way to an active assimilative phase and, after the collapse of the structures of Soviet authoritarianism, to a proactive phase. If this collapse provided new opportunities, however, it also created major pressures and incentives for the rise of organized criminality. In addition, criminals in Russia had available certain resources and capabilities that meant that they were able to take advantage of both push and pull factors and become major players in post-Communist Russia.

Opportunities

Periods of transition and turmoil generally provide enormous opportunities for criminal activity. As Durkheim argued almost fifty years ago, most societies have regulatory mechanisms to restrain criminal behavior through both formal sanctions and social norms, 'but when society is disturbed by some painful crisis or by beneficent but abrupt transitions' it becomes incapable of enforcing restraint – at least temporarily.[10] This underlines one of the most important elements in the best case assessment of Russian organized crime – the emphasis on the weakness of the state and, in particular, the inability of the state to provide contract enforcement. This is only one form of weakness, however. As important as the inability of the state to fulfill certain positive functions that are necessary for the development of a flourishing market economy, is its inability to prevent criminal actions from taking place. While the first weakness is reflected in the failure to provide a legal and regulatory framework to facilitate the transition to, and management of, the new economic system, the second is manifest in the weaknesses in the legal system. Although there is an article of the Criminal Code covering banditry, this has not been used very much against criminal organizations and has generally been regarded as inadequate to deal with the new criminal organizations that have emerged during the transition to the market economy. Moreover, for a variety of complex reasons – ranging from crass political considerations to genuine concerns about how best to balance human rights considerations against the powers of the state – there is not yet in place comprehensive legislation against organized crime in Russia. Moreover, as the Main Economic Crime Directorate of the MVD has noteu, 'there are still no criminal penalties for phony businesses, fictitious bankruptcies and other socially dangerous practices in a market economy'.[11] As well as providing penalties for these activities, legislation directed against organized crime should also allow law enforcement to target criminal organizations *per se* and provide for measures such as witness protection and use of informants that would enhance the capacity of law enforcement to respond more efficiently to organized crime.

The legislative vacuum, however, is compounded by weaknesses in law enforcement. In analyzing Russian law enforcement, it has become common-place – and rightly so – to comment on the paucity of basic equipment, such as cars, telecommunications and computers. Similarly, the fact that law enforcement officials are poorly paid makes them highly vulnerable to the temptation of corruption. Yet the deficiency of law enforcement goes beyond the lack of equipment and pay. Law enforcement agencies have little experience in dealing with financial crimes, whether fraud or money laundering. Yet this is one of the areas of criminal activity where sophistication and specialized expertise are most needed. In short, the learning curve associated with capitalism has proved to be both very steep and very difficult for law enforcement to climb. This is one reason why – as Yuriy Voronin points out in his succinct but telling analysis – organized crime in Russia pervades much of the economy and goes way beyond the supply of illicit goods and services which is the staple of criminal organizations elsewhere.

Incentives and Pressures

Organized crime tends to develop amidst political chaos, economic dislocation and social upheaval. Russia has been subject to all three in the 1990s. The early stages of the transition, accompanied as they were by hyper-inflation, the move away from a full employment economy, and the inapplicability of the old rules and the uncertainties and inadequacies of of the new, helped to provide an environment in which criminal organizations could prosper. The collapse of the command economy also brought with it the collapse of a variety of social and economic safety nets that had distorted Soviet economic life but also provided some reassurance for the average Soviet citizen. The growth of inflation and unemployment meant that new ways had to be found to make a living. Moreover, many groups that had once had an exalted status in the society now found themselves poorly paid and with little prospect of improvement in their economic condition. In such circumstances, organized crime provided an important source of revenue. For a society that had long been used to black markets and evasion of the ostensible norms of behavior, the new conditions were highly propitious for the emergence of criminal organizations. These organizations were able to find a steady stream of recruits as younger men facing unemployment or poor prospects sought to emulate those with Western cars, cellular telephones and, considerable money – that is, those involved in criminal organizations. The result is that organized crime has become pervasive, as the Yuriy Voronin illustrates.

Resources

Even with all the opportunities and the incentives and pressures, however, Russian organized crime would not have attained its current levels had certain kinds of resources and capabilities not been available for exploitation. In this connection it is hard to disagree with the worst case analysts when they observe that organized crime in Russia had a very good breeding ground in the old Soviet system. Not only were patterns of corruption established – with links between the *nomenklatura* and the criminal entrepreneurs who operated the black markets proving especially important as the basis for much criminal activity in post-Soviet Russia – but also many people became adept at circumventing state authorities. As Mikhail Yegorov has noted: 'The growth of criminal associations in the former USSR was due to the state command system of government and its result – the shadow economy. The numerous efforts in the sixties and seventies to change economic laws by force encouraged the expansion of the underground market and the creation of a substantial criminal potential. Illegal industrial and commercial structures appeared. Major thefts became widespread in the state and public sectors of the economy and official corruption became common. A new social stratum emerged, comprising people with large amounts of illegal capital'. [12] Many of these people were able to put this capital to use in the new capitalist economy.

As well as providing practice in 'beating the system' the Soviet period was one in which traditions and sources of criminal governance were established and developed. The 'thieves professing the code' were important figures in the Soviet Union's criminal world, and the fact of their imprisonment helped to develop the bonding mechanisms that added to their authority both inside and outside prison. The thieves provided arbitration and guidance in the criminal world, offering governance and order in a milieu that is often thought of as totally disorderly. Not surprisingly they subsequently brought their experience and traditions into the new economic and political system, posing a challenge that was all the more serious now that the traditional constraints on them had also been removed. Indeed, the confluence of factors that came together after the collapse of the Soviet Union was an ideal one for organized crime. The constellation of favorable circumstances was evident in the speed with which criminal organizations developed, the extent of their development, and the scope of their activities.

The Dimensions of Russian Organized Crime

The Growth of Russian Organized Crime

According to the published figures on Russian organized crime there has been a constant growth in the number of criminal organizations. The figures have inexorably moved upwards from 3,000 in 1992 to 5,700 in 1994 and, according to the most recent reports, about 8,000 in late 1995 and early 1996. At first glance, these figures seem to tell a straightforward and highly disturbing story – the number of Russian criminal organizations has been increasing and, therefore, the threats they pose are also growing. When examined critically, however, the figures on the number of Russian criminal organizations pose questions rather than provide answers. The most fundamental question is 'what do they mean?'. When posed starkly like this, there are many possible answers:

- The increase in numbers is symptomatic of the increasing power of Russian organized crime. It reflects a criminal empire that is expanding constantly and extending its reach into more and more legitimate economic enterprises.

- The increase in numbers reflects the fact that there are fissiparous tendencies in many Russian criminal organizations with the result that a considerable number of them are splitting into smaller groups. The increase in numbers reflects a process of fragmentation rather than expansion.

- Another possibility is that the criteria for categorizing groups as criminal organizations have become more inclusive. What, for example, is the minimum size for inclusion? Similarly, it is necessary to ask whether the term has been extended to incorporate many of the ancillary services which tend to develop around criminal organizations and which often act as connections to the licit world, which that are not formally part of the criminal organizations themselves. In this connection, it is worth considering the extent to which Western assistance in combating Russian organized crime has created incentives for threat inflation on the part of Russian law enforcement.

• The increase in numbers is a reflection of more efficient policing and, in particular, better intelligence and analysis. The police are looking more closely at Russian organized crime and are obviously seeing more, but this does not necessarily mean that there has been a real increase as opposed simply to an increase in what is visible. The difficulty is that there is not a standard base-line to determine whether the problem has increased or the appraisal of the problem has become more accurate.

• Many of these groups are the equivalent of relatively small and unimportant street gangs in the United States and reflect a process of emulation whereby more and more groups are being formed at a local level. Such groups do not have close links with the bureaucracy and are generally engaged in petty criminal activities rather than major enterprises.

Compounding the difficulty of assessment is the fact that these explanations are not mutually exclusive. Moreover, it is not entirely clear whether these figures incorporate or omit those organizations that have supposedly been arrested or disrupted, and disbanded during the last several years. Even allowing for these ambiguities and uncertainties, however, it is clear that Russian organized crime is extensive. Moreover, the figures themselves do not reveal the extent to which there has been a process of consolidation among individual organizations – and there are certainly reports of development of loose associations of distinct groups – within what may well be a broader phenomenon of fragmentation. The implication of this is that in the final analysis the number of Russian criminal organizations may matters rather less than the predominant relationships among the various groups.

The Structure of Russian Organized Crime

While the term Russian organized crime has become extremely popular, it is in fact grossly over-simplistic in encapsulating a highly complex and diverse phenomenon that is not exclusively Russian, is not always well organized and is not invariably criminal in all its aspects. Indeed, it is far more accurate to speak of Russian criminal organizations than to use the term Russian organized crime. Rather than being monolithic, organized crime in Russia is highly diverse and fractured, with ethnic divisions, divisions based on territorial and sectoral control, and generational splits.

One of the most important organizational principles is ethnicity and 'ethnic criminal groups have been identified in practically all regions and more than 20 major cities'.[13] There are also divisions between those who have established symbiotic links with officials, and those who want to do this but have not yet succeeded. In addition, there are several different categories of groups in terms of their scope or range: some are purely local or domestic, while others have transnational linkages. One aspect of this, of course, is role specialization. As one Russian sociologist has noted,

> The largest and most influential groups have claimed the principal spheres of activity. For example, the Solntsevo gang 'runs' the gambling business; the Kazan gang is in charge of loans; the Chechens handle exports of petroleum, petroleum products and metals, banking operations, and the trade in stolen cars; Azerbaijani groups are into the drug business, the gambling business and trade; Armenian gangs deal in car theft, swindling and bribery; the Georgians are partial to burglary, robbery and hostage-taking; the Ingush's areas are gold mining, trade in precious metals, and weapons deals; and the Dagestanis are involved in rape and theft.[14]

Along with this has gone, the 'territorial division of Russia into "zones of influence"'. Operating in Krasnodar Territory are a Kemerovo gang (Novorossiisk), an Omsk gang (coastal region), Chechen and Abkhaz groups (Krasnodar), and some others. In St. Petersburg, there are three major gangs: Tamboy, Chechen and Kazan gangs, which control the whole city. 'The five major crime groups which are active in Moscow have divided up the municipal districts in accordance with their official administrative status'.[15]

An excellent analysis of the major groups with details of their leaders, number of members, and major activities is provided in Guy Dunn in what is one of the most detailed accounts of Russian criminal organizations to appear in a Western publication. The role specialization that Dunn discusses in passing is sometimes helpful in limiting conflicts. Furthermore, it does not preclude cooperation among at least some of these groups, especially when there are benefits from joint activity. As noted above, there have been continuing reports that some organizations have formed into large loose associations. Common and cooperative arrangements include contributing to a common pool of resources which is used to support the families of those in prison, for bribery and corruption, and for support for new enterprises.

At the same time, there has been enormous competition among the groups. The sources of such competition have included territorial rivalries and personal animosity among criminal leaders. One important division which has resulted in open conflict has been that between the thieves professing the code and the new generation of criminals who do not respect the traditions, are more entrepreneurial in their approach, and in some cases have become 'authorities' because of wealth rather than status accrued through time in prison and conformity with the criminal code, especially the principle of non-cooperation with the state or its representatives. Not only are the thieves less dominant in the Russian criminal world than might have been expected, but they have also suffered considerable attrition. Among those who have been killed are Globe, Arsen, Givi, Bobon, and Banin (nicknamed Bandit). If many of those who were killed were Slavs, there were also casualties among other ethnic groupings including the Georgian criminal authority Pipiya and the Chechen criminal leader known as Sultan. The implication is that overlapping the rift between new authorities and the old criminals professing the code is a continuing struggle for dominance between the Russian or Slavic groups and those from the Caucasus.

In some respects such conflict between different groups reflects the powerful bonding mechanisms within particular criminal organizations, bonding mechanisms that provide the basis for trust in a milieu without formal laws and rules. Ethnicity provides one such mechanism, as does territoriality, and the common experience found in functionally based groups such as the karate or sportsmen organizations that are a feature of organized crime not only in Russia but elsewhere in the former Soviet bloc.

From one perspective this diversity is a weakness of the criminal world in Russia. Although conflict sometimes spills over and claims innocent victims, it is better to have groups competing with one another than to have a process of consolidation into larger groups that are even more formidable. At the same time, the very diversity and complexity of Russian criminal organizations makes concerted action against them even more difficult. So does the fact that many of the groups have infiltrated licit business and established inroads in key sectors of the licit economy.

Infiltration of the Banking Industry

The Russian banking system faces many problems that have little or nothing to do with organized crime and drug trafficking. In order to develop a banking system appropriate for a market economy, further changes and reforms have to be made not only in the structure of the banking sector but also in procedures and in the underlying norms and values. Difficulties resulting from the old banking system

> include the unhealthy relationships among the legislative apparatus, state enterprises and banks; the poor payments system; the overspecialization of banks; the values, incentives and habits of

Soviet-trained bank personnel; the dual monetary circuit; regulatory confusion; the lack of tools to affect monetary policy; the legacy of bad loans to enterprises; the absence of information, expertise and technology available to the banking system; and the banks' role in collecting taxes .... Problems resulting from decentralization can be divided into those due to decentralization in Russia and those due to the break-up of the USSR. In Russia, these include the breakdown of links among banks, the reinforcement of longstanding ties between banks and local politicians, power struggles within individual banks' vertical chains of command, the proliferation of 'wildcat' banks, and the rise of organized crime in banking. [16]

The implication of this assessment is that the infiltration of criminal organizations is far from being the only problem facing Russia as it tries to develop a banking sector appropriate to a functioning and effective market economy. Establishing a clear relationship between the central bank and the commercial banks, providing the central bank with sufficient instruments to control the money supply, implementing new practices based on accurate evaluations of credit risks and modernizing procedures and attitudes are all essential. Yet only limited progress can be made in these other areas, so long as criminal organizations have a major influence on banking operations. The disruptive effect of organized crime was manifest in December 1993, when Russia's major commercial banks suspended their work to mark the funeral of the Chairman of Rosselkhozbank, Nikolay Likhachev, who had been killed by organized crime. The chairmen of the country's main banks, including Promstroybank, Mozbiznesbank, Vneshtorgbank, Kredo Bank, Unikombank, Sberbank Rossii, Most-Bank, Bank Menatep, Mezhdunarodnyy Sberbank, and Tekhnobank, voiced their outrage at what was the latest in a long series of murders of bank officials. They also expressed their alarm at the absence of effective steps by law enforcement to identify and apprehend the killers, something which they believed destabilized the socio-political situation in the country. There was also in the declaration a sense of frustration because although the state had repeatedly declared its resolve to fight against organized crime, it had 'gone no further than issuing loud statements ... while actually distancing itself from a solution to this most acute problem and thus provoking the further criminalization of Russian business'.[17] These sentiments seem to have been validated rather than challenged by subsequent developments: from 1994 to July 1995 there were 30 assassination attempts against top banking officials, 16 of whom were killed. These killings, along with the earlier ones, were an important indicator of the efforts by criminal organizations to infiltrate the Russian banking system and take over control of particular banking institutions.

Criminal ownership of banks is not unprecedented. In the late 1970s José Antonio Fernandez, one of the main importers of Colombian marijuana into the United States, used several fictitious companies 'to put a small bank in Florida ... under his control. It operated as a giant laundry until 1984'.[18] If the Russians cannot claim responsibility for innovation, however, they have nevertheless turned this technique into an art form. In August 1995 the MVD All-Russia Scientific Research Institute estimated that criminal groups control over 400 banks and 47 exchanges.[19] An even more pessimistic assessment was made by Professor Lydia Krasfavina, head of the institute for banking and financial managers, who estimated that 70 to 80 per cent of private banks in Russia are controlled by organized crime.

The control of banks is an important asset for criminal organizations in several ways, not the least of which is that it facilitates money laundering through the banking system – both by Russian criminal organizations and those from elsewhere. It could be argued, of course, that there has been no need for control: the absence of effective legislation against money laundering has made it easy for criminals to pass the profits from drug trafficking, arms trafficking and other criminal activities through the banks. Certainly, the laundering process itself is much simpler than in the United States or Western Europe where great pains have to be taken to obscure both the origin and the ownership of money. There is no real requirement to clean the money. Questions about the origin of money are simply not asked. Possession is regarded as sufficient.

The crucial point about control over banks, however, is that it provides a long term advantage and considerable protection in the event that serious regulations are eventually imposed by the Russian government. While banking is not the only way in which money is laundered – several other economic sectors are also used extensively for laundering, including the advertising industry and the entertainment industry – with criminal organizations establishing or acquiring banks of their own, even stringent legislation would not necessarily lead to a serious clamp down on money laundering. It is not necessary to worry too much about suspicious transaction reports when one owns the bank.

Where the banks are controlled directly by a criminal organization, of course, it is also possible for the organization to use at least part of the capital resources of the bank for its own purposes. Even in those cases where they do not have direct control, however, criminal organizations demand preferential credit. Indeed, one of the reasons why there has been so much violence in the banking sector is that some managers have resisted such demands – and have paid the penalty for so doing.

Organized crime's influence over the banking sector also helps to facilitate both extortion and corruption. It facilitates extortion by providing details of businesses and thereby helps to identify potential targets for blackmail. In cases where businessmen have been engaged in tax evasion, they often find it preferable to pay the criminals than to pay the government. Similarly, access to the banking industry provides resources that facilitate the corruption which criminals use to manage and reduce the risks posed to them by law enforcement. Not surprisingly, in this climate, foreign firms have expressed qualms about operating in Russia. Yet, as Joe Serio points out in his analysis in this collection of essays, the threat to foreign firms is often exaggerated. Certainly with some care, and close adherence to the principles and practices skillfully outlined by Serio, firms operating in Russia should be able to avoid serious interference from criminal organizations

Not all the consequences of criminal control over an important part of the banking security are wholly negative. This is particularly true of money laundering. Laundered cash, has become an important part of the economy and has helped to cushion some of the effects of the shock therapy, while also providing money for budding entrepreneurs. Yet these positive effects cannot obscure the negative consequences. It is difficult for the government or the Central Bank to ration credit and control the money supply – two tasks that are essential for effective macro-economic management – when the banks have their own agendas, in many cases motivated by the desire to facilitate or extend criminal activities.

Moreover, there are many banks that are crudely violating the law 'On the Bases of the Tax System in the Russian Federation'. According to that law, a bank may open current accounts only after the client undergoes an accounting at the tax inspectorate. Violation of this rule leads to commercial structures not paying taxes on their profits. In St Petersburg, instances of this occurring were brought to light in 21 of the 35 existing banks. Indeed, there have been efforts to deal with some of these problems, with the detection of an increasing number of crimes in the banking sector, more bank officials being charged with criminal behavior, especially in relation to the provision of credits, and a greater willingness to impose sanctions against banks which do not abide by the rules. Not surprisingly, the effort to impose greater regulation on the banking industry has met with considerable resistance and may have provoked retaliatory measures. On March 18, 1996, for example, shots were fired into the home of the Chairman of the Russian Central Bank, Sergei Dubinin, leading to speculation that this was because the Central Bank had angered criminals by revoking the licenses of commercial banks which had violated banking regulations.

Infiltration of Industry

It is not only the banking industry that has suffered from the infiltration by criminal organizations. Control over banks is a great source of intelligence for criminal organizations, allowing them to identify targets for extortion – especially businesses that have evaded tax and would find it cheaper to pay a 'criminal tax' than be reported to the authorities. Both domestic and foreign firms have been targets, with the criminals demanding about 10 percent of the turnover. Although there have been reports that extortion methods have become increasingly sophisticated with the criminal organizations offering to provide protection in return for a share of the profits, and actually placing their members in key positions in firms, the continued use of violence against businessmen suggests that the notion that businesses seek out criminal organizations for contract enforcement provides only one part of the picture. During 1995, for example, several high officials in the aluminum industry were killed as part of what was clearly an effort by organized crime groups to establish a high degree of control over a highly lucrative export industry. It followed a pattern in which criminal organizations have often joined with entrepreneurs and corrupt officials in exporting large segments of Russia's raw material base.

Contract Killings

Events in the aluminum industry have been part of a wider pattern of criminal activity in Russia characterized by the increased prevalence of contract killings. According to one estimate there were about 100 of these in 1992, but during 1993 somewhere around 250 took place. In January 1996 Tass suggested that such killings had now reached around 500 a year. Earlier reports, however, suggested that in Moscow at least, there had been something of a decline from one a week to one a month. Even if the figure of 500 a year is correct, such killings are only a small proportion of the murders in Russia – in 1992, for example, there were 319 murders in Yekaterinburg, but only 20 of them had the characteristics that led law enforcement authorities to classify them as contract killings. Their importance, though, is far greater than their number.

This is partly because of the people who tend to become victims of contract killers. Several categories of victim are readily identifiable: bosses of the criminal world who are killed as part of the struggle for power among criminal organizations – and whose death may result from business rivalries, personal animosities, or even such motives as revenge or professional jealousy; businessmen or bankers who resist hostile take-overs by criminal organizations; and journalists, law enforcement officers, officials, and politicians who are serious about exposing and eliminating corruption. As one commentary observed, 'After 1992 orders began to be placed for elimination of "recalcitrant" bureaucrats, prominent commercial dealers, entrepreneurs, and bankers, with the aim of penetrating their business'.[20] In effect, the use of contract killing has been extended from an instrument of intergroup warfare to an instrument used to punish or eliminate those who were willing in one way or another to stand up to criminal organizations. Such a pattern was evident in Kuzbass. Initially contract killings were confined to 'crime bosses' as part of a struggle for power and motivated by such factors as revenge.

> But then the chairman of the council of Kuzbass entrepreneurs fell victim to a contract killing. Next came a series of assassination attempts on enterprise directors ... among the victims were M. Gerasimenko, director of Sibir, a large ore processing factory; A. Skovpen, finance director of the Kemerovo chemical giant Azot; director of Kyrgayskaya mine V. Pishchenko; V. Pak, finance director of the Kuznetsk metallurgical production complex, and his wife. An assassination attempt was made on the head of Chernigovskiy strip mine V. Zabolotnov; director of the Belovskiy strip mine was wounded.[21]

Sometimes such killings can be understood as part of an effort to infiltrate and control a particular industry or a particular firm. On other occasions, they are used as a protective measure. There have been several incidents, for example, in which 'officials ordered assassination attempts on fighters against corruption, who were trying to uncover abuse'.[22] The killings themselves are generally done by professionals – many of whom have a background in the armed forces, with Afghan veterans particularly prominent, or the security services.

Drug Trafficking
Drug trafficking in Russia has become a major activity, involving not only well-publicized links with Colombian cocaine traffickers, but also the supply of opium, heroin and marijuana from Central Asia and the Golden Crescent. In addition, there have been several major cases involving large-scale trafficking in synthetic drugs. While much of the trafficking is carried out by individuals or small groups, there is clearly a great deal of activity structured and controlled by larger criminal networks. The networks in Russia itself are linked with those in Central Asia and have become adept at both marketing and ensuring a regular supply of narcotics. In 1994, 3,126.74 kilograms of all kinds of drugs were seized in 418 separate incidents; during 1995, 6,457.3 kilograms were seized in 767 incidents.[23]

While the increase can be accounted for in part by greater efficiency in interdiction and continued improvements in law enforcement techniques, it also reflects what appears to be an expanding market in Russia as well as the growing use of Russian territory in the transshipment of drugs to Western Europe. While the problem has been exacerbated by the fact that Nigerians have also been very active in their effort to exploit what they see as an important new market, the indigenous organized crime groups have found drug trafficking to be a highly lucrative activity. While some organizations specialize, others combine drug trafficking with activities such as car theft, prostitution, extortion and fraud. Indeed, one of the strengths of organized crime in Russian is that it has so many different dimensions and engages in such a wide range of activity.

Nuclear Material Trafficking

The issue which has aroused the greatest trepidation is that of nuclear material smuggling. The lack of security at some nuclear facilities as well as doubts about the accuracy of the Russian inventory have provided opportunities that disgruntled workers in the nuclear industry have been willing to grasp. The possibility that workers, either through economic need or because they are victims of intimidation, could offer weapons grade material to criminal organizations provides the basis for nightmare scenarios that range from large scale environmental damage to nuclear terrorism or nuclear extortion. The prospect of an alliance between criminal organizations and pariah states is yet another dimension of the issue. What remains uncertain, however, is the extent to which nuclear material trafficking is a core activity of Russian criminal organizations. For the most part nuclear material trafficking has been the preserve of amateur smugglers rather than well established criminal groups. Yet, there is some evidence that criminal organizations have been involved on a limited basis in this activity. Moreover, as Rensselaer Lee points out in his trenchant analysis of this issue in this volume, there are several insidious developments which need to be taken into account in any balanced appraisal of this issue.

Corruption

Criminal organizations are generally concerned with maximizing profits while minimizing the risks they face from law enforcement. One way of minimizing risk is through the widespread use of corruption. Bribery of officials can be used to minimize enforcement efforts, to obtain counter-intelligence which can neutralize genuine enforcement efforts, or to ensure that enforcement does not result in prosecution or conviction. In a sense, corruption is a way of keeping the state weak and acquiescent. Not surprisingly, therefore, the issue has loomed increasingly large on the agenda even though corruption has still not been legally defined in a way that makes it easy to prosecute. Much corruption, of course, is relatively small-scale and not necessarily connected to the activities of organized crime. Yet this contributes to an atmosphere in which principles are far less important than profits and which criminal organizations can therefore exploit for their own purposes. It could be argued, of course, that there is nothing new in all this, and that the old patterns which existed in the Soviet Union are simply being revised to fit the new circumstances. Yet, there is a crucial difference: it is increasingly the criminal organizations which determine the 'rules of the game'. In the old Soviet system the government used the black market as a safety valve, tacitly acknowledging the role of those who operated in this market. In the new system, those nominally in power may become little more than puppets for organized crime. In post-Soviet Russia, corruption is designed not to overcome the inefficiencies of state control of economic life, but to protect criminal organizations from law enforcement. As the political elite has been forced to accommodate those who have both the power to hurt and the wealth to purchase support, a new type of symbiotic relationship has emerged in which organized crime is the dominant force Indeed, systemic corruption as an instrument of organized crime has helped to maintain a congenial environment within which the groups can continue to act with impunity. The danger, therefore, is that Russia is increasingly providing a safe home base within which organized crime can function unhindered and from which it can increasingly engage in transnational activities.

The Transnational Dimension of Russian Organized Crime

Although many Russian criminal organizations are local in character, other groups are heavily engaged in transnational activities and, in some cases, have significant links with criminal organizations elsewhere. Russian criminal organizations are known to be active in Germany, the United States and Israel, as well as in Holland and Belgium. In addition, Cyprus has become a major recipient of the profits of Russian criminal activity, while there is considerable concern in London about laundering through British financial institutions. In the United States, Russian criminals have been involved in lucrative fuel tax evasion schemes as well as in health care and insurance fraud. Extortion of athletes, car theft, and contract murders have also been engaged in by criminal organizations. Although Brighton Beach is regarded as the main center of Russian organized crime in the United States, Russian criminal networks are active in Florida and in California. Seattle and the North West of the United States are also becoming major venues for Russian émigrés and increasingly important in terms of trade with the Russian Far East, much of it through Vladivostok. As elsewhere, the illicit is likely to accompany the licit. What makes the problem all the greater, of course, is that United States law enforcement has relatively few experts on Russian organized crime and will find it difficult to replicate its successes against the Italian Mafia. Another problem which arises is that it is not always clear – as James Finckenauer and Elin Waring point out so effectively in their contribution – whether the issue is Russian organized crime or simply Russian crime that is organized. This theme is also picked up in the report on organized crime that makes up the documentation section. This analysis suggests, among other things, that Russian criminals are particularly effective at fraudulent activities. One of the most infamous of these is the fuel gas scam. In his detailed and incisive article Alan Block peels away some of the intricacies of these schemes while also showing how the Russians were able to exploit an industry that was already rife with corruption.

This is far from an exhaustive survey of Russian organized crime, as it has dealt neither with specific activities, such as counterfeiting, nor with the corrosion of institutions such as the military, which is increasingly described as a mafia in uniform. Nevertheless, the discussion has given some flavor of the extent to which criminal organizations have infiltrated political and economic life in Russia. The extent to which organized crime poses a threat to the processes of democratization and privatization must now be examined, and an attempt made to assess the validity of the worst case and best case assessments of Russian organized crime.

An Appraisal and Prognosis

Organized crime in the West has generally revolved around the supply of illicit goods and services. In Russia, it runs far deeper than this, partly because in the midst of a protracted and complex transition process, there is not a clear demarcation between what is legal and what is not. This has enabled Russian criminal organizations to become a very powerful force in the social, political, and economic fabric of post-Communist Russia and to combine organized crime and white collar crime. Ironically, the growth of organized crime has benefitted enormously from the reform process while at the same time posing a threat to that process. While this appraisal may be close to the worst case assessment, it differs from it in the sense that the situation is not as hopeless or as irretrievable as the worst case assessment suggests. Indeed, there are several areas where the worst case assessment is an exaggeration. There is, for example, a real threat from nuclear material trafficking – but to portray nuclear material smuggling as a major activity of Russian organized crime is to misrepresent what is first and foremost an opportunist activity engaged in by a wide variety of groups and individuals. This is not to deny that there is an urgent need to take actions designed to inhibit organized crime involvement in this activity. But this has to be part of a more comprehensive program designed to reduce the opportunities for, and to increase the risks of, nuclear material smuggling.

Another element where the worst case assessment of Russian organized crime distorts through exaggeration is the role of ex-KGB operatives. It is clear that former KGB operatives are among the more important players in the Russian organized crime scene, especially regarding contract killing. To convey the impression that Russian organized crime is controlled by either former KGB members or its successor organizations, however, is to ignore the divisions, the rivalries, and the complexities that characterize organized crime in Russia. Similarly, while the thieves in law retain some importance, they are not leading criminal entrepreneurs. Moreover, as discussed above, their high status in the criminal world has been challenged by the new criminal authorities who do not believe that spending time in jail – one of the major credentials for thieves professing the code – is a badge of honor. Not surprisingly, the new authorities are resistant to direction from those whose period in jail they regard as the result of incompetence rather than professionalism. In short, Russian organized crime is a multi-dimensional phenomenon that is not subject to simple characterization or simple control. Indeed, there is a central irony in the worst case assessment in that, by reducing the complexity of Russian organized crime, in some respects it actually underestimates the problem.

Similarly, the 'meetings at the summit' need to be considered very carefully. The very language used to describe these meetings among criminal bosses is extremely misleading. Characterizing such meetings as summits gives them a dignity and an importance which they do not have. When there are summit meetings between heads of government, those involved have both the authority and the responsibility to speak for their states. When leaders of Russian and Italian criminal organizations meet, do they have a similar authority to speak for Russian or Italian organized crime *per se*? The way these events are typically described, they do. Yet, how realistic are such descriptions. When there are 8,000 Russian criminal organizations, do they vote for their delegates? Even if the delegation is chosen in a more manageable fashion by criminal authorities and thieves professing the code, how is the choice made? And to whom do the delegates report on their return? Given that Russian organized crime is not a monolithic criminal conspiracy, but a complex, sprawling, largely undisciplined phenomenon, then the idea of cooperation between Russian and Italian organized crime as such is nonsense. This is not to deny that some Russian criminal organizations cooperate with some Italian criminal organizations. While this is not something to be complacent about, however, it is far from the establishment of the kind of global criminal conglomerates envisaged in the worst case assessment.

The other deficiency of the worst case assessment is that it fails to acknowledge the positive functions of Russian organized crime. And without understanding the roles which organized crime in Russia fulfills in the society and the economy, it is impossible to determine how it can be controlled or reduced. One of the strengths of the best case assessment is that it does incorporate an understanding of the positive functions that criminal organizations fulfill. Yet, apart from Diego Gambetta, who acknowledges that the positive functions of organized crime make it even more difficult to control and eradicate, proponents of the best case see these functions as a temporary phenomenon caused by incomplete reform, market distortions and the inadequacies of the state. In their view, as the remaining distortions and controls are removed from the market and the state becomes increasingly comfortable in a role that combines facilitation with regulation, then the opportunities for organized crime will diminish. The free market will triumph.

The brief survey of Russian organized crime offered above, however, suggests that the best case assessment suffers from a fixation with both the virtues and the power of the market. It also fails to acknowledge the capacity of organized crime to perpetuate itself even when some of the market conditions that contributed so much to its emergence have disappeared. As suggested above, the symbiotic relationships which have developed in Russia are likely to perpetuate the weakness and acquiescence of the state in criminal activities. Consequently, criminal organizations may well be more enduring than the best case assessment acknowledges. Because economists see the issue almost exclusively in terms of market forces, they tend to ignore the process whereby criminal organizations become deeply entrenched and to underestimate the task of removing or eradicating them. Organized crime in the United States, for example, survived the change in market conditions brought about by the end of Prohibition. Similarly, contract enforcement was one of the major functions of the Mafia in Sicily in the nineteenth century but became less important when the Italian state itself became strong enough to fulfill this task. Yet, the Mafia remained deeply entrenched in Sicilian society. There is also something slightly optimistic in referring to 'normal Western levels' in an era when organized crime seems to be extending its activities in most Western countries.

Another problem with the best case assessment is that there are several ways in which organized crime can undermine the reform process. Simply because organized crime groups are entrepreneurial capitalists does not necessarily mean that they facilitate the transition to a market economy. To interpret organized crime in Russia as a positive force overlooks the long term threat posed to the integrity of political and economic institutions and to social norms. Violence against businessmen and bankers can deter the foreign investment that is crucial to its economic future, while organized crime can have a dampening effect domestically by hampering economic competition and stifling legitimate entrepreneurship. It is difficult for legitimate entrepreneurs to compete with those who have ready access to large financial resources obtained through illicit means. An additional cost is that protection payments by legitimate businesses are passed on to consumers in the form of higher prices, something that has a particularly severe psychological impact on populations long accustomed to price stability, and already suffering the effects of inflation. Moreover, when organized crime takes over particular sectors of the economy it proves very difficult to dislodge, as is evident in the United States where organized crime still has considerable influence over the construction industry, especially in New York, and over the waste disposal industry. In sum, penetration of the economic system is one of the most serious and long term consequences of organized crime, undermining the integrity of financial institutions and constricting business opportunities.

It is not something that is easily eradicated. Nor are the problems only economic. To argue that organized crime is somehow a progressive force in states in transition is to ignore its impact on not only social and economic life but also political power. In states in transition, organized crime facilitates the consolidation of the position of entrenched elites based not on democratic support but on the power to coerce and intimidate. Additionally, a state in which organized crime has become one of the dominant forces is also a state in which respect for law is likely to be minimal. The symbols of wealth and power displayed by organized crime will prove very attractive and lead to even more emulation than currently exists. Recruitment is easy as illicit routes for advancement promise far greater and more immediate rewards than legitimate avenues. In short, the problem is unlikely to go away and could get worse. Louise Shelley's analysis in this collection is unequivocal on this, arguing very persuasively that the authoritarianism of the Soviet state has been replaced by the authoritarianism of organized crime in Russia.

One possible response to this, of course – and one that is certainly consistent with the best case assessment of Russian organized crime – is that the licit market will prove irresistible and that there will be a gradual legitimization of criminal capitalists. Although the first generation of capitalists are more concerned with capital accumulation than with the means of achieving it, they will want their sons and daughters to be legitimate, with the result that there will be a gradual transition from illicit to licit business. Support for this thesis can be found in the phenomenon of ethnic succession in organized crime in the United States – and the way in which the traditional mafia has declined in importance. Such a process could be assisted by the development of effective rules and regulations to govern the economy. The theory here is that unregulated capitalism in which illicit business looms largest will give way to a more regulated form of capitalism that is dominated by licit business. In short, there will be a gradual cleansing process.

The alternative model of the Russian future – and the one suggested by the analysis of Russian criminal organizations and their activities offered here – is that organized crime could become the dominant force in Russian society. Once criminal organizations have consolidated their position within the society then it is very difficult to remove them, especially when symbiotic relationships have been established with the political and economic elites. In the Soviet Union there was a symbiotic relation between black marketeers and the *nomenklatura*, but it was a symbiosis that was dominated by the state – Rawlinson's active assimilative state. The danger for Russia is that the symbiosis is increasingly dominated by the criminal organizations – the proactive phase. In essence, the prognosis here is the reverse of that outlined in the previous paragraph: instead of the legitimization of criminal capitalism and criminal organizations by the licit economy, the process moves in the opposite direction, with corruption becoming an all-pervasive phenomenon leading ultimately to a collusive relationship between the Russian state and Russian organized crime. Gloomy as this prognosis may be, it is ultimately rather more compelling than the expectation that Russian organized crime will simply disappear or decline. To expect such an occurrence, rather like Dr. Johnson's second marriage, is the triumph of hope over experience.

NOTES

1. Claire Sterling, 'Redfellas', *New Republic*, Vol.210, April 11, 1994, p.19.
2. Ibid.
3. This is a major theme of Claire Sterling, *Thieves World* (New York: Simon and Schuster, 1994).
4. See the interjection by Arnaud de Borchgrave in the discussion between Peter Grinenko and Claire Sterling, in Frank Cilluffo and Linnea P. Raine (eds.), *Global Organized Crime: The*

New Empire of Evil (Washington: Center for Strategic and International Studies 1994).

5. Jim Leitzel, *Russian Economic Reform* (London: Routledge, 1995), p.43.
6. Aleksey Voyevodin: 'Who Is the Master of the House?: Crime, Terrorism and the Economy in Russia', *Literaturnaya Rossiya,* [in Russian] No.42, Oct. 21, 1994, pp.5–6.
7. Ibid.
8. Diego Gambetta, *The Sicilian Mafia: The Business of Private Protection* (Cambridge Mass.: Harvard University Press, 1993).
9. Leitzel, op. cit., p.45.
10. Quoted in Richard Lotspeich, 'Crime in the Transition Economies', *Europe–Asia Studies,* Vol.47, No.4 (June 1995), pp.555–590, at p.569.
11. V. Zakalyuzhnyy, 'Economic Crime Is Still on the Rise' Moscow *Ekonomika I Zhizn* [in Russian], Feb. 1996, No.5, p.34.
12. Vladimir Nadein: 'Russian Mafia Alarms America', *Izvestiya* [in Russian] May 28, 1994, pp.1, 5.
13. Izvestiya Analytical Center, 'Criminal Russia' *Izvestiya,* Oct. 21, 1994, p.5.
14. Olga Kryshtanovskaya, 'Russia's Mafia Landscape – A Sociologist's View', *Izvestia,* Sept. 21, 1995, p.5. Condensed text.
15. Ibid.
16. From an interview with the chairman of the Russian Central Bank, Viktor Gerashchenko, 'The Russian banking system: Institutional Responses to the Market Transition'.
17. 'Bankers Deplore Mafia Murder of Bank Chairman' *ITAR–TASS,* World Service in Russian, 1510 GMT, Dec. 6, 1993.
18. Eduard Dorozhkin: '"Money Laundering": Theory and Practice', *Moscow–Stolitsa* [in Russian] No.24, June 1994, p.24.
19. *Izvestia,* Analytical Center, op. cit.
20. Ibid.
21. Ibid.
22. Ibid.
23. These figures are from Ministry of Interior reports.

Russian Organized Crime: A Brief History

PATRICIA RAWLINSON

Almost overnight, Russian organized crime has become the focus of attention for academics, international law enforcement agencies and the world media. Cold War ideologists see its proliferation as a vindication of their struggle against the 'evil empire' of communism manifested by endemic corruption, a failed centralized economy and totalitarianism. Others see it as a by-product of a difficult transition to the market, exacerbated by the chaos of the economic reforms instigated by Gorbachev. Federico Varese looks at Russian organized crime in the light of another ideology, that of the Mafia. Using Gambetta's model of Mafia as 'insurance' agents, suppliers of a much sought after commodity – protection – in an environment devoid of trust where property rights remain crude and undefined, Varese applies the same model to Russian organized crime. As property ownership developed only during and after *perestroika*, any forms of criminal activity prior to that time were 'in fact, instances of "organized" corruption involving mainly top state officials'.[1] Hence we have two major approaches which represent a common perception of the phenomenon: Russian organized crime as communism and Russian organized crime as 'Mafia'.[2] Both perceptions explain Russian organized crime as 'alien', as operating outside the legitimate norms of Western liberalism, whether as political ideology or criminal behavior. If however we look at the history of organized crime in Russia, how the nature of Russian society under both the Tsarist and Soviet regimes was conducive to such forms of criminality because of the conditions of its legitimate structures, irrespective of its ideological base, then we can understand why it spread so quickly and why it has also successfully emigrated to cultures outside the former USSR. Alan Block writes of organized crime in America: 'The history of the phenomena of organized crime is but a part of the social history of the US'.[3] The same is true in Russia where the history of organized crime is both a component and reflection of the turbulent social history of Tsarist Russia and the Soviet Union. What emerged as organized crime under Gorbachev was the consequence of a long history of Russian politics and society.

This article examines the history and development of organized crime in Russia from Tsarism to the end of Soviet socialism in 1991. Within this context it presents two hypotheses. First, that there exists a pattern of behavior and interaction between organized crime and the dominant culture which is not based on ideology but on the condition, that is, the measure of strength, of what we will call the legitimate structures.[4] The second hypothesis states that it has been the *response* of the legitimate structures towards the presence of organized crime which, up to a crucial point, has determined the latter's development. Organized crime, unless of a political nature as in certain types of banditry, needs to interact with the legitimate structures in order to expand its activities. At various stages of this interaction, the legitimate structures, or a part of them, are the dominating force behind the dynamics of this interaction. A study of the history of Russian organized crime is in fact an appreciation of the changing nature of this interaction between legitimate and illegitimate.

The Chameleon Syndrome

The study is presented within the framework of a model entitled the Chameleon Syndrome, so called because of the ability of organized crime, through its interaction with the legitimate structures, to merge with and eventually play a proactive role in the Russian state.[5] The model recognizes four stages of development in the relationship between the legitimate structures and organized crime in Russia (see Figures 1a and 1b). The first stage, *reactive*, describes organized crime when it operates outside of, or contiguous to, the legitimate structures. At this point the dominant system is politically and economically stable and has little or no need to compromise or negotiate.[6] Politically motivated banditry, youth gangs and organized groups at a primitive stage of development fall into this category. The second stage, the *passive assimilative*, indicates the first phase of negotiation or compromise. The dominant system has weakened, particularly in the economic sector, and seeks to acquire from illegal sources that which cannot be gained legitimately.

If not actively engaged with the illegal suppliers, it turns a blind eye to those who are, on condition that such a relationship ultimately benefits the legitimate structures. This phase is particularly pertinent to the evolution of the shadow economy, marked *inter alia* by low level bribery and corruption.

The third stage, the *active assimilative,* describes the penetration of organized crime into the legitimate structures to the point where it is has the opportunity to act with a degree of autonomy. The transition from passive to active assimilative is difficult to discern and the most threatening to the legitimate structures as it is beyond this point that they begin to lose control of the 'negotiating' process. Organized crime now has a direct effect on the condition of the legitimate structures. Money laundering, high levels of

FIGURE 1a

THE RELATIONSHIP BETWEEN LEGITIMATE STRUCTURE AND
ORGANIZED CRIME IN RUSSIA

Bandits, Pugachev, etc. *Vory v zakone* (I) (Less sophisticated gangs, teenage groups)	REACTIVE	Tsarist autocracy Soviet totalitarianism
Vanka Kain War of bitches (1940s) *Vory v zakone* (II) Black market–*tsekhoviki* early 1970s	PASSIVE ASSIMILATIVE	Tsarist autocracy Soviet totalitarianism Quasi-totalitarianism
Growth of shadow economy *Tsekhoviki* increase economic base	ACTIVE ASSIMILATIVE	Nepotism and mass corruption in Central– Asian republics (late 1970s). Slowing down economic growth.
Mass money laundering into new economic ventures co-operatives, joint ventures		*Perestroika* Democratization
Active role in privatisation Foreign business contracts Political figures bought Media manipulation Infiltration into banking	PROACTIVE	End of Gorbachev era 1991 August coup Yeltsin and 'new' Russia

FIGURE 2b

Bandits, teenage groups No desire or ability to negotiate and break into the legitimate structures	REACTIVE	Usually strong. Political and economic stability. No need to negotiate
Integration into *legitimate* structures, usually as informant or low level bribery. Restricted level of money laundering	PASSIVE ASSIMILATIVE	Subtle weakening of structures, e.g. economic slump, law enforcement not in full control. Prepared to negotiate. on prescribed terms.
Integration now more controlled. Bribery moves into higher level of *legit* structures. Money-laundering widespread Active and significant participation in *legit* economy.	ACTIVE ASSIMILATIVE	Political and economic stuctures significantly weakened Power vacuums. Grey areas between *legit* and *illegit* increase. Negotiation strength on a par with organized crime.
Significant control of *legit* structures, particularly economic and law enforcement. Manipulation in politics	PROACTIVE	Anomie Acquiscence replaces negotiation.

bribery and an active presence in the legitimate economy mark the activities of organized crime at this phase. The final stage, *proactive*, indicates that organized crime has become the major power-holder. It has penetrated all the structures of power, including the media, and no longer needs to negotiate on the terms favored by the dominant system.

These stages do not indicate a natural progression for every organized crime group. Some groups never develop beyond the reactive stage, others find immediate entry into the active assimilative phase. That these stages exist at all depends ultimately on the condition of the legitimate structures.

Defining Organized Crime

To avoid the ideological constraints placed on defining organized crime by the more orthodox interpretations (I have in mind the President's Commission on Law Enforcement and Administration of 1967, which defined organized crime as 'a society that seeks to operate *outside* the control of the ...people and their governments[7] – italics mine), the paper restricts itself to a broad, structural definition, focusing on the *how* rather than the *who* of Russian organized crime. The following definition, given by Moscow academic Luneev, is the most appropriate for this purpose. Organized crime comprises:

- a financial base for 'communal tasks';

- a hierarchical structure;

- a clear division of labor;

- strict discipline operating vertically and based on prescribed norms and laws; and

- strict punishment which can include the elimination of apostates.[8]

These characteristics are applied to a group which operates over a period of time and not just for the occasional job.

Russian Society – The Inheritance

A study of organized crime demands that we find its roots rather than simply consider the prolific foliage of the present. This therefore takes us back to Tsarist Russia, as much a cause of the excesses of Soviet totalitarianism as were the idiosyncrasies of its leading protagonists, such as Lenin and Stalin. A marked continuity of political and social culture links two seemingly opposite regimes.

Tsarist Russia

'If there is any one single factor which dominates the course of Russian history, at any rate since the Tartar conquest it is the principle of autocracy'.[9] At the beginning of the nineteenth century, while most Western European states were making tentative moves towards liberal democracy, Russia remained fixed in a feudal system in which most of the population were serfs. Neither the legislature nor the economy had complete autonomy and the notion of representative institutions was anathema. The Tsar's authority was absolute. The first real threat, an abortive palace coup, known as the Decembrist Revolt of 1825, only served to intensify the autocratic machine, by stepping up censorship and by the creation of the Third Section, a surveillance network of Tsarist informers. Some reforms advocated by the Decembrists and subsequent groups of liberalists were eventually effected (for example, the Emancipation of the Serfs in 1861 and the judicial reforms of 1864 which introduced *inter alia* open hearings, the election of judges and a jury system for criminal cases). But constitutional reform remained as elusive as ever. The response to Tsarist intransigence was an escalation of revolutionary activity which culminated in the assassination of Alexander II in 1881 and ultimately the Revolutions of 1905 and 1917.

The impact of centuries of autocracy on the country's legitimate structures is pertinent to the development of a certain type of consciousness conducive to deviance and criminality. The centralization of power weakens other state structures, in particular the criminal justice system. Even after the 1864 reforms a desired legal impartiality could not exist in an environment of endemic corruption, motivated to a large extent, by sycophancy, lack of tenure and arbitrary policy-making, all of which are the consequence of authoritarian rule. What emerged was a parody of justice and a deep cynicism towards codified rules. Defense lawyer V.A. Maklakov commented in 1905, 'No, the law is not honored in Russia! Before the eyes of everyone, openly, the law is violated, lawlessness flourishes, and this embarrasses nobody, no-one thinks about it.'[10]

The law operated as an instrument of the strong, providing little or no protection for the vulnerable. In many ways deviance became a means of survival for the peasant, an attempt to redress the inequities of a life that was sufficiently tough at the best of times. A psyche evolved which, as the eighteenth century traveller, the Marquis de Custine, noted, allowed the peasants to 'compensate themselves by artifice what they suffer through injustice'.[11]

What manifested in the peasantry as artifice was practiced as corruption in the bureaucracy. Bribes, back-stabbing and sycophancy were endemic, as was corruption a condition 'from which my country groans',[12] wrote Prince

Shcherbatov. These conditions were famously satirized in the drama *The Government Inspector* by the nineteenth century writer Gogol. Further, the absence of tenured employment, where promotion was based more on appeasement than merit, encouraged an elaborate practice of 'window dressing'. It became known as *pokazhuka*, or Potemkinization,[13] named after the courtier Prince Potemkin, the architect of the frontispiece villages constructed to dupe the short-sighted Catherine II. (To the horror of the Prince, she had insisted on seeing for herself his false claims of village development along the Volga.) Truths and falsehood, the legal and illegal, were separated only by blurred and often indistinguishable boundaries. And even when clearly defined, the criminal justice system was too corrupt to uphold justice, the executive too dependent on the Tsar to effect positive changes.

The absence of a significant middle-class, which might have helped to temper the growing tensions between revolutionary groups and the Tsar in the second half of the nineteenth century, was most keenly felt in the economic sector. In the 1880s and 1890s Russia experienced an industrial boom which brought the country into fourth place in world production of minerals and raw materials. But the potential of its middle class remained stymied by dependence on the Tsar for the maintenance of high tariffs which discouraged Russian businesses from adopting the advanced economic theories and practices of their Western counterparts. Further, the industrial boom was heavily supported by foreign investment, including German banks and industrialists. This made Russia's decision to enter the First World War even more disastrous and brought the country near to economic collapse. This was to prove a dangerous inheritance, even more so as the new regime's claim to legitimacy stood on an ideology based on economic performance.

Soviet Russia

Lenin and the Bolsheviks were products of Tsarist Russia, their thinking and conduct inescapably shaped by the system they sought to destroy. Their inheritance included the vestiges of an autocracy which pervaded all the legitimate structures, and the social chaos which accompanies most revolutions. The inception of the new regime was achieved using the draconian measures advocated by autocracy. Only months after Lenin's declaration 'We shall not allow the police to be re-established!',[14] the Cheka (the Extraordinary Commission for Combating Counter-revolution and Sabotage), more brutal than any of its Tsarist counterparts and the predecessor of a line of feared organizations such as the NKVD and the KGB, was established. So too was the legislature, as corrupt as it had been previously, to become abused and manipulated to an extent and an extreme never before witnessed in the history of Russia. But it was in the economic sphere that Lenin and his successors found themselves caught up in ideologically awkward compromises, from the New Economic Policy (NEP) right up to *perestroika*. Conflict between ideology and reality was most felt in the gulf between prescribed quotas and actual productivity, between increasing demand and decreasing supply. The corruption and guile which had been a ubiquitous feature of Tsarist Russia was to become an essential prop for Soviet Russia. Right from its inception, the foundation upon which the superstructure of the new regime was built proved to be weak, and in that weakness called forth all manner of abuses of power by a regime which claimed the dubious soubriquet of 'socialist'.

The crisis of legitimacy which confronted the Soviet government was more chronic than that suffered by Tsarism. The authoritarian rule of the two systems severely weakened the legitimate structures within each, but a justification of force and absolutism found greater acceptance and legitimacy in the amorphous claims of divine right by a people still steeped in religion than it did in the more materialist ideology of Marxism. The events of 1917 were as much a convergence of apostasies as the emergence of revolutionary ideals. Tsar Nicholas II had failed to meet the Russian people's expectation of strong monarchy, 'seeing in invincibility the criterion of legitimacy',[15] but the backlash for the most part was aimed at the personality rather than the status of the Tsar. Opposition to the new regime was widespread. The Civil War of 1918–21, armed resistance to the expropriation of property, and violent opposition to Stalin's even more violent collectivization program, were hardly the indicators of a nation unanimously swept along by revolutionary fervor. The claims to legitimacy of the new ruling elite lay in economic performance. Economic failure meant political failure. It was almost inevitable, given the weak infrastructure, that sooner or later the new government would have to compromise its ideological stance without having to admit failure or a permanent deviation from the stated goals. What began as a temporary means of alleviating shortages, a negotiation with structures outside the dominant economic system, that is, with the penumbral world of the second and shadow economies, became an eventual cause of those shortages and the nemesis of a system it was supposed to support, thus paving the way for the burgeoning of organized crime from the late 1970s.

Banditism

Up until the 1930s the most common manifestation of organized forms of criminality in Russia had been of political banditry. Organized crime in the purely economic sense was not officially recognized until the Resolution 'On the creation of inter-regional sub-divisions of the Ministry of the Interior of the USSR in the fight against organized crime in May 1990'.[16] In the Criminal Code of the Russian Socialist Federation of Soviet Republics (RSFSR) of 1928, Banditism, under Article 77 in the section headed 'state crimes' was defined as: the organization of armed gangs having the intention to attack government or public enterprises, institutions, organizations or private individuals, and in like manner, the participation in such gangs and the carrying out of such attacks.[17]

Up to the 1970s it is possible to identify two types of banditry: that which operated outside the legitimate structures – *reactive* – and that which formed some degree of alliance with them – *passive assimilative*.

Banditry – The Reactive Stage

Banditry in its more common usage occurred in pre-industrial cultures and consisted of those 'peasant outlaws who the lord and state regard as criminals, but who remain within peasant society, and are considered by their people as ... fighters for justice, perhaps even leaders of liberation'.[18] It was particularly endemic in Russia in the seventeenth and eighteenth centuries. Amongst the numerous leaders of bandit groups, *razboiniki*, Stenka Razin and Emeleyan Pugachev, are the most famous. Both have been immortalized in Russian folk song and literature. Don Cossacks motivated by the harsh conditions imposed upon the Volga communities as serfdom spread across the country (and in the case of Pugachev as pretender to the throne), they led rebellions against the landlords or *boyars*. These were, in Hobsbawm's terms, 'social bandits', symptomatic of social discontent rather than social disorder. Both Razin and Pugachev were executed by monarchs confident in the support of the aristocracy and peasant population. The brutal response was a sign of strength and therefore legitimacy. Russian history has shown that liberalism is an unpopular concept evoking a violent backlash against its adherents.

It would be a century after Pugachev's death before another wave of armed resistance emerged to challenge the Tsar. Once again banditism took a revolutionary form, but this time it was well organized, orchestrated at times from abroad, and began to form alliances with members of the criminal underworld. The new movement was encouraged by the exiled leader of the Bolsviks, Vladimir Illich Lenin. Armed robberies, aimed at banks, post offices and mail trains, were carried out in what was termed 'exes', the expropriation of private property, a violent form of fund-raising for the illegal Communist Party. Amongst the bandit leaders, and mastermind of the Tiflis post-office robbery, was a bandit who went by the alias Koba, known better by his other alias, Stalin.[19] Their own experience of banditry alerted the Bolsheviks to its dangers. They knew the strategies, strengths and tactics of armed resistance, hence set out to eradicate, using the full might of the Cheka, the bands of counter-revolutionaries which sprang up across the country after 1917. This wave of anti-revolutionary banditism, which accounted for the definition in the Criminal Code quoted above, spread across what had now become Soviet Russia as a real threat to the Bolsheviks. Organized groups, comprising dispossessed factory owners and/or White sympathizers, adopting names such as 'Hurricane', 'Avant-garde' or 'Commune of Moroz', bombed factories and carried out armed raids on appropriated property. The official line described them as 'anarchist groups [which] attracted criminal elements and under the flag of anarchism began to rob stalls, depots, shops and private flats'.[20] Most politically embarrassing was the formation of the 'Petrograd Militant Organization', initially comprising sailors from the port of Kronstadt, who were the most active supporters of the revolution in its early days. Disillusioned with the tactics of the new regime and the perceived betrayal of revolutionary ideals, the sailors mutinied, and after their defeat, formed their undergound association which eventually attracted former White army officers, members of the aristocracy and intellectuals opposed to the Revolution. Its members were accused of colluding with foreign bodies, and of conducting operations from Paris – a dark reminder for Lenin that history has a habit of repeating itself.

This was to be the last reactive relationship between large groups and the legitimate structures on such a scale, certainly until the wave of nationalist unrest which emerged in the late 1980s. However, a non-political rejection of the dominant system did occur amongst a group of individuals from the criminal underworld. They constructed their own society based on norms and codes strictly adhered to by its members and severely punished if betrayed. The leading figures were known as *vory v zakone*, or 'thieves-in-law', successors of the old criminal underworld of pre-revolutionary Russia. According to Gurov the term *vory v zakone* began as common usage in reference to recidivists at the beginning of the 1930s when their codes of behavior were first formalized.[21] Amongst the numerous rules were a total rejection of Soviet society which forbade their members to have a family, to fraternize with public groups or to act as witnesses in court trials. Typical of most sub-cultures, they employed a particularly rich criminal argot known as *fenya* or *blatnaya musica*. Although the *vory* did not operate as an organized, hierarchical and stable group, decisions were made and 'sentences' of apostates were passed by a special 'court' *sud* comprising the most experienced and respected professionals. Their relevance to the development of organized crime lay in the creation of a structured criminal underworld which would be able to withstand the brutalities of Stalin's regime and provide a base upon which more sophisticated and collaborative forms of criminal behavior could evolve. Their unwillingness to conform to the Soviet system and their acceptance of the risks of living outside it gave them almost heroic status in the eyes of many ordinary Russians. Solzhenitsyn, who 'co-habited' with the *urki*, as they were known, in the labor camps, was less kind in his assessment. 'All their "romantic bravado"', he wrote in *The Gulag Archipelago*, 'is the bravado of vampires'.[22] Nevertheless the thieves themselves believed in their honour. 'Thieves' solidarity was worth more than money', declared one, and despite the romanticism so despised by Solzhenitsyn this would have appeared to be the case up until the Great Patriotic War (1941–45) when a bloody split, discussed below, occurred in the criminal underworld.[23]

Idealism, revenge, or a general feeling of alienation are the main characteristics of those groups which operate outside the legitimate structures. By their very nature political bandits, members of the underclass and youth gangs, are going to be reactive, as are the legitimate structures in their response. There are clear losers and only one winner in this relationship. Compromise is seldom sought as the cost for either side is too great, whether as a loss of ideals or of status. These rebels or revolutionaries offer no direct advantages to the legitimate structures. The latter respond at best with a reluctant tolerance if the effort to pursue these types of offender is not commensurate with the gains achieved by their attempted prosecution, or more commonly, seek to eradicate what is perceived as being a threat to the status quo. It is rare for organized criminal activity – with the exception of youth gangs and certain forms of terrorism – to operate in this way these days. Most organized crime, as many types of business, is motivated purely by self-interest and the rapid acquisition of large profits.

Bandits – Passive Assimilative

Not all criminal activity is violently dismissed by the authorities and it is contingent upon the role that members of criminal groups might play as to how they will be treated by the legitimate structures. Compromise or negotiation between the legitimate structures and the criminal world is an age old practice most commonly employed in the use of informers. Although this involves an element of risk on both sides it is the informer who takes the greater risk as he is acting against the interests of his colleagues and in breaking the rules of his 'society' can expect violent reprisals. On the part of the legitimate structures, (*sic*) law enforcement, the need to use informers is an indication of a weakening of their position, a sporadic compromise needed to achieve an otherwise unattainable goal. Hence the essential aim behind any form of compromise or negotiation is that the legitimate structures remain in control, that the power of negotiation lies firmly on their side. More oblique forms of compromise include 'turning a blind eye' to criminal activities in return for some kind of reward: 'We will allow you the criminal to function insofar as there are advantages to be gained by doing so'. The stronger the dominant system, the less likely this will occur. But if a society is weak, if corruption is extensive, if the line between legal and illegal is constantly blurred, oblique forms (in fact, any forms) of compromise are going to be more common. The danger lies in the extent to which the legitimate structures can remain in control of these negotiations which become increasingly commonplace.

This next stage in the development of organized crime, the passive assimilative, where compromise is made between the legitimate and illegitimate structures, began in Russia, not with a group but with an eighteenth century thief Ivan Osipov, known by his underworld alias Vanka Kain. According to Dixelius and Konstantinov, Kain represented 'one of the predecessors of contemporary extortionists and bandits', on account of his willingness to collude with the authorities and use their cover to protect his extortion racket.[24] Kain's criminal career began in childhood and eventually brought him into the Moscow underworld. He was required, as were all new recruits into the criminal community, to pay a subscription, *paya*, and give an inaugural address in criminal argot,[25] initiation rites which demonstrated loyalty to the group. After his arrest for theft in one of the Moscow markets and his subsequent escape from prison, Kain, for some unknown reason, changed career and worked for the local regular police as an informer, *donoschik*. In his first night of employment, he is said to have been responsible for the arrest of 32 criminals. Kain received no payment for his work but was allowed regularly to extort money from his erstwhile colleagues and the local merchants. But his position was by no means autonomous. When the new chief of police decided his career was over and that his activities were more of an embarrassment than a help to the authorities, Kain was arrested in 1741.

Up until the mid to late nineteenth century, little is known about the history of organized crime but it is safe to assume that, like the gangs which roamed the slums of St. Petersburg and other growing cities, it remained as localized hooliganism claiming its victims from the laboring poor or the reckless merchant who happened to find himself on the wrong side of town. From the two decades of intense industrialization until the Revolution economic crime flourished in the changing socio-economic conditions and offered new opportunities to the criminal underworld. Pick-pockets, swindlers, robbers and forgers found profitable trade in the new economic climate seeking to increase their acquisitions through more structured forms of activity. Criminal *artels*, in St. Petersburg known as the Choirs, *khory*, became a feature of the entrepreneurial spirit, loose associations which met to discuss how crime as a *trade* could best evolve in the changing environment. Like their Soviet successors, the aim was to collaborate wherever it was profitable to do so. The Soviet regime's brief lapse into market relations, Lenin's New Economic Policy (NEP), gave the *artels* a temporary reprieve and together with a new breed of profiteer, the despised NEPmen, they plied their trades relatively undisturbed – until that is, Stalin's rise to power and the brutal crackdown on economic and 'anti-state' criminals, now perceived as one and the same thing. Recidivists, *artel* members, anarchists, NEPmen, all became absorbed into the rapidly changing structure of the underworld. By 1930 the *vory v zakone* emerged as the elite sector. What united these disparate groups, however, was not the strength of the *vory* but the brutality of the Stalinist regime and one of its most infamous institutions, the labor camps or *gulags*.

One Day in the Life of...

'The prison makes possible, even encourages, the organization of a milieu of delinquents, loyal to one another, hierarchized, ready to aid and abet any future criminal act'.[26]

Prisons, 'those universities of crime', and labor camps became a society within a society, a microcosm of the increasing brutality of a regime which had pushed the back parameters of even the worst excesses of Tsarim. Life inside Stalin's ignominious legacy, the labor camps of Solzhenitisyn's *The Gulag Archipelago* or Marchenko's *My Testimony*[27] exposed the best and the worst of the human condition. The camps gave birth to a cruel hierarchy of inmates, where cunning and experience determined ranking and survival. This was the time of the *vory* and the *pakhany*, the cream of the criminal elite. The honor accorded them by other inmates from the underworld was expediently acknowledged by the prison employees, who used the hardened criminals within this incarcerated hierarchy to maintain control over those prisoners perceived as the most dangerous to society, that is, the politicals, broken victims of Stalin's repression.

The thieves' code of honor was maintained in the camps but remained exclusive to professional criminals. Open collaboration with the authorities (beating the life out of politicals was not perceived as collaboration) remained one of the more serious transgressions, though a number of inmates preferred to opt for an easier life by working for the camp guards, even if they risked abuse or getting their throats cut. The tension between the so-called *zakony*, loyal, thieves and those who, because of their apostasy, became known as 'bitches' (*suki*), reached its peak during and after the Great Patriotic War.[28] Desperate for manpower at the front, the authorities made a deal with the thieves (politicals were considered too much of a risk) by offering them freedom if they would fight for the Motherland. Many accepted, the more realistic amongst them realizing it was simply a matter of choosing how and where to die rather than a genuine option for freedom. Those that did survive the war were sent back to the camps to face a hoard of revengeful *zakony*. The 'War of the Bitches' accounted for years of conflict between factions in the underworld which achieved a reduction in membership of the thieves' world more efficiently than the authorities could ever have done.[29] It left a vacuum previously inhabited by traditional criminals, a vacancy in the underworld which was to be filled by the newly convicted, products of post-war society who would establish their own norms based more on self-interest than idealism.

The social fall-out from the Great Patriotic War had significant repercussions in the criminal underworld beyond the above-mentioned conflict. The Soviet Union sustained massive fatalities of both the fighting and civilian population, leaving many of the younger generation homeless or orphans. The only option available to those without support was to turn to crime – and so camp and prison numbers began to swell with new inmates who had little cause to respect traditional rules and codes. Further, the post-war years had seen an increase in banditism, serious crimes and treason. These new elements merged into large groups, one of the most famous being the *Polsky Vory*, which set out to challenge the authority of the traditional *vory*.[30] They adapted the thieves' code to their own way of life, in some instances flagrantly defying conventionality by collaborating with the prison authorities against the old *vory*. By the beginning of the 1960s the reign of the traditional *vory v zakone* was practically over. The gulf between the legitimate and the illegitimate began to disappear as new aims and relationships brought the politically powerful and the criminal elite into the same arena.

The Burgeoning of the Shadow Economy

> Our revolution is the only one which not only smashed the fetters of capitalism and brought the people freedom, but also succeeded in creating the material conditions of a prosperous life for the people. Therein lies the strength and invincibility of our revolution.[31]

Stalin's confidence in the performance of the economy was not shared by everyone. Even in the early 1950s before his death in 1953, it was evident that Soviet industry was running into difficulties A study published by Joseph Berliner in 1952 on the informal organization of Soviet firms, based on a survey taken from the first wave of post-war immigrants from the USSR, pointed to the existence of a penumbral world of facilitators and alliances upon which the efficient running of the economy rested.[32] A whole vocabulary to describe these informal practices of management and workers had made its way into unofficial common usage: *blat,* having the right connections; *ochkovtiratel'stvo,* 'pulling the wool over someone's eyes', akin to the Tsarist Potemkin device; *krugovaya poruka,* mutual support between officials in such activities as fiddling accounts, pocketing pay-offs or illegally gained 'extras'. So too had a penumbral workforce emerged, the most effective member being the *tolkach* or fixer, a wheeler and dealer who negotiated the exchange of necessary goods or equipment which would enable firms to meet their official quotas. Centralized planning, the cornerstone of Soviet socialism, was malfunctioning. To admit as much meant to admit a failure of the Communist Party and so the great deception, the building of propagandist frontispieces to hide economic inadequacies, became a full-time task for many of the bureaucrats and workers. It also exacerbated the continuous problem of shortages and poor quality products. The Soviet consumer, like the factory manager, had to seek alternative sources of supply, outside the dominant mode of production. Many consumers stole directly from the state, from their place of work, and such was the environment and general mentality, that the artifice upon which survival had rested for centuries made it all seem so normal. As Simis commented, 'The truth is that the mass of the population does not look upon theft from the state as real theft'.[33] And yet the idea of stealing from one another was unthinkable. The philosophy behind such practices was based on a logical principle: the people are the state, state-owned property belongs to them, so how can a man steal from himself? But as demand continued to outweigh supply the population had recourse to another source: the growing black market.

The burgeoning unofficial economy employed hundreds of individuals, who worked in a variety of jobs such as *speculyanty* or profiteers who sold whatever goods they could get their hands on, *fartsovshchiky* or foreign currency dealers, *putanky* hard-currency prostitutes, the foreign visitors' foray into the black-market. By 1990 official estimates admitted that 50 percent of Soviet citizens purchased a variety of goods from *speculyanty.*[34] The real figure was much higher, for as Yuri Kozlov commented: 'We were so accustomed to the shadow economy that it was impossible to live a normal life without black market goods and services'[35]. The Soviet economy found itself in a Catch-22 situation. It needed the black market to provide what the legitimate market was failing to produce and so pre-empt any potential disorder arising from shortages, but the more dependent the legal sector became on the black market the less it produced. A total symbiosis between the two sectors was now unstoppable: 'in the West the shadow economy cohabits with the official (in various alignments). In the USSR it is intrinsic to the official economy becoming its circulatory system, its brain, its nucleus'.[36] Economic performance, that litmus of legitimacy, was in deep trouble.

These individual entrepreneurs described here were, however, the bottom end of the black market hierarchy, opportunists whose lives were spent ducking and diving the system, paying bribes to hotel doormen, to low level members of the police, *militsia*, and spending the profits they made on creating a small impression on the small minority with whom they dared share their successes. They were the visible elements of the black market, the subjects of sporadic media exposure condemning society's 'parasites'. But in the growing game of profit acquisition they were merely pawns, the weaker partner of the unsigned contract with the legitimate structures which exercised an arbitrary discretion when dealing with those unfortunate to fall out of favor or whose contacts were not sufficiently strong – to block prosecution. The real players, however, lived quietly and undisturbed, a condition only achieved because of the *krysha* (protection) they received from their official patrons, members of the Party structures. Together they formed an alliance which would help to bring the country to its knees, an economic disaster waiting to happen and given an inadvertent final push by Gorbachev's reforms.

Communists and Criminals

A new breed of criminal emerged with the new breed of Party official. Profits replaced the idealism of the old *vory*, as power and prestige replaced commitment to the ideological goals of the Bolshevik fathers. The completion of the transition to full communism was put back to a nebulous time in the distant future. Even the Party leadership could not keep up the charade that under the present conditions the aspired-for Utopia was readily achievable. The Brezhnev-led government (1964–82), described in less than subtle manner by Vaksberg as 'ignorant cynics incapable of dissimulation, vulgarian self-seekers',[37] is remembered as a period of political profligacy which gave rise to the economic stagnation, *zastoi*, of the late 1970s. The endemic corruption which spread throughout the Party structures, particularly the *nomenklatura* or elite, has been well documented not only by Vaksberg in *The Soviet Mafia* but by other writers of the time including Chalidze in *Criminal Russia* and Simis in *USSR: Secrets of a Corrupt Society* and needs little elaboration here. What is of relevance, however, is the formation of a direct alliance between organized criminal groups as suppliers of commodities and services to the political elite and the patronage offered in return. And yet, despite the high level connections of certain criminal groups, they were still unable to operate with the degree of autonomy that was to become a significant feature of organized crime in the second half of the 1980s. Individuals like Sokolov, the head of Moscow's most famous food store, who supervised and amassed huge profits from the sale of caviar and other luxuries to speculators, as well as supplying the tables of his protectors, have been singled out as examples of how the Brezhnev 'mafia' operated, of the greed and corruption that marked the Kremlin in the decade of decadence.[38] But like the *speculyanty*, Sokolov turned out to be simply a pawn, albeit a bigger one, passively assimilated into the system under the patronage of the Brezhnev circle. When that circle collapsed, so too did Sokolov's business. The ruling elite, whichever individuals that might constitute, retained sufficient power to dictate the activities of its criminal partners. Hence the anti-corruption campaign led by the new General Secretary and former head of the KGB, Yuri Andropov, could result in the execution of Sokolov and incarceration of many of that circle which had colluded with high-ranking officials. Sokolov and his type were just the tip of the iceberg, the 'who' of organized crime rather than the 'how'. This one-off patronage of individuals and their entourage represented only the symptoms of an illness already well advanced. The roots of organized crime had spread quietly and rapidly in the flourishing world of the *tsekhoviki*, the new entrepreneurs, underground factory managers who were refining their skills and expertise for market relations, suppliers to the growing demand for unobtainable goods and inexpendable components of the Soviet economy. As business improved, 'according to the laws of the market' they merged into larger associations. It was still easy enough to eradicate them but was it desirable, since they represented the very foundations upon which the legitimate economy now rested?

The Black Trinity

Varese's contention that the 'mafia' as racketeers, appeared when private property became available is indeed true. But private property need not be legal. As the *tsekhoviki* and other *del'tsy*, businessmen, began to amass their fortunes during the 1970s, over a decade before *perestroika*, they became a target for criminal gangs, the less sophisticated illegal groups. In effect, muscle became a defining part of the evolution of the underworld. The heads of these gangs, employed in the business of gambling, prostitution, narcotics, and various other forms of contraband, extended their activities, like their famous predecessor, Vanka Kain, into extortion. They demanded money from the illegal entrepreneurs, either by direct physical threats or through the kidnapping of relatives, particularly children, of the businessmen. There was little the *del'tsi* could do, even with the patronage of the legitimate structures. No-one dared to admit collaboration in illegal activities. A compromise was made between the crime bosses and entrepreneurs. Criminal groups offered bodyguards to the underground businessmen, who were becoming targets for rival firms and 'sorted out' any potential competition. In return, crime bosses were allowed to invest in business and, in certain instances, take a seat on the 'board of directors'. By association, Party members, government employees and law enforcement workers became enmeshed and profited from the new alliance. But as long as the Communist Party remained the sole source of authority in the USSR, despite the growing influence of the underground business world, the power base of the relationship between the legitimate and illegitimate structures would rest with the former. However with the erosion of authoritarianism and a greater emphasis on market-style economics, the balance was soon to tilt in the opposite direction.

The Transition: From Passive to Active Assimilative

'And this is how it has turned out now. A thief-in-law works as the head of a co-operative, as a businessman, acting legally ... To be "in law" for us meant simply to be a professional thief.'[39]

When Gorbachev became General Secretary in 1985, economic growth was estimated by some Western observers to have come to halt, even as far back as 1978.[40] Gorbachev was well aware of the economic crisis facing his country. Unlike his predecessors, though, he attempted to do something about it. With hindsight many of the reforms introduced under the heading of *perestroika* appear to have been misguided and ill-informed, but in the prevailing atmosphere of secrecy, duplicity and corruption it was impossible to gauge accurately the extent of economic decline and the best remedy for it. Gorbachev saw the need for an acceleration of economic growth, *uskorenie*, which was to be supported by a more productive input from the labor force. One of the biggest obstacles to achieving this was the high level of alcoholism which cost the economy millions of roubles each year. Gorbachev's solution was to cost it even more and line the already swollen pockets of the business underworld. The introduction of the anti-alcohol campaign in 1985 was about as popular and successful as Prohibition had been in the United States during the 1920s And, like its American counterpart, it also provided organized crime the opportunity to accrue vast profits from bootlegging or *samogon* (homebrew). Underground vodka factories sprang up across the republics as networks of distribution outlets were established and racketeers found new businesses to extort. The quality of drink was often very poor and even fatal, but for an alcohol-thirsty nation the issue of safety was of minor consideration. However, the swelling ranks of underground businesses and organized criminal groups were still faced with the problem of how to use their vast profits effectively without attracting the attention of the uncorrupted members of law enforcement. As it turned out, Gorbachev's subsequent reforms were to become a bespoke package for money laundering and a welcome mat for organized crime into the legitimate world of economic prosperity.

The Law on State Enterprises (1987) was an attempt to break with the cumbersome state control over state enterprises by allowing the latter more independence from central and branch administration, a first step along the path towards private ownership. From this law, numerous experiments with management were conducted, including the creation of joint-stock companies which gave state employees the right to become shareholders of up to 49 percent of their enterprise. It was also used as an enticement to foreign business to invest in Soviet enterprises as a means of increasing the flow into the country of much needed hard currency. By mid April 1988 there were 35 established joint associations of which 31 were with foreign partners.[41] Control of the joint ventures remained within Soviet jurisdiction and initially allowed the foreign partner only 49 percent of the holdings. Although it was hardly an attractive deal for the foreign side, a cautious interest brought many firms from capitalist countries into contact with Soviet economic life, anticipating a more rapid move towards a full market economy. The opportunities for the expansion of organized criminal activity were endless. Not only did the criminals have access to funds that could be invested in creation of new joint ventures, a process facilitated by connections with the bureaucracy, but they were also able to launder their profits as hard currency in bank accounts held in the West through their foreign partners. Many of these new entrepreneurs displayed a surprising knowledge and expertise in the workings of the market, much to the amazement of capitalist businesses which had been led to believe that the Russians were grossly naive in the workings of the market. Many Western businessmen were confronted with enthusiastic entrepreneurs operating from relatively modern offices containing the odd fax machine and computer. Few foreign partners stopped to think how such expertise and technology had been acquired in a system which until recently had forbade any form of market activity. If they did suspect, as an interviewee from a large British firm once admitted, there was an instant justification for turning a blind eye by asserting that business, no matter what the background or *modus operandi* of its employees, was essential for the economic development of the USSR.[42] Legitimization, one was assured, would happen when the market was sufficiently developed.

If joint ventures were a passage to the West for the crime boss/business director, the cooperative movement provided a fertile domestic base for the further development of business and the rapid growth of racketeering. Black money was invested in setting up businesses after the Law on Cooperatives in 1988 lifted restrictions on the type of economic activity permissible, other than that forbidden by law, removed the ceiling on profits and size of cooperative (formerly it had been restricted to one or two people) and set no price controls. It also allowed cooperatives to set up joint ventures with foreign firms. As with so many of the reforms implemented within a heavily bureaucratic and corrupt system, bribes had to be paid, by those who could afford to, in order to register the cooperatives. Also having the right 'connections' became all-important, as most goods, including food for the numerous new cooperative restaurants, could only be obtained from the black market or at highly competitive prices from reliable sources. Cooperatives could operate at any level, from the small hairdressers on Leninsky prospect to the huge firm 'Association of the 21st Century' which opened one of the first private banks in Moscow. Size was often an indicator of criminal involvement. Filming *Moscow's Mafia's Millions* for British TV's Channel 4 in August 1990, I was sent to take a pre-interview with the head of the aforementioned 'Association' which had offices in the Intourist hotel, sponsored one of the local football teams and had recently signed a lucrative construction deal. A reluctant five minutes was allowed for the interview during which time it was, in arrogant tone, made clear that the head of the cooperative was not simply a director but the *President* and that such a powerful firm as the Association was 'its own, *svoyo*, government'. It was a telling conversation. Businesses had become powerful enough not only to run their own affairs, independent of the state, but to compete with it. (Nor did they need to show the traditional deference to the authorities in the presence of a foreign journalist.) The balance of power had tipped onto the side of the organized criminal associations. They had now become actively assimilated into the legitimate structures, a joint venture in itself between legal and illegal. The unresolved murder in 1989 of one of a growing number of investigative journalists looking into organized crime, Vladimir Glotov, was yet another indicator of the increasing power of Russian criminal associations at this level.

Racketeering was also to become a lucrative and rapid growing industry in the new climate of legalized private wealth accumulation. Cities were divided into patches run by the ruling groups. Names like Solntsevo, Chechentsy, Dolgoprudny, Lyubertsy became constant features in the Russian press, the names of the top Moscow gangs who also branched out into car theft and the spare parts trade, illegal drugs and small weapons. Leningrad too had its share, boasting famous *vory* such as Feoktistev, the Vassily brothers and, more recently, Malishev and Kumarin. Local businesses and stall holders which proliferated under *perestroika* usually paid without complaint, having little faith in the *militsia* as a source of legal protection. Protection rates varied according to the business and predicted profit margins. One street trader who had handed over nearly half his week's takings to local racketeers, described the 'humanity' of his illegal tax-collectors as they offered him a special discount on account of his physical disability.[43] Private taxis were also a popular target for racketeers particularly as many of their clients were foreigners who paid, albeit illegally, in the much coveted hard currency. By 1989, according to the Ministry of the Interior (MVD), the number of criminal groups exposed was up by 60 percent on the previous year, implying a huge increase in the number of gangs rather than MVD successes.[44]

Organized crime as racketeering lies on the border between passive and active assimilative in the Chameleon model. It has still not integrated into the legitimate system to the extent that it becomes difficult to identify. Because of its distinct imagery – heavy built *buiky* (bulls) bodyguards, ostentatious clothing and cars – it has become the focus of Western media attention, inviting analogies with Chicago of the 1920s and 1930s, a dangerous detraction from the more powerful influences of organized crime. The endemic presence of organized crime on the cusp between passive and active assimilative is undoubtedly inimical to the economic health of Russia and any state in which it operates, but it has not been absorbed into the dominant system to the extent that it can dictate its own terms. Even when the more enterprising groups branched out into other businesses, such as running hotels, casinos, prostitution, or exporting illegal arms, drugs, scrap metal and so on, unless they had reached the active assimilative stage they were still subservient to a degree to the legitimate structures. Although they can afford to pay off certain members of the criminal justice system to ensure lighter sentences or contacts with the outside world, crime leaders, *avtoritety,* such as Feoktistev, Malishev, and Kumarin (head of the Tambov gang in St. Petersburg), have all served (or continue to), their time in prison, the very fact of which indicates a vulnerability in the relationship with the legitimate structures not apparent with organizations like the Association of the 21st Century. Malishev, like one of his American counterparts, Al Capone, was even arrested on a comparatively trivial charge; in his case of carrying a firearm, in Capone's, on charges of tax evasion.

From Active to Proactive

Active assimilative involves a symbiosis between the legitimate and illegitimate structures. At this juncture the boundaries between legitimate and illegitimate become indiscernible. After the abrogation of Article 6 in 1990, which gave the Communist Party political monopoly, the dictates of economic power took over from that of political power. As the Party machinery began to crumble, power vacuums were filled by those with access to wealth. Overnight economic strength had more clout than political connections, especially as the new Russia seemed set on pursuing a path of reform towards the free market. Not surprisingly there was a scramble by former members of the political elite to invest in the economic sector. The compromise of former times, turning a blind eye to crime or even collaboration on prescribed terms, now became a fully active partnership on equal terms with criminal groups. When Russia committed itself to full scale market reform after the August coup of 1991, the end of the Soviet Union, it could only employ the expertise necessary for that from the former black market sector, that is from the ever-sophisticated criminal associations which had become the entrepreneurial base of the new Russia. Privatization, banking, a media run by advertising, stock markets: all these elements of capitalist economies are now controlled to a large degree by criminal enterprises. As too are many of the politicians who stand as people's deputies. Patronage has now become the province of the economic lords. But does domination of a system by organized crime necessarily lead to its eventual legitimization as many Western observers believe?[45]

Western *Naïveté* or Ideological Expediency?

'We told ourselves that Russians, given a genuine choice, would grab democracy with eager hands. And we were convinced that capitalism and a free-market economy would provide the motor for Russia's transformation'.[46]

Many of us were desperate to believe that the end of communism (few even considered that the Soviet experiment with communism was in fact nothing like that advocated by Marx) was a vindication of capitalism, that it was the *ideological* make-up of the Communist Party rather than a culture built on weak foundations that was the cause of the rapid growth of organized crime. Few are prepared to admit that the continuing influence of organized crime might be as attributable to the nature of a distorted market as encouraged by capitalism as it is to distorted Marxism experienced in Russia. The existence of organized crime in Russia today should be an opportunity to question our assumptions not just about the nature of this type of crime, whatever its ideological environment, at the end of the twentieth century, but about the changing nature of the market and business *per se*. The history of organized crime in Russia, in its different metamorphoses, has been a history of responses by the legitimate structures to the presence of the former. The weakness of those structures which evolved under authoritarian regimes accounted for the readiness to compromise with entities outside the dominant system. Russia's fate has been to exist constantly with these weaknesses. But could it happen in seemingly stable capitalist states?

In most Western capitalist states the strong presence of civil society and the gradual evolution of a market economy within stable legal parameters have allowed the dominant structures to contain organized criminal activity. This containment, however, is contingent upon maintaining the strength of the legitimate structures. With the advance of technology, the globalization of the economy and the dominance of market forces in all spheres of life the control factor becomes more problematic. Economic recession, too, has become a reality for many wealthy states initially complacent in their optimism for growth. An increasing ability to compromise with 'grey' or even 'black' business practices and structures is in evidence. The BCCI affair, the Securities and Loans scandal, and arms to Iraq débâcle, are just a few examples of growing trends in international business. How near are we to negotiating with organized crime – and we can include the growing tendency by estate agents world wide to sell property of suspected Russian criminals or to city banks to accept large transactions from dubious businesses on the justification that it is impossible to verify the source – in the present climate of economic insecurity, as the weakened structures of the USSR did? Organized crime cannot operate or develop in a vacuum. Its development is dependent initially on the environment in which it operates, until it has reached a point at which it becomes a cause rather than effect. Vincenzo Ruggiero, in his study on organized and corporate crime, comments on the effects of mutual interaction between legitimate and illegitimate business: 'learning processes appear to cross the boundaries of social groups, as criminal know-how is transmitted to a variety of actors. In other words, techniques are exchanged and skills enhanced within an economic arena inhabited by legal, semi-legal and illegal businesses'.[47]

Conclusion

There is little evidence to support the theory that organized crime in Russia will eventually legitimize itself as the market becomes more established. On the contrary we are witnessing, again in the words of Ruggiero, 'the mafiazation of business'. By concentrating on the ideological rather than the structural, by denying the growing partnerships between legitimate and illegitimate motivated by a weakening of legitimacy through economic crisis and uncertainty, we in the West are also turning a blind eye. The rapid decline of the Soviet regime was based on economic inefficiencies. Few could have predicted that such a decline would have occurred so quickly and so finally. There is no room for complacency therefore on the side of capitalism. It would do us well to pay heed to Russia's recent experience, to reassess our perceptions of both organized crime and capitalist business and gain at least some wisdom from the Russian maxim which states: 'The sad fate of our country is to show the rest of the world how not to live'.

NOTES

1. Federico Varese, 'Is Sicily the future of Russia? Private protection and the rise of the Russian Mafia', *European Journal of Sociology*, Vol. 23, No.2 (1994), pp.224–258.
2. The term 'mafia' is inappropriate for the activities of Russian criminal groups, although it has now become common usage. Despite the presence of hierarchies and a clear division of labor, organized crime in Russia does not have the strict codes observed in the more traditional forms of mafia groups. There is also a rapid turnover of personnel at the bottom end of the hierarchy suggesting a less organized structure than in, for example, Italy. The problem of identifying many groups in Russia as mafia in the present climate of legislative ambiguity further cautions against the use of a term which some academics would argue has a very dubious semantic base in any case.
3. Alan Block, *Space, Time and Organized Crime* (New Brunswick: Transaction Publishers, 1994), p.57.
4. The term 'legitimate structures' refers to the political, economic and criminal justice system..
5. The model forms part of the author's thesis entitled 'Hunting the Chameleon: the problems of identifying Russian organized crime' being completed at the London School of Economics..
6. By the term 'negotiate' I am referring to any interaction, whether passive or active, prompted by either partner..
7. US President's Commission on Law Enforcement and Criminal Justice, *Task Force Report: Organized Crime* (Washington DC: US Government Printing Office, 1967). .
8. A. Dolgova and S. Dyakov (eds.), *Organizovannaya Prestupnost'* (Moscow: Yuridicheskaya Literatura, 1989), pp.25–26.
9. Hugh Seton-Watson quoted in Stephen White, *Political Culture and Soviet Politics*, (London: Macmillan, 1979), p.22 .
10. Samuel Kucherov, *Courts, Lawyers and Trials under the Last Three Tsars* (New York: Frederick Praeger, 1953), p.238.
11. Marquis de Custine, *Empire of the Czar* (New York: Anchor Books, 1989), p.125.
12. Prince Scherbatov, *On the Corruption of Morals in Russia* (London: Cambridge University Press, 1969), p.255.

13. Count Potemkin's village fronts were a resounding success. According to Martin Walker in *The Waking Giant*, even Gorbachev was a victim of this duping technique. Determined to see how the average Soviet citizen lived, he visited a supposed 'normal' family only to discover, purely by chance, the Communist Party crest on the bottom of a cup. The whole situation had been set up, thus defeating the object of the visit which was to discern the real living conditions of the Soviet people. In this environment it was practically impossible for Gorbachev to assess with any accuracy the extent of the problems facing the Soviet Union..

14. V.I.Lenin, *Collected Works*, Vol.24 (Moscow: Progress Publishers, 1964), p.107.

15. Richard Pipes, *Russia under the Bolshevik Regime 1919–1924* (London: Harvill/Harper Collins, 1994), p.492.

16. A. Dolgova and S. Dyakov (eds.), *Organizovannaya Prestupnost' 2* (Moscow: Kriminologicheskaya assotsiatsiya, 1993), p.279.

17. *Ugolovny Kodeks RSFSR* (Moscow: Yuridicheskaya Literatura, 1987)..

18. Eric Hobsbawm, *Bandits* (London: Penguin, 1972), p.17.

19. Robert C. Tucker, *Stalin as Revolutionary 1879–1929* (New York: W.W. Norton & Co. 1973), ch. 3.

20. D.L. Golinkov, *Krakh vrazheskovo nodpol'ya* (Moscow: Izdatel'stvo Politicheskoi Literatury, 1971), p.76.

21. Alexander Gurov, *Krasnaya Mafia*, p.104.

22. Alexander Solzhenitsyn, *The Gulag Archipelago*, Vol.2 (London: Collins & Harvill Press, 1975), p.238.

23. A. Gurov and V. Ryabinin, *Ispoved' 'vora v zakone'* (Moscow: Rosagropromizdat, 1991), p.8.

24. Malsolm Dixelius and Andrei Konstantinov, *Prestupnyi Mir Rossii*, p.44 .

25. Ibid., p.27.

26. Michel Foucault, *Discipline and Punish. The Birth of the Prison* (London: Penguin, 1991), p.267.

27. Anatoly Marchenko, *My Testimony* (Middlesex: Pengiun, 1971).

28. The Great Patriotic War is the name given by the Russians to their involvement in the war against Hitler's Germany (1941–45).

29. Dixelius & Konstantinov, op.cit., p.75–81.

30. Eduard Maksimovsky, *Imperiya Strakha* (Moscow: Zelenyi Parus, 1992), p.98–99.

31. *History of the Communist Party of the Soviet Union* (Moscow: Foreign Languages Publishing House,1939), p.341.

32. Joseph S. Berliner, 'The Informal Organization of the Small Firm', *The Quarterly Journal of Economics*, Vol.LXVI, No.3 (Aug.1952), pp.342–363.

33. Konstantin Simis, *USSR:Secrets of a Corrupt Society* (London: J.M.Dent, 1982), p.177.

34. B.Vasil'iev, 'Zloveshchee ciyaniye "chornovo" rinka', *Ekonimika i Zhizn*, No.47 (Nov. 1990), p.8.

35. A. Dolgova and S. Dyakov (eds.), 1989, op.cit., p.144.

36. K. Ulibyn, 'Znakomaya neznakomaya', *Tenevaya Ekonomika* (Moscow: *Ekonomika*, 1991), p.7.

37. Arkady Vaksberg, *The Soviet Mafia* (London: Weidenfeld & Nicolson, 1991), p.19.

38. Ibid., pp.205–215.

39. A. Gurov and V. Ryabinin, *Ispoved' 'vora v zakone'*, p.8.

40. Anders Aslund, *Gorbachev's Struggle for Economic Reform* (London: Pinter Publishers, 1991), p.17.

41. F. Lukyanov, 'Sovmestnye Predpriiatiia–god 1988' *Izvestia*, 5 May 1988, p.3.

42. Informal interview with a British businessman in Leningrad July 1990.

43. Interview, July 1991.

44. *Argumenty i Facty*, No.22, 2–8 June 1990.

45. Edward Luttwak, 'Does the Russian mafia deserve the Nobel prize for economics?', *London Review of Books*, 3 Aug. 1995, p.7.

46. Stephen Handelman, *Comrade Criminal. The Theft of the Second Russian Revolution* (London: Michael Joseph, 1994), p.xvi.

47. Vincenzo Ruggiero, *Organized and Corporate Crime in Europe*, (Hants: Dartmouth Publishers, 1996), p.154.

The Emerging Criminal State: Economic and Political Aspects of Organized Crime in Russia

YURIY A. VORONIN

The old order in Russia has broken down but, as yet, there is little to replace it. Russia has become a country where chaos is a constant, where narcotics and nuclear materials are suddenly for sale. As if these dangers are not worrisome enough, the real nightmare scenario involves Russia's ruthless organized crime syndicates and corrupt government officials working in league to create not so much a new market economy but actually a new criminal state. It is a state in which attempting to ascertain where gangsterism ends and the government begins is impossible, a state wherein the laws of criminal clans turn out to be higher than human laws.

Around 8,000 criminal formations comprising an estimated 100,000 now operate in Russia. Many of these groups have organized themselves into loose criminal confederations, perpetrating crimes such as extortion, drug dealing, bank fraud, arms trafficking, export of contraband oil and metals, and smuggling of radioactive materials and components. During 1995 the shadow turnover of capital across the country reached 45 trillion roubles – almost 25 percent of the gross national product. The liquidation of the Communist Party of the Soviet Union put an end to the solidity of the old state power and to a strict hierarchy of opportunities for legal and illegal enrichment by bureaucrats at different levels. But in the new Russia a close correlation has developed between the political weight of an office and its importance in the redistribution of property. The vast new opportunities and the sharply increased temptation to 'grab everything', combined with juridical chaos in the regulation of economic relations, could not fail to bring about a qualitative growth of corruption which acquired new, more dangerous and refined forms. Most of these acts of corruption go beyond the 'ordinary' abuse of power, actually merging with the criminal activities of the underworld. The extent is staggering. About 20,000 crimes connected with corruption are recorded in Russia every year now, but experts are sure this figure is less than one percent of the real scale of corruption. A poll of businessmen in the capital revealed that several thousand bribes are given and taken in Moscow alone in one day. Corruption has taken particular hold today in such spheres of the economy as the export import sector, involving commodities such as oil. One-fifth of this strategic raw material that was exported in 1995 took the form of contraband. The motor-vehicle business, real estate, land deals, banking are other areas where corruption occurs on a huge scale. Specialists calculate that because of this there is 300 billion dollars worth of capital of Russian origin in foreign banks, and we are therefore essentially donors of a mutinous economy.

Following the lead of world-class criminal organizations everywhere, Russian syndicates are amassing considerable muscle and are already well-equipped with sophisticated weapons and advanced communications. Furthermore, the criminal underworld is exploiting Russia's military-industrial complex to gain access to an unusual array of talent, including former police officials, military specialists, and university-trained chemists, managers, and economists. Many MVD operatives assume also that almost every one of the organized criminal groups has its own high-ranking official who provides protection and support. Especially advantageous in this connection is a deputy, inasmuch as he can directly influence or block a legislative decision which is dangerous to his employers. And locally, in remote areas, one public servant is, at times, more powerful than the authorities in Moscow.

There is a broad consensus among specialists that Russia has witnessed the emergence of large mafia empires which control whole spheres of the economy and industrial production. In this sense, today in Russia there are two levels of racketeering. The first is inhabited by street thugs. They are basically low-level muscle who extort payoffs for 'protection' to small businesses. The far more profitable level, known as 'the roof', is peopled by traditional crime bosses, along with some of Russia's emerging entrepreneurs who have a driving ambition to make the most of new opportunities in order to get rich quickly. Many of these entrepreneurs have shed their Communist Party cards en route to becoming wealthy monopoly financiers. Businesses that deal with these groups are brought under the 'roof'. If they cannot afford to develop their own security forces, protection is provided. More important, they can find connections and access to lucrative contracts – all for a hefty cut, of course, typically about 30 percent and sometimes up to 70 percent of profits. Further activity of criminal groups in the industrial, financial and credit systems is to be expected. Penetration is increasing and it is clear that banks and commercial structures are becoming part of the system for laundering criminal capital. This is why the shooting of prominent bankers and businessmen is certain to continue, and could even intensify. The artificially created chaos in the settlements and payments sphere will continue to stimulate the growth of shady financial transactions.

It has become clear that idealistic expectations about life after the downfall of the totalitarian regime have not been met. The fact that any significant social changes which break down the established and customary mode of life require the transformation of the previously acquired system of values and the creation of new models of economic and political behavior was not taken into account, at least initially. Unfortunately, the collapse of Communism did not lead automatically to democratization and the transition to a competitive capitalist economy. Instead, domination by the Communist Party was replaced by the controls of organized crime. State ownership of the economy was exchanged, in fact, for control of the economy by organized crime groups which have a monopoly on existing capital. Labor markets once controlled by state planning and submissive trade unions are instead subject to the intimidation of organized crime which is already a major employer.

The Criminalization of the Economic System

Since crime in general – and organized crime in particular – is a product of economic, political and other social processes, it is impossible to explain the parameters of crime without studying and interpreting these processes.

Organized crime and corruption are the price that must be paid for Russia's experiment with free enterprise. While other nations have also experienced high crime rates during periods of acute social and economic change, the Russian experience is distinctive. Organized crime in Russia took root in the fertile irrationalities of a planned economy and prospered in the vast black and gray markets that emerged in the last three decades of Communist rule. The distinctive feature of contemporary Russian organized crime is its inseparable connection with phenomena of past Soviet life, especially the shadow economy. The 'socialist' economic system could not have existed without the shadow economy, which acted as a substitute for the market, and was one of the main means by which the totalitarian regime exercised power. Under these conditions, the law and the rules of the bureaucratic apparatus existed as though in parallel worlds: in the world of semblance and in the world of reality. Such a situation erased the border between legal and illegal actions by any holder of official powers. All of this was combined with the lack of an independent judicial system and the fictitious character of the institutions of legislative power.

Shady economies have existed in all countries and in all periods. In the majority of cases, however, organized crime thrives only through traditional criminal sources of revenue: drugs, gambling, weapons, and prostitution. In the new Russia, in contrast, organized crime flourishes well beyond these areas – it wields power over all the economy. This is a particularly tragic feature of modern Russian reality. Organized crime has deeply infiltrated the economy during the crucial transition from a centrally planned system to a free market – a transition accompanied by a fundamental reorganization of the structure of Russian society. The problem is that disassociating the further economic development of the Russian state from the continued pervasiveness of organized crime could prove impossible. The economy has become dependent on illegitimate rather than legitimate economic activities; and the rise of private property has become inextricably linked with the protection offered by organized crime.

Consequently, most new Russian capitalists operate mainly in the so-called 'gray zone' that exists between the underworld and the official world. Today in Russia there is nothing at all that is completely 'clean'. It is virtually impossible to make money in Russia without breaking the law. Even apparently legitimate entrepreneurs find it difficult to muster the necessary capital for new enterprises and all too frequently must borrow funds from mobsters at extortionate rates of interest. Criminal support for businesses is becoming a precondition for their existence. Even the more powerful entrepreneurs in Russia are businessmen who are forced to break the law and who earn money from their powerful connections. There are several reasons for all this.

First, the monopolization of power has resulted in the formation of a state administration that seeks to derive benefits from businesses. As a result, economic bodies within the state and government structures are attempting to preserve their privileged positions throughout the period of capitalist reform. Indeed, between 25 and 30 percent of money obtained from criminal economic activity is used to nourish corrupt relations with government and state officials. Instead of fighting against corruption, modern political leaders simply announced the elimination of the state's role as an active agent in economic life. The resulting vacuum has substantially cleared the field for criminal economic behavior.

The second important factor is that many of the investors who are participating in privatization were created from shadow economic activity – speculation, racketeering, extortion, looting and so on. It is hardly surprising, therefore, that Russia's privatization process is turning many of the country's prime assets over to swindlers and thieves. According to estimates made by the Ministry of Internal Affairs (MVD), more than 40,000 enterprises were either established by or are now controlled by criminal organizations in Russia. From 70 to 80 percent of private and privatized firms and commercial banks are forced to pay criminal groups, corrupt officials and racketeers. The result of this criminalization of the economic system is the tendency to match economic policy to the specific economic interests of criminal structures. This, in turn, prevents much-needed reforms in the material and technological bases of production.

The Intertwining of Crime and Politics

In the highest echelons of Russian government, crime and politics are often indistinguishable from one another. Crime in the post-Soviet era, in other words, is often a continuation of politics by other means – but carried out by the same persons: the functionaries, security and police officials and others who run the state. Professional criminals commonly manipulate police and customs organizations, military establishments, and financial institutions. Furthermore, the tentacles of organized crime apparently extend to the highest levels of government. Parliamentary bodies are riddled with *de facto* criminal syndicate representatives, who diligently block or water down any significant anti-crime legislation. This inflicts considerable damage on the authority of the state and hinders the establishment of the rule of law. The penetration of organized crime into Russian governmental structures also has a corrosive effect on citizens' perceptions of democracy. Opinion polls indicate declining confidence in the transition to democracy.

The larger criminal syndicates are eager to transform their wealth into political influence. But as Russians increasingly identify free market democracy with organized crime and corruption, they will turn toward much less congenial forms of governing. This might result, first of all, in the future election of more authoritarian governments (and presidents too). On the other hand, the alternative political power of organized crime is poised for future growth because criminal groups have the resources to fund candidates in elections at the local and national levels. Consequently, organized crime is increasingly likely to undermine the electoral process and forestall the emergence of a viable multi-party system.

Besides this, organized crime is undermining the establishment of laws needed to move towards a carefully regulated market economy. Corrupt officials and legislators with ties to organized crime impede the introduction of legislation that might circumscribe organized crime activity. From 1993 until 1996 the legislative framework needed to combat organized crime – including banking laws, regulation of securities markets, insurance laws and such specific measures as laws against corruption, organized crime, money laundering, as well as provisions for a witness protection program – has been impeded by corrupt legislators. The result is that Russian prosecutors still lack the legal tools to strike at the leadership of criminal organizations.

One more damaging result is that the old danger for the West stemming from the 'evil empire' has been replaced by Russian mafia penetration of Western economies. Russian gangs have been responsible for a wave of violent crime in Central and Western Europe and in the United States. The smuggling of Russian resources abroad has depressed world prices for commodities. Crime syndicates in Russia are exacerbating the international proliferation of advanced weaponry and dangerous radioactive substances. Such syndicates are also assuming a more prominent role in the global traffic in illicit drugs. Russian criminal enterprises are exporting their operations and networks and are collaborating with foreign criminal organizations. More generally, Russian organized crime imperils the emergence of a legitimate economic and political order in post-Communist Eurasia.

Combating Organized Crime

Implicit in the preceding analysis are several crucial questions: could the Russian government's fight against organized crime merely be a factional war among organized criminals, whereby certain ones are eliminated to protect the turf of those in power? Could this struggle also be an attempt by members of the investigational hard core of the former Soviet state – the bureaucracy, military, and so on – to perpetuate themselves in power at the expense of legitimate entrepreneurs and democrats? The evidence strongly suggests an affirmative answer to both questions. The Russian government's responses to date are characterized more by rhetoric than substance, while those initiatives that have been taken reflect a basic misunderstanding of the causes, dynamics, and consequences of the criminal sector in the country.

There have been some indications that the Russian government has woken up to the growing threat. Some members of the government have called for an urgent program to fight organized crime. Thus far, however, the government has done too little too late, with the result that it has been no match for the mafia. There are several reasons for this:

• First, organized crime, thanks to the corruption of the bureaucratic apparatus and to the constant powerful financial infusions it received from its activities, began to acquire the means to spy on the Ministry of Internal Affairs, the procurator, and even the courts.

• Second, law enforcement organs, for various reasons, were deprived of many of their most experienced professionals. One reason for this was the allure of the commercial sector, which often provided these professionals with income several times their meager salaries.

- Third, although the government is continually restructuring and reorganizing law enforcement agencies, a truly serious reform that would improve their work has simply not occurred. The resulting tensions, distractions, and demotions demoralize the ranks. Law enforcement agencies also suffer at the mercy of the lingering ideological prejudices of Soviet jurisprudence. Many activities that are required for a market economy to function remain illegal or unprotected by legislation; other activities that are considered unlawful according to Western norms, such as organized crime, are not specifically prohibited. Under the existing system, police may arrest a group of felons caught in criminal acts, but the lack of Western-style conspiracy laws means police cannot prosecute the criminal leaders so long as they did not participate directly in the crimes. Moreover, Russia has no independent judiciary and no way of tackling more sophisticated varieties of white-collar crime. Current laws offer no means of impounding the records of fraudulent companies or checking the criminal provenance of banks accounts. Even if such provisions existed, their enforcement would be doubtful.

- Fourth, because it is able to operate with such a high degree of impunity, organized crime has become a major impediment to the development of civil society. Social organizations, which, in principle, should oppose the onslaught of organized crime and corruption, in many cases support them – partly because they have become so established that they provide a certain kind of stability. Indeed, when organized crime controls much of the economy of a particular area, it often contributes to the infrastructure of the community. Organized crime groups pay for the construction of hospitals and schools as a form of insurance against collaboration of community members with law enforcement. Many organized crime figures in Russia sponsor sporting events and are associated with philanthropic groups. Corrupt banks contribute to educational and other community projects on a regular basis. In essence, this is all evidence that the nascent civil society is being corrupted from within. Many mafiosi are involved in charity work and social protection programs. Charitable organizations in Russia have become increasingly embroiled with organized crime. These organizations and societies are directly engaged in commercial activities. Half the staff in these businesses are disabled and this legally exempts the companies from paying certain kinds of taxes. But it is not necessary to have disabled staff to gain exemption; fake agreements can be signed and symbolic wages paid to non-existent personnel. Legally, profit from businesses owned by charities and other public organizations is not liable for tax if .

it is used to fund the ostensible activities of these bodies. This makes them an attractive channel for laundering money.

Just one example connected to my native town, Yekaterinburg. Boris Yeltsin used to run this town. The new czar is a former soccer star named Konstantin Tsyganov. Police and fellow gangsters say Tsyganov's crime organization controls 60 percent of this rich industrial region, with branch operations in Moscow. Tsyganov's men make regular deliveries of food, tea, and medicine to Yekaterinburg's overcrowded jail. The warden, who says the state has slashed his budget so severely that two inmates have died from the poor conditions, shrugs and accepts the booty. Tsyganov is something of a Russian Robin Hood. His thugs allegedly extract up to a third of the profits from businesses struggling to establish themselves. Yet, after he was arrested on extortion charges, invalids, pensioners, and the local soccer team wrote letters of protest, extolling his philanthropy and demanding his release. All said they could not survive without his largesse.

In other words, social organizations which, in principle, should be contributing to the development of civil society have already been neutralized or co-opted by criminal organizations. Criminal networks are exploiting societies, associations, funds, and unions. This helps them in several ways: 'dirty' money becomes clean, necessary protection is created for criminal associations, symbolic actions create a more favorable climate of public opinion, Russian 'godfathers' are made to appear as saviors of the homeland, and political channels for promotion of representatives of criminal structures to organs of government power are secured.

- Fifth, it is also clear that organized crime has supplanted many of the functions of the state, and currently represents the only fully functioning social institution. For instance, organized crime provides many of the services that citizens expect from the state – protection of commercial businesses, employment for citizens, mediation in disputes. Indeed, in the absence of a functioning commercial order, businesses rely on the mafia to collect debts and to resolve disputes with suppliers and competitors. Private security, mostly run by organized crime, is replacing state law enforcement. Approximately 100,000 private law enforcers presently operate without any regulation. And recent Russian sociological research indicates that businessmen willingly pay protection as a cost of doing business effectively in relative safety. In a sense, the development of Russian organized crime can be understood as a result of the government's social policy. And the ultimate consequence of all of these circumstances is that in Russia organized crime has in fact replaced a largely dysfunctional state.

Conclusion

Organized crime fighting in Russia is more than a matter of law enforcement: the political, economic, and human rights dimensions are central. Organized crime-fighting should be linked with a general strategy designed to promote irreversible reform, something which over five years after the Soviet collapse remains elusive. Under these conditions, the struggle against organized crime presupposes first of all the establishment of a non-contradictory legal basis for economic relations and the further development of judicial protection for all kinds of property. If this is not done, the demands for unrestricted expansion of powers of punitive bodies and the hardening of measures of criminal punishment will be substantiated. This reveals the political essence of the problem of organized crime in Russia: will the bureaucracy consolidate its power under the banner of the struggle against organized crime, or will society realize the real danger involved in arbitrary law and concentrate its efforts on developing institutions for civil control over the activities of the power structures and the bureaucracy? The answer to this question depends on many factors.

Whatever the case, the first objective is to drive organized crime and corruption out of government structures. Without this first step, everything else is lost. If Russia remains unwilling to prosecute and punish politicians, bureaucrats, judges, and police from the lowliest to the most powerful, then everything else is a waste of time and effort. Robber barons and corruption must not be accepted as necessary evils in the transition to democracy and a market economy. This is not to overlook the difficulties in Russian society of coping with organized crime and especially corruption (there were 17 million state officials in the USSR, while Russia now has 18 million). What is urgently needed for the struggle against organized crime is the fastest possible legal reform. In today's legal language, for example, the concept of corruption does not exist. The concept has not been defined – and without clear categories and definitions it is virtually impossible to fight corruption. The more elusive the concept, the more difficult it is to contain. The other main requirement is for a criminological assessment of the laws, edicts and decrees being adopted. A reliable and effective system for combating organized crime and corruption can only be built upon a solid legal and regulatory foundation.

In addition, the West must act to bolster Russian efforts to combat organized crime and corruption. A significant proportion of Western financial aid to Russia, which now comprises mostly export credits and IMF stabilization loans, should be redirected to crime-fighting purposes. Appropriate areas for international assistance include helping Russians draft effective anti-racketeering legislation, reforming Russia's antiquated judiciary, equipping police forces with vehicles, computers and communications equipment, and training police in investigation techniques. In part, this is a matter of Western self-interest. The extension of Russian criminal activities beyond the borders and the penetration of Western economies by Russian crime syndicates pose threats to Western countries that, while less significant than those facing Russia itself, are still serious enough to encourage greater cooperation. Agreements must be concluded between Western and Russian governments on information exchanges, extradition, asset sharing, and other legal matters. Such agreements are no guarantee of success in the struggle against organized crime; in their absence, however, failure is certain.

Major Mafia Gangs in Russia

GUY DUNN

When our society is so chaotic, how is it that our crime is so organized?
A proverb for the new Russia

The emergence of the Russian mafia is the major development in transnational organized crime in the 1990s. According to the Interior Ministry, the number of mafia gangs in Russia has grown from 785 in 1990 to more than 8,000 by mid-1996. As many as 120,000 people are believed to be active members of these gangs, though other sources estimate that more than three million people may be involved.

Several factors characterize the Russian mafia: its ruthlessness and propensity to use overwhelming violence, and its ability (and willingness) to operate abroad. Although all mafia organizations increasingly operate on a world stage, Russian groups appear to have particular advantages in this respect. First, the fact that the Red Army was stationed in many European (and African) countries means that gangs often had contacts abroad which they were able to exploit when they turned to criminal activities. Secondly, there are Russian émigré communities across the world, and – as with the Sicilians in New York or the Chechens in Moscow – organized criminal groups tend to flourish when they come from close-knit ethnic minorities in an alien society. An estimated 110 Russian mafia gangs now operate in more than 44 countries worldwide.

The other major distinguishing feature of the Russian mafia has been its aptitude for business and economic crimes. Russian mafia gangs may have emerged by carrying out traditional heavy-handed activities – such as extortion, prostitution and debt-collecting – but they have not been afraid to expand their range of activities. Russian gangs emerged as capitalist reforms were being introduced in Russia. Not only has this enabled them to take advantage of the mass privatization program, but it has also effectively allowed them to become the driving force or major entrepreneurial spirit behind the economy. Unlike the Italian Mafia, for instance, which has emerged like a cancerous growth on the side of an already functioning market economy, the Russian mafia is inseparable from the Russian economy. The Russian mafia controls an estimated 50,000 companies and accounts for up to 40 percent of Russia's GNP.

The official figure of 8,000 Russian mafia gangs is alarming, but essentially meaningless. First, although the recorded number of these gangs may continue to rise in the short term, it is likely to fall in coming years as smaller gangs join together to ward off larger groups. In addition, some of these gangs are little more than a small *ad hoc* group of people who occasionally work together for criminal means; they have no set structure and cannot be defined as organized.

Only about 30 of these gangs are truly large organizations with a broad range of operations. It is these gangs which are moving more and more into economic and business spheres and which are increasingly operating abroad.

This paper presents detail in a systematic manner about the leading mafia gangs currently active in Moscow, St. Petersburg, Yekaterinburg and Vladivostok. These gangs are the largest and most powerful criminal organizations in Russia and operate abroad. The information on the gangs is based on research derived largely from a series of confidential briefings with well-placed sources – including local and international policemen, Interior Ministry officials, prosecutors, crime reporters, regional and city government officials and business personnel – together with Control Risks' own extensive specialist database. The sensitive nature of the article means that all interviewees wish to remain anonymous and this article will contain no footnotes.

Structure of Russian Mafia Gangs

Before examining these major gangs, it is useful to look briefly at their structure. Although there is no set structure for a Russian criminal gangs, the following is probably the commonest one for the larger groups:

Leader – who in turn will have excellent contacts in industry, national and local governments, etc.

Deputies of Various Sections – strategist, economic adviser, banking consultant, industry specialists, heads of racketeering, drug smuggling, security, counter-intelligence, etc.

Team Leaders – accountants, bankers, car traders, extortionists etc.

Soldiers – smugglers, bodyguards, pimps, hitmen, etc.

In addition, the following characteristics are shared by most major gangs:

- a hierarchy enforced by strict disciplinary sanctions

- restricted membership, sometimes based on family or ethnic ties

* tight secrecy and compartmentalization

* the uninhibited use of intimidation and violence.

Major Gangs in Moscow

There are an estimated 150 mafia gangs operating in the Russian capital. Of these, 20 of them are well-armed, relatively large organizations, but only six of them wield real power. These six main mafia gangs are the three Chechen gangs (the *Tsentralnaya, Ostankinskaya* and *Avtomobilnaya*), and the *Solntsevskaya, Podolskaya* and *21st Century Association* organizations.

One of the main reasons for the drop in the number of important gangs is their increasing sophistication. While in the past extortion was the major activity, the gangs are now more interested in financial and business operations, which offer more opportunities for profit; only a few gangs have the resources to carry out such financial operations. Extortion is still carried out (in fact is rising), but is no longer the larger gangs' primary concern.

The Three Chechen Gangs

Size. The total number of members of these three gangs is difficult to assess. It has been as high as 3,000, but it is currently reckoned to be about 1,500 people (largely because many Chechens have returned to their homeland to fight the war there). Because of the close links between the Chechen gangs, it is difficult to break down these numbers into individual gangs.

Leading 'authority'. Nikolai Suleimanov ('Khoze') who came to Moscow in the early 1980s helped set up most other Chechen crime bosses and was considered to be the leading 'authority' until he was shot dead in December 1994. 'Aslan' and 'Lechi the Beard' are considered to be the new authorities.

Nominal leader. Overall control of the *obshak* (see below) is held by 'Musa Starshii'. Through his control of the *obshak*, he is perhaps nominal leader of the Chechen gangs in Moscow (although 'Khoze' certainly enjoyed greater authority when he was alive). Musa Starshii was in hiding in Chechnia in 1993–94 for the alleged shooting of 21st Century Association (see below) boss Amiran Kvantrishvili; he only returned to Moscow after Amiran's brother Otari was also killed.

Other key figures. The leaders of the former Lazanskaya gang, Khozha N.

and Ruslan A., both enjoy considerable authority in Chechen crime circles. The former acts as a go-between between the Moscow community and Chechnia where he allegedly has links to the highest echelons of power.

United financial source (the 'obshak'). All three gangs maintain a single *'obshak'* (the term for pooled criminal resources). The money from the *obshak* is used for paying lawyers, bribing officials as well as supporting their fellow countrymen currently serving prison sentences. The *obshak* is thought to contain billions of roubles at any one time.

Shared security departments. The Chechen groups also share a 'security and intelligence' department. This is headed by Akhmet M. and 'Vakha Mladshii', the brother of Musa Starshii. This department deals with corrupt officials to provide information on possible operations against the gangs and to keep abreast of the activities of competitors.

Links with corrupt officials. The Chechens allegedly have links and contacts at the highest level in both the Moscow city government and the national government. The Chechen gangs are also thought to maintain particularly close contacts with the Moscow Regional Department for Organized Crime (RUOP) and the Moscow Department of the FSK (the former KGB).

Links with other gangs. Smaller groups in Moscow, such as the Lobnenskaya, Kazanskaya and Baumanskaya are generally loyal to the Chechens.

International operations. Chechen gangs mainly operate in Germany, Austria, the UK, Poland, Turkey, Jordan, the Netherlands the former Yugoslavia and Hungary. Main operations are banking, car smuggling, illegal oil deals (including to Serbia), drug smuggling and prostitution.

Tsentralnaya Gang

Headquarters. Moved from Uzbekistan restaurant to the Belgrade and Zolotoye Koltso Hotels.

Leader. 'Lysiy'. Having studied in Moscow, he was set up in his first 'business' by Khoze in 1987.

Areas of city where active. As its name suggests, the gang is active in the centre, although not exclusively. Nor does it have a monopoly on central areas of the city.

Main operations. Counterfeiting, financial swindles, drug and arms smuggling, extortion, kidnapping, prostitution, 'importing' of foreign consumer goods and food, smuggling and exporting of raw materials, and control of many hotels, casinos and restaurants.

Ostankinskaya Gang

Headquarters. The Ostankino Hotel.

Leader. Magomed O. He came to Moscow as a student. He set up in the Ostankino Hotel, using it as the meeting-point for Chechens transporting goods. He now controls almost all the Russia–Transcaucasia road transportation business.

Areas of city where active. Controls the area around the Ostankino Hotel, but has influence over other areas such as the Moscow section of the Yaroslavl Shosse northern road.

Main operations. Domestic and some international road haulage including the smuggling of goods into the northern Caucasus (including Chechnia, circumventing Russia's effective blockade). Other operations include the extortion of money from transportation companies near Moscow and drug- and arms-smuggling.

Avtomobil'naya Gang

Leader. Khoze was the leader before he died. It is not known who replaced him although it might be Tsentralnaya's leader, 'Lysiy'.

Areas of city where active. In all the main car markets and showrooms in Moscow, including at Leninsky Prospekt, Ulitsa Mytnaya, VDNKh, Tverskaya, Yuzhny Port, Danilovsky and Begovaya.

Main operations. Legal and illegal car trade, including import and export, theft, smuggling and sale of cars, including from abroad, extortion of money from other car showrooms, including from foreign companies.

Other Major Moscow Gangs

The Slav groups (Solntsevskaya and Podolskaya) are the natural enemies of the Chechen gangs. In 1990–91 Slav gangs waged a vicious 'war' against the

Chechens under the guidance of one of the most important Russian mafiosi, 'Yaponets' (meaning 'The Japanese'). Feuding between the two sides continues; more Chechens were killed in both 1993 and 1994 than during the 'war'. Most of the later killings, however, were over battles to win contracts and business, rather than as the result of an actual strategic 'war'. One such battle took place over the Allianz car showroom in early 1994 between a Slav gang and the Avtomobilnaya gang; the Slavs won.

Solntsevskaya Gang

Size. 3,500–4,000 members (largest single gang in the country). It also is the best equipped, with at least 500 Kalashnikovs, 1000 TT and PM pistols, several dozen *Uzi* rifles, some anti-tank weapons and grenade launchers (of the RPG–22–I Mukha type).

Leader. The leader is probably 'Mikhas', a former engineer who has spent at least five years in prison.

Other key figures. Mikhas's deputy is 'Avyora'. Other key figures are 'Tashkent Dato', Dzhemal K. and Beslan D. Yuri R. is the main financial expert. Yaponets, who was arrested in New York in late 1995, also has close connections to the group. Sergei Timofeev, 'Sylvester', was the gang's leading authority before he was blown up in his car in central Moscow in September 1994; rumours persist that he staged his own death and is now living abroad.

Main areas of city where active. It enjoys exclusive control in the district of Solntsevo, but has operations elsewhere, notably in the centre and the south of the city.

Main operations. Drug production, smuggling and distribution (notably of synthetic drugs, such as tri-methyl fentanyl and methadone), arms and car smuggling, extortion, prostitution; kidnapping; running hotels and restaurants, retail, banking, investment, economic crime.

International operations. The gang is particularly active in Germany, Austria, Poland, Belgium, the United States, the Czech Republic, Italy and the United Kingdom. Its main operations include car, drug, arms and antiques smuggling, as well as illegal trading in oil, metals and other raw materials. Some sources indicate that the gang is involved in the transit of

South American cocaine through Russia into Europe and the United States. It is thought to have links with the Cali cartel; these links were set up by Yaponets who went to New York to set up American operations for the gang.

Podolskaya Gang

Size. About 500 members. It is a relatively new gang, only emerging as a strong organization in the last five years. It is well armed with about 200–300 Kalashnikovs and has a reputation for ruthlessness, organization and discipline.

Leader. Probably Lalakin ('Luchok').

Other key figures. Luchok's closest aides are 'Rospis' and 'Kremen'. The gang's main authority is allegedly 'Zakhar' who also has links to the Balashikhinskaya gangs (see below).

Areas of city where active. It is based in small suburb of Podolsk, where it enjoys exclusive control. It has operations elsewhere, including control of about 25 percent of the street trade and prostitution in the center of Moscow.

Main operations. Extortion, kidnapping, prostitution, gambling, financial swindles, money laundering, drugs and arms smuggling; the import and sale of food, electronic and consumer items; and the illegal production of food and spirits under pirated brand names. It controls several casinos.

International operations. It imports and exports goods to countries all over the world, but its main activities are believed to be in the Netherlands. Its main operations there is the production of counterfeit food and drink products for sale back in Russia. The gang also is believed to deal in illegal oil products and in arms and drug smuggling. Before his arrest, Yaponets tried to help the gang extend its operations in the United States.

21st Century Association

History. The 21st Century Association was established in Moscow in 1988 as an 'umbrella' organization for a number of newly created co-operatives. It rapidly became regarded as a criminal gang, mainly because of its brutality in extortion, and skill at high level corruption schemes. In recent years it has extended its activities to concentrate on business activities. It is one of the most powerful criminal organizations in Russia.

Size. The gang is believed to be able to draw on the resources of up to 1,000 members nationwide (more in times of crisis). It has operations in 18 Russian regions and abroad.

Leaders. 'Anzor'. Anzor, a Georgian, is a graduate of the elite Soviet Diplomatic Academy of the Ministry of Foreign Relations. He trained as a lawyer and has links with the higher echelons of society. The Association's vice president is believed to be Joseph K.

Other key figures. The Association's two most infamous members were the Kvantrishvili brothers, Amiran and Otari. They were two of Russia's most ruthless criminals but were killed in internecine feuding with Chechens in Moscow in 1993 and 1994 respectively (see above). Otari's funeral procession, attended by many leading politicians, brought Moscow to a stand-still.

Links with corrupt officials. The 21st Century Association's leadership prides itself on its close ties with corrupt individuals in regional and municipal administrations. However, one informed source remarked that its 'scandalous reputation' has hindered its attempts at making contacts at the highest levels of national government.

Main activities. The Association's operations are diverse. It carries out extortion, kidnapping, prostitution and other traditional mafia activities. It controls several hotels, casinos and restaurants. However, it is also increasingly moving into the business arena and now offers insurance, investment, banking and pensions services. It is increasingly active in the oil industry and has set up several charities (allegedly to take advantage of legal and tax loopholes). The 21st Century Association is believed to control as many as 100 companies nationwide and has founded several charities for ex-sportsmen and military personnel.

International operations. It has operations in seven countries (in the United States and in western Europe).

Smaller Gangs in Moscow

There are about 20 important smaller gangs in Moscow. By national standards they are very rich, but in Moscow they cannot compete with the larger Slav and Chechen organizations. When major conflicts arise, these gangs must take sides with one or other of the large gangs.

Details of the *Pushkinskaya* and *Balashikhinskaya* follow. Other such organizations include the *Lyubertsyskaya,Odintsovoskaya, Domedovskaya, Khimkiskaya, Koptevo-Dolgoprudnenyskaya, Sokolnikiskaya, Zhdanovskaya, Izmailovoskaya, Pokrovskaya, Lyublinskaya, Azerbaijanskaya, Mazutinskaya (Georgian), Chekhovskaya, Shchelkovoskaya* and *Ingushskaya* gangs.

Pushkinskaya Gang

Size. About 70–100 members.

Leader. 'Papa'. He has been the leader for a long time. He is believed to be in hiding from the Russian authorities in Israel, but still controls operations through his deputies.

Areas of city where active. The suburbs of Lesnoi, Pravda, Pushkino, Mytyshi and the Moscow section of the Yaroslavl *shosse* (road) up to VDNKh.

Main operations. Production and sale of contraband alcohol (mainly vodka).

International operations. Its main international operations are in Israel. The gang also has links within the United States, mainly through the Russian mafiosi Dmitri B. (who was arrested by the FBI in 1994).

Balashikhinskaya Gang

Size. No more than 50 members. The gang has weakened dramatically following the killing of two of its leaders 'Gera' and 'Sukhoi' in 1992, and of its paramount leader 'Frol' at the beginning of 1994.

Leader. 'Zakhar'.

Other key figures. Zakhar's deputies include 'Vovan' and 'Sapog'.

Areas of city where active. The suburb of Balashikha and nearby regions in the North East of Moscow.

Main operations. Controls bars in several hotels, as well as the so-called Northern Market. It also controls several retail outlets and is increasingly involved with distributing material.

International operations. None known at present.

Major Gangs in St. Petersburg

St. Petersburg is generally considered to be Russia's most crime-ridden city. In April 1994 the US consulate even advised American citizens to avoid travelling to the city because of rising crime; it later (sensibly) retracted the advice.

Crime levels are so high because of St.Petersburg's strategic position. As a busy port lying in close proximity to western Europe, it is proving to be an ideal conduit for smuggling operations. Violence between rival gangs is common as they vie for control of the city's major transit points. Several bombs in the city in late May 1996 indicated that a mafia turf war between several of the city's leading gangs might be about to resume. Such turf wars have proved extremely violent in the past; in February 1994 seven corpses were found in the back of a Mercedes in the city centre. A month earlier ten people were killed in a shootout nearby.

There are four major gangs in St. Petersburg (Tambovskaya, Vorkutinskaya, Malishevskaya and Kazanskaya) and are some of the largest in Russia. Detailed information on these gangs has been the hardest to obtain and verify.

Tambovskaya Gang

Size. 1,500 (though twice as many people are associated with the gang in a looser sense).

Leader. Little is known about the leader, though it appears that he is or was the official head of an oil company.

Areas of city where active. Unclear at present, but probably has operations throughout the city.

Main operations. Drug production and selling, protection rackets, prostitution, kidnapping, contraband alcohol production, car trading, arms dealing and selling oil.

International operations. Drug and arms smuggling, car smuggling and trading in raw materials (perhaps including nuclear materials). Main operations in Finland, Sweden, Germany, Netherlands and Poland. May be involved in the snuggling of illegal immigrants.

Malishevskaya Gang

Size. 1,500–2,000 members. The police believe that the number of 'drifters' connected to the gang fluctuates between 3,000 and 5,000 over different periods of time.

Leader. 'Malishev'. Little is known about Malishev's background. He was arrested in December 1992 for carrying an illegal firearm, but 'bought' his freedom. He has been in prison several times since, but continues to lead the gang from there.

Areas of city where active. The southwest of the city (mainly in the Krasnoselski, Kirovski and Moscovski regions), but has operations elsewhere.

Main operations. Drug production, prostitution, car dealing, abduction, arms dealing and extortion.

International operations. Drug and arms smuggling, car theft and smuggling. Main operations in Germany, Baltic States, Finland, Sweden, Norway and Germany. May be involved in the smuggling of illegal immigrants.

Vorkutinskaya Gang

Size. 2,000.

Leader. Unclear at present.

Areas of city where active. Unclear at present, but probably has operations throughout the city.

Main operations. Drug production and dealing, prostitution, protection racketeering, kidnapping, contraband tobacco and alcohol production, car-smuggling, arms dealing.

International operations. Drug and arms smuggling, car smuggling and running prostitution rings. Main operations in Finland, Sweden and Germany.

Kazan'skaya Gang

Size. 1,000–1,500 (the make-up of this gang changes constantly with members travelling to and from Tatarstan all the time).

Leader. (?) 'Gzhizhevitch'. He was recently arrested but is believed still to be leading the gang from within prison.

Areas of city where active. The north of the city (mainly in the Vyubertski, Primorski and Kalininski regions), but has operations elsewhere.

Main operations. Extortion, car stealing and trading, drug dealing, kidnapping, prostitution, arms dealing.

International operations: Unclear, but probably involved in car, drug and arms smuggling operations.

Smaller Gangs

The most important smaller gangs are the Arkhangel, Murmansk, Kavkaz and Volgod gangs. These gangs tend to have a couple of hundred members and specialize in operations such as extortion, kidnapping and drug dealing. They do not operate independently but either pay tribute to one of the four top groups or work as an arm of the stronger structures. The Kavkaz gang specializes in hostage taking, particularly of children.

The major ethnic gangs are the Chechen, Azerbaijan and Dagestan gangs. These ethnic gangs are not as powerful as they are in Moscow and they all have less than a hundred members. Their main sphere of activity is running the fruit and vegetable markets.

Major Gangs in Yekaterinburg

Yekaterinburg is one of the most criminalized cities in Russia. Violent crime in particular has risen sharply this year. The organized crime situation in Yekaterinburg has degenerated into total anarchy since the weakening of the two main gangs – the Uralmashskaya and Tsentralnaya – which for several years had provided a certain equilibrium in the criminal world. Now there are far more smaller-scale gangs striving for influence in the criminal world, meaning that a full-scale war is almost permanently underway.

Uralmashskaya Gang

Size. At its peak in 1990-1992 there were 500 members. Today there are about 50 central figures serving the gang, though another 100–150 old allies can still be mustered in case of necessity.

Leader. Konstantin T. He took over after his brother Grigory T. was murdered in 1992. Konstantin has been forced to go into hiding recently because of official investigations into his activities; his leadership has been weakened as a result.

Other key figure. The second most important figure is (?) Mayevski, who has recently been arrested but still co-ordinates activities from prison.

Areas of city where active. Mainly around the large Uralmash factory on the city's outskirts.

Main operations. Economic crime, banking, smuggling raw materials and metals, extortion, real estate manipulations, arms smuggling, prostitution and (allegedly) nuclear material smuggling.

International operations. Uralmash allegedly has operations in Cyprus, the United States, Poland, Germany, China. Main operations are smuggling of metals, arms and drugs.

Tsentral'naya Gang

Size. It is impossible to say how many members the gang has today, since for the moment its activities are extremely limited.

Leader. It was Eduard K., before his arrest in Brussels by Interpol on extortion charges in September 1994. The new leader is not known.

Areas of city where active. Traditionally the city centre.

Main operations. Gambling, prostitution, metal-smuggling, trade, extortion, drug and arms smuggling. It controls several hotels.

International operations. Hungary and Belgium. Main operations are weapon smuggling and extortion in Hungary and 'legitimate business' in Belgium. Unclear how much these operations have been affected by Kazaryan's arrest.

Afghantsy Gang

Size. About 15–20 permanent members and up to 200 drifters. Most members are Afghan war veterans.

Leader. Vladimir L. and Viktor K. Both have criminal records, for rape and extortion respectively.

Areas of city where active. In and around the Central Market.

Main operations. Extortion, selling cars and petrol, drug smuggling.

International operations. Drug smuggling in Afghanistan.

Siniye [Blues] Gang

Size. Gang of former prisoners. Impossible to give size because numbers fluctuate as members go back and forth to prison.

Leader. 'Severyonok'. A former convict.

Areas of city where active. City outskirts and nearby towns and villages. Currently bidding for city centre. The *Siniye* gang forced Chechens out of Yekaterinburg in 1993 by using a stolen tank to attack the Chechen HQ.

Main operations. Protection racketeering.

International operations. None.

Azerbaijan Gang

Size. The number of members changes constantly, with a migrant population travelling between Yekaterinburg and Azerbaijan.

Leader. The Azeris do not have a leader, since they represent a community rather than a very well structured crime gang.

Areas of city where active. Their base is in the military settlement of Torchemeto, near Yekaterinburg, though they are highly active in the city itself.

Main operations. Drug and arms smuggling. They use profits to fund fighting in Nagorno-Karabakh.

International operations. None (excluding in Azerbaijan).

Major Mafia Gangs in Vladivostok

Crime levels in Vladivostok were relatively low until 1992. Prior to that, Vladivostok was closed to (almost all) foreigners and had a strict entry–exit regime for Russians. The loosening of this control led to the influx of criminal groups hoping to take advantage of the newly lax border regulations with China and the possibilities for trade with Japan and the Korean peninsula.

Mafia gangs soon infiltrated and took over the lucrative trade in Japanese used cars brought into Vladivostok and the Primorye region's eight other warm-weather ports. The open borders with China also allowed mafia gangs to extort money from the Chinese traders selling their goods in the city's markets.

Vladivostok's mafia gangs are still trying to consolidate their positions and they have a reputation for using excessive violence. This violence has resulted in Vladivostok being referred to as 'The Wild East'.

Although organized crime levels were previously low in Vladivostok, they were not non-existent. For example, Yaponets (see p.68) originates from Vladivostok and set up one of the first gangs there. In addition, a German businessman, who – because of official contacts – had had limited business operations in the city in 1977, told Control Risks that he had received an extortion demand then.

There are nine major mafia gangs in Vladivostok. Largely because of the short time that they have been operating, none of them is particularly large or powerful. The gangs are identified by the nickname of their present (or former) leaders. The gangs' territory is not divided up by physical boundaries within the city, but in terms of the businesses they control.

Mikho's Gang

Size. About 100 full-time members (though it can draw on the support of about another 200–250 drifters).

Leader. 'Mikho'. He has a college degree in economics and is described by police as 'very smart'. He has been in prison for stealing state property. He allegedly has excellent connections with several gangs in Moscow.

Other key figures. Yevgeny V., who is a *vor v zakone* and is based in Komsomolsk-On-Amur, 400 kilometres to the north of Vladivostok. Yevgeny has a crime empire that deals in smuggling, trading and selling Chinese manufactured clothing and electronic goods. Yevgeny acts independently, but would always come to aid of Mikho in time of necessity.

Main operations. Extortion, prostitution, smuggling of clothes and goods from China, arms and drug smuggling. The gang also manages the illegal hiring of cheap Chinese labour.

International operations. As well as its operations in China, the gang is believed to run prostitution rings in Macao and smuggle cars from Japan. It is not known whether the gang smuggles arms and drugs abroad.

Kostenaya Gang

Size. About 60 members, but access to another 150 drifters.

Leader. 'Kosten'. The oldest of the gang leaders, he ran one of the few gangs in the city during the Soviet period; he extorted money from sailors who received part of their salary in hard currency. He has been imprisoned for black-marketeering.

Main operations. Trading in cars and electrical appliances, drug-smuggling and drug production and prostitution.

International operations. Drug smuggling from China. In particular, it trades in the performance-enhancing drug ephedrine, a byproduct of prescription drugs ephedrine produced in China.

Kovolskaya Gang

Size. Uncertain, but no more than 20 members.

Leader. 'Kovol'.

International operations. Very little is known about this group except that in 1992 its members travelled to Japan in an attempt to set up contacts with the Yakuza. The Vladivostok police claim that the meeting was at Kovol's initiative. It is not certain what operations were agreed upon, though it may have been to confirm plans to swap Japanese cars for Russian guns.

Makorskaya Gang

Size. Unknown, but no more than 40–60 members. Most of them are former athletes, usually martial arts experts.

Leader. 'Makor'. Makor is a former kick-boxer who has been in jail for hooliganism and extortion.

Other key figures. Anatoly K. (former USSR kick-boxing champion).

Main operations. Extortion, prostitution, contract killing and arms running. They run a local sports club.

International operations. Unknown, gun running suspected.

Trifonskaya Gang

Size. Not very large, perhaps 30–40 members. A new gang and has no 'drifters'.

Leader. 'Trifon'. Trifon is in his twenties and has no criminal record. He is a former athlete.

Main operations. The gang is only just establishing itself and its only reported activity to date is running protection rackets.

Pogonyalo Gang

Size. About 50 members.

Leader. Alexei A.

Main operations. Extortion, car trading.

International operations. Believed to be behind car smuggling operations from Japan.

Anashkinskaya Gang

Size. About 50 members. The gang was severely weakened following the arrest of seven members, including its leader, in an arms raid in 1994.

Leader. The new leader is Andrei V. following the arrest of its original leader, 'Anashkin'.

Main operations. Extortion, prostitution and arms-running.

International operations. It is believed to run prostitution in Hong Kong and Macau, and may be behind arms-running to Japan in exchange for used cars.

Bachurinaya Gang

Size. About 20 members.

Leader. Sergei B. He was arrested in 1994 on drugs charges, but is believed to have 'bought' his freedom.

Main operations. Prostitution, drug smuggling and protection racketeering, mainly of the Chinese stall-holders in the city's markets.

International operations. None.

Mitischenskaya Gang

Size. Up to 50 members.

Leader. 'Mitischen'.

Main operations. Car trading, extortion and prostitution. The gang was first identified in mid-1994 when some of its members broke a US customs seal on cargo load heading for Louisiana (USA); the cargo turned out to be American cars which the gang allegedly resold for 200,000 dollars.

International operations. Car smuggling from Japan.

Smaller Gangs

In addition to the above groups, smaller crime groups from Tajikistan, Uzbekistan and Azerbaijan are beginning to set up in the city. The Azerbaijan gang is the most powerful of these; they are believed to have contacts with the Yakuza to coordinate drugs and car smuggling.

APPENDIX
Russian Mafia Activity in Europe

By mid-1996 there were an estimated 8,000 mafia gangs operating in Russia. The activities of these gangs have played a major part in the tripling of the crime rate in Russia since 1989. As well as the more traditional mafia activities, such as protection racketeering, extortion and prostitution, these gangs are increasingly turning to more sophisticated business activities: an estimated 50,000 companies in Russia are controlled by the mafia. Going into partnership with one of these 'front' companies is one of the biggest risks of doing business in Russia – or with Russians abroad. The increasing sophistication of the gangs' business activities has meant that they are expanding their operations from their cities of origin to elsewhere in Russia and, increasingly, abroad. The Russian Interior Ministry claimed in June 1996 that about 110 mafia gangs operate abroad, either in co-operation with foreign partners, or independently. Most of these are permanently based abroad. The Interior Ministry has information about up to 7,000 people who are believed to act abroad, though the real number is likely to be much higher. Russian mafia gangs are believed to be operating in more than 44 other countries. These include: Austria, Belgium, Bulgaria, Canada, China, Cyprus, the Czech Republic, Finland, France, Germany, Greece, Hong Kong, Hungary, Israel, Italy, Japan, the Netherlands, Poland, Spain, Sweden, Switzerland, Turkey, the United Kingdom, the United States and former Yugoslavia.

Activity in European Countries

Austria

Russian mafia gangs are active in Vienna and elsewhere in Austria, where they specialize in prostitution and economic crimes. Russian gangs control about 700 prostitutes in Vienna, a business that officials believe could be worth about $300m per year. Control of such lucrative operations can lead to internecine feuding. Sergei Hodzha-Akhmedov, a Russian who was shot dead in his car in the city on 20 September 1994, was believed to be a mafia member controlling car-smuggling and prostitution rings. More sophisticated Russian gangs also exploit Austria's lax banking and tax laws. The Solntsevskaya gang, the largest mafia organization in Russia, has based its western European headquarters in Vienna largely for this reason. Solntsevskaya is increasingly jettisoning its more rudimentary activities, such as racketeering, in order to concentrate on more profitable business operations. Other Russian organizations, such as the shadowy 'business' XXXX, are headquartered in Vienna. XXXX, which initially made its money smuggling metals out of Russia, allegedly concentrates on drug smuggling and is believed to launder its money through Austrian banks. In early November 1995 the Austrian authorities clamped down on XXXX and deported 70 of its 80 employees. The authorities were forced to act after receiving complaints from several banks.

Belgium

Russian mafia groups are active in Belgium, where they specialize in prostitution and pornography rackets. Gangs lure Russian and other eastern European women to Belgium to work as prostitutes, often with the false promise of a job and a work permit. When the women arrive in Belgium, they find themselves trapped in prostitution. Russian gangs in Belgium also concentrate on economic crimes. Their major area of operation is Antwerp, though they also operate in Brussels. There are so many Russians in Antwerp that Falcoplein Square in the center has been dubbed 'Red Square'. Antwerp's port has a reputation for being a major smuggling base. The city's diamond dealers, many of them Russian Jews, have links to many Russian gangs and are allegedly among the world's most experienced in the art of laundering money and dodging taxes. Several Russian groups have been uncovered recently, among them a group headed by Boris N., a leading mafia boss, who was charged with racketeering, drug trafficking, conspiracy to murder and association with Russian Jewish criminal groups. In 1989–93 N's group was centered on companies owned by Antwerp Russians, as well as affiliates in Moscow, Berlin, Odessa and Warsaw. He was heavily involved in laundering money illegally obtained through drug and arms smuggling.

Cyprus

Cyprus is a popular location for money laundering, as well as a destination for capital from Russia; by 1996 about $1.3bn was estimated to arrive in Cyprus from Russia every month. These dealings are extremely profitable for Cyprus, and the country has refused a request from the Russian Central Bank (RCB) to consult it before granting licenses to Russian companies. There are an estimated 2,000 Russian companies in Cyprus. Many of these are small and were opened simply as a means of keeping hard currency in offshore bank accounts – where they are safe from inflation, low interest rates and the unstable ruble. The main attraction of Cyprus is its double-taxation agreement with Russia. As well as facilitating money laundering, companies are used as transit points from which to pour money into other countries, such as the London property market. A wave of bomb attacks in late 1995 in Limassol is believed to be partly connected to growing internecine violence between rival Russian gangs. The bombings, in which several people were killed, followed the deportation of several Russians from Cyprus in previous months for extorting protection money from compatriot businesses.

Czech Republic

The Czech Republic suffers from similar problems to most other former Soviet bloc states. Russian gangs have used links forged during the Soviet years to set themselves up in Prague; they have since laundered money by buying up Czech companies. Some 3,000–4,000 organized criminals, mainly from Russia, are believed to be operating in Prague. The gangs tend to concentrate on extortion and protection rackets, drug and arms trafficking, armed robbery and money laundering. Five Russian and three Ukrainian members of a gang were arrested and charged with possession of arms and stolen foreign vehicles in December 1995. Prague also is a major transit point for drug smuggling: 70 per cent of drugs entering Germany come through the city. Russian gangs often use Prague as their base in central Europe; they also occasionally use the city as a meeting point. The gangs have great power and access to officials. A leading Russian mafia member was erroneously released from Prague's Ruzyne prison in late October 1995 after the authorities were fooled by a bogus fax from the district court demanding his immediate release. The fax bore the court's official stamp and the correct evidence number. The Russian, who specializes in extortion, remains at large. He was responsible for an incident in mid-May 1995 in which more than $12,000 was extorted from the foreign-run Blue Duck Restaurant in the city center. In a separate incident in December 1995, the head of the Interior Ministry internal investigations department (Ministry Inspectorate), Vladimir Nechanicky, was dismissed for alleged links with Russian organized criminal gangs. Nechanicky had apparently tipped off leading Russian mafia leaders – including 'Mikhas', the leader of Russia's Solntsevskaya gang – that they were to be arrested when they visited the city in May 1995. There is increasing internecine warfare between rival gangs. A Russian was killed and three were injured in a gun battle between Armenian and Russian groups at a McDonald's drive-in restaurant in south-east Prague in November 1995. The incident is believed to be connected to the deaths of two Russians whose bodies were discovered in their car in a nearby area a few days later. The men had been shot in what appears to have been a classic mafia killing. Both incidents appear to have been the result of a debt dispute between the two gangs.

Finland

Russian gangs are increasingly active in Finland and there has been an influx of ethnic Russians in the 1990s: more than 50,000 now live there, concentrated in Helsinki. The Finnish police have concluded that Russian groups already control theft rings (notably of cars), prostitution and the smuggling of vodka, arms, drugs, illicit pharmaceuticals and precious metals. Russian gangs are reported to control the traffic in hashish and marijuana in Finland. Russians have taken over clubs and restaurants to launder illicit proceeds. Stolen cars (usually luxury Western models) are often taken to Russia. Russian gangs also have set up protection rackets to extort money from businesses. However, violence in public places, such as bombings and shoot-outs between feuding gangs, remains rare in comparison to Russia. Helsinki's Police Commissioner, Tomas Elfgren, has called for the establishment of a Nordic (leading to a European) register of known Russian organized criminals to help combat crime. Former members of the Soviet/Russian former KGB and GRU intelligence services and the military are believed to be involved in organized crime in Finland.

France

Russian gangs control prostitution rackets and some bars and night-clubs in Paris and other major cities. They also have used banks and other financial institutions to launder money. However, generally speaking, Russian mafia activity in France is relatively low-key. Many Russians use France as a base for holiday homes and even residence. The average Russian visitor to France spends ten times more than an average German, British or Japanese visitor – much of this 'spending' money may have been gained illegally.

Germany

About 50 Russian criminal gangs are believed to operate in Germany. About 20 of these come from the Moscow region, others originate from Krasnodar, Rostov and Kemerovo. Many of the Russians now operating in Germany were stationed in former East Germany in the Soviet era, and thus already have contacts there. Germany is a popular place for mafia bosses to live since from there they can control operations throughout western Europe.

It is estimated that Russian criminals are responsible for one-third of all crimes committed in Germany. The main areas of activity include prostitution and car theft, as well as extortion, drug-related offenses, currency counterfeiting and the trade in arms and radioactive materials. The German Federal Police (BKA) estimates that at least 10,000 Russian women are forced to work as prostitutes in the country. Economic crimes also occur. For example, the Semyenov gang from Krasnodar fraudulently removed $750,000 from Russia and transferred it to a clearing account in Hamburg in early 1994.

The Russian mafia in Frankfurt tends to concentrate on economic crimes. Other types of activity, such as extortion and prostitution, are not as common in Frankfurt as they are in eastern German cities. Nevertheless, in a well-reported case in August 1994, four prostitutes, their pimp and his wife – all from St Petersburg – were killed in Frankfurt in a suspected internecine mafia feud.

Hungary

Russian mafia activity in Budapest is relatively high. Gangs tend to use contacts fostered when the Red Army had bases there. More than 1,000 Russians deserted from the Red Army during the last week before its withdrawal in 1991 – many to set up criminal operations. Russian groups have tended to concentrate on the theft and smuggling of cars, prostitution and protection racketeering.

Russian gangs have divided up much of Budapest's night-life among themselves. This leads to occasional violence; at least three Russians were killed in an internecine mafia feud in Budapest in early 1994. In another incident in October 1995, a Belarussian was kidnapped from his home in Budapest by a Russian mafia gang. The gangs demanded a ransom of $30,000 from his father, a Minsk businessman. The victim was released after a tip-off, and the gang members were arrested when they tried to pick up the ransom. The victim was alleged to have had links with the Russian underworld.

Russian mafia gangs in Budapest are beginning to specialize in economic crime, which has increased considerably (see Hungary). Banking regulations are lax, and the country has long had a reputation as the white-collar crime capital of eastern Europe. Russian organizations also have laundered money by buying up Hungarian companies in the privatization program.

Italy

There are believed to be at least six Russian mafia gangs operating in Italy. One of these is the Ingush gang from Moscow (which is closely connected to the Chechen gangs), another is from the Central Chernozem belt; the rest are from the Urals.

Their areas of specialty include theft, robbery, arms and drug smuggling, economic crimes and extortion. Some of these operations are carried out in conjunction with the powerful Italian Mafia groups. For example, Russian gangs smuggle arms to Italy, from where the Italian Mafia smuggles them to Bosnia-Herzegovina. The Russian gangs are most powerful in Milan, where they are carrying out some sophisticated economic crimes.

Netherlands

Russian gangs operate in the Netherlands, especially in Amsterdam, in increasing numbers. As well as taking advantage of liberal drug laws to use the Netherlands as a transit-point for smuggling narcotics, Russian gangs specialize in prostitution and pornography. Many of the women and boys working in Amsterdam's red-light district come from Russia and eastern Europe and have Russian mafia members as pimps. Russian gangs also are heavily involved in smuggling stolen cars, especially from eastern border towns such as Hengelo.

As elsewhere in western Europe, the more sophisticated Russian gangs are carrying out more complex business and economic crimes. The level of money laundering and currency counterfeiting is high. Counterfeiting of goods also is a problem; the Pushkinskaya gang, based in Moscow, produces counterfeit Stolichnaya vodka in the Netherlands for resale in Russia.

Poland

Poland suffers from many of the same problems as Hungary and the Czech Republic. In addition, Russian mafia gangs are primarily responsible for the high level of car crime in Poland. In 1995 car theft in Poland rose fivefold compared to 1994 – itself a fourfold increase on the 1989 level. There also has been a dramatic increase in the number of armed car-jackings by Russian gangs; at least 20 foreigners were held up by armed thieves while driving in and around Warsaw in January 1996.

Most stolen cars are taken to Russia, where there is a ready market for such vehicles. An estimated 20 per cent of all foreign-made cars driven in Moscow are stolen property. The vehicles that are most popular with thieves are expensive German makes (such as Mercedes, BMWs and Volkswagen Golfs) or four-wheel-drive vehicles. On average, a Mercedes driven in Warsaw is likely to be stolen within just over three months. Less high-profile foreign cars (including Volvos and mid-range Japanese makes, for which there is reportedly no market in Russia) are less likely to be stolen.

Spain

Russian mafia activities in Spain are relatively low-key, mostly for geographical reasons – criminal gangs are as yet simply too busy in countries closer to Russia. However, there is some activity: many Russians own residences in Spain, especially in Marbella and other coastal resorts. Some economic crime by Russian mafia groups has been recorded in Madrid, but most Russian businesses in Spain have based themselves in the south so as to be close to tax-lenient Gibraltar.

Sweden

Russian mafia activity also is increasing in Sweden: gangs use Sweden as a transit-point when smuggling refugees into the West. They charge up to $3,000 per person for this profitable activity, which is known as 'criminal tourism'. Gangs have set up a large underground industry for false or stolen passports, visas and other travel documents. For example, in December 1992 and January 1993 almost 600 refugees, mostly Kurds, landed on Sweden's southern island of Gotland.

A Russian mafia gang also made an attempted kidnapping in Sweden in August 1993 – the only known incident of Russian gangs targeting Westerners for kidnapping outside Russia. The attempted abduction was of leading Swedish industrialist Peter Wallenberg. Three Russians and a Swede of Polish extraction, armed with pistols and a grenade, were arrested outside Wallenberg's holiday villa on the island of Varmdo, near Stockholm, after Wallenberg had become suspicious and notified the police. A fifth suspect, another Russian, was arrested later. Estimates of the planned ransom vary from $0.5m to $30m. A one-person submarine had been prepared for Wallenberg's abduction.

Switzerland

Russian mafia gangs operate in Switzerland only in a business sense. Like Italian gangs, they do not like to carry out extortion and other activities in countries where they launder much of their money. Russian gangs have increasingly taken advantage of lax Swiss banking laws to launder large amounts of money. They are believed to have displaced Colombian drug cartels as the major users of Swiss bank accounts. Even 'registered' transfers of money from Russia to Switzerland have doubled since 1992 (up to $4bn). The real figure is much higher: most money is pumped into Switzerland from other countries, such as Cyprus. It is not uncommon for Russian mafia gangs demanding protection money in Russia to ask that monthly payments be made straight into Swiss bank accounts.

United Kingdom

Russian mafia gangs are interested in London for two main reasons. One is that they use the City, Europe's financial capital, as a base for money laundering. There were 300 reported dubious transactions connected to Russia in 1994, and this figure continues to rise rapidly. Three people (including two Russians) were arrested in London in May 1995 after attempting to launder 32m ($51m) of alleged Russian mafia money over an 18-month period – one of the largest single laundering operations ever run in the United Kingdom. Chechen mafia gangs are particularly active in London. Russian gangs are also interested in the United Kingdom for a more personal reason. Many mafiosi are keen to keep their families out of Russia and have bought homes in the United Kingdom to house them. The United Kingdom is popular because of the perceived excellent (primarily private) education facilities. Moreover, high property prices in London make purchases of houses and flats a good way of laundering money.

Major Russian Mafia Activities against Business in Europe

The threat to business from Russian mafia activities abroad can be divided into two types: security threats and business risks. Security threats, such as extortion, car theft and kidnapping, pose a potential hazard to all companies. Business risks include more sophisticated economic crimes, which are most likely to impinge on banks and other financial institutions.

Security Threats

Extortion

Apart from petty crime, extortion is the most common crime in Russia: the police register up to 700 cases of racketeering each month. An estimated 80 per cent of all (local and foreign) companies have received extortion demands. The true figure is probably even higher: many businesses are unwilling to reveal that they have been approached by criminal groups for fear of reprisals.

There are fears that Russian mafia gangs will soon begin to carry out extortion abroad on a similar scale. Extortion cases by Russian gangs have been reported in Hungary, the Czech Republic, Poland, Germany, Israel, Cyprus, the United States, the United Kingdom, Finland, Belgium and several other countries. Most reported cases involve Russian gangs putting pressure on companies owned by compatriots. There have been only one or two reported instances where Russians have targeted a major multinational company outside Russia. Those companies that have been targeted outside Russia so far appear to have been chosen because they have offices in Moscow. However, this could change as Russian gangs become more established abroad.

Russian gangs use extortion as a means of controlling the targeted company – not simply to squeeze payments out of a company in return for protection. They often demand to be paid in stocks or shares and as a result quickly force themselves into the financial heart of a company. In Russia there are many instances of extortionists acquiring such large interests in a company that they have ended up on the board of directors. Several case studies illustrate the types of demand made as well as the growing international capability of Russian gangs.

• In November 1995 the local partners of a German multinational in St Petersburg brought an uninvited Russian to a joint business meeting. At the end of the meeting, the man offered the company guarding services. These were declined. A few days later four men burst into the flat of one of the company's German employees, beat him up and demanded protection money. The multinational withdrew the German and his family to Berlin. Two weeks later, a gang of five Russians arrived up at the German's flat in Berlin. The company found alternative accommodation for the German and has employed a reputable security company to guard its premises in St Petersburg.

• In May 1995 two foreign executives and the Russian manager of a major contracting company visited Budapest to discuss a business venture with a Russian company based there. After the two foreign executives had left Budapest, the Russian manager was approached by the representatives of the Russian company, who told her that they expected her to organize a one-off payment of about $35,000 from the contracting company. The woman managed to get away from the gang and maintained a low profile in Budapest for several days before flying back to Moscow, thinking that she had escaped. However, on returning to her flat she found her mother lying in a pool of blood, barely alive. The gang's Moscow arm had visited the flat several days earlier and had seriously assaulted the mother.

• In February 1995 a British finance company withdrew its manager after he had been targeted in an extortion bid by a gang in Moscow. Several days after his return to London, the man was visited at his home by a Russian who informed him that his organization had a long reach and that it was not too late for an agreement to be achieved. The company provided a 24-hour bodyguard for its employee and has drastically curtailed its operations in Russia.

• In February 1994 several mafia members visited the Moscow offices of a leading US company and demanded that it pay them about 15 per cent of its monthly turnover. The gang appeared to have detailed knowledge of the company's affairs, and had brought details of a Swiss bank account into which it wanted the money to be paid. An agreement was allegedly reached, but two months later the multinational's Prague offices were visited by a group of Russians offering protection. They had detailed knowledge of the extortion demand paid in Moscow and appear to have been the Prague section of the Moscow gang.

The Threat of Extortion and How to Deal with it. There are no hard-and-fast rules for dealing with extortion demands. However, carefully constructed resistance should be possible. Many companies pay the first demand made, gain a reputation for being an easy target, and end up receiving further demands in other cities and even other countries. Although reaching some sort of financial agreement with a gang should be considered only as a last resort, all demands should be taken seriously. Violence has been used against companies which refuse to pay.

Russian gangs will ask for an initial payment of just one ruble or a few dollars. Some companies pay such demands to have the gang leave their offices, and to gain some time. However, this is a mistake. Under mafia law, this token payment signifies that the business has come under the *krysha* (roof) of the gang: not only is it difficult to extricate the company from the arrangement at a later date, but local security companies will automatically double their prices if they know that a payment, however small, has been made.

Each case should be dealt with on its merits, and a contingency plan should be drawn up in advance to deal with the problem when it arises. Once a demand is made, companies must assess the situation and clarify their objectives.

Kidnapping

In Russia, gangs regularly kidnap local business figures. Kidnapping of foreigners also is increasing as gangs become aware that foreigners can command larger ransoms than locals. About 20 foreigners were abducted in Russia in 1995; they were all released unharmed. (Other unreported kidnaps may have taken place.)

There have been very few incidents of attempted kidnaps by Russian gangs abroad. Russian gangs have targeted compatriots in the United States, Poland, Hungary and the Czech Republic. There have been several short-term abductions of employees of small business operations in Germany, usually to back up an extortion demand. The only abduction of a foreigner that could be termed a traditional kidnap and ransom case was the attempted abduction of Wallenberg (see Sweden).

The threat of kidnapping for foreign executives could increase as Russian gangs become more established and realize that they can obtain greater ransoms for foreign victims. Many companies respond to this threat by taking out kidnap and ransom insurance policies, which usually provide specialist crisis management advice before and after an incident.

Car Theft

Russian mafia gangs are heavily involved in car theft and the smuggling of cars, particularly in Poland, the Czech Republic, Hungary, Germany, Austria, Belgium and the Netherlands. A large number of stolen vehicles either end up on the black market in Russia or are shipped back to the West to be resold.

Elaborate smuggling networks have been set up, with cities such as St Petersburg and Tallinn (Estonia) being used as distribution or transit centers. Stolen vehicles are usually provided with false registration documents and license plates. The gangs are believed to have bought' border and customs guards in certain countries in order to facilitate smuggling. In some cases, vehicles are simply rented in western Europe and driven east. The number of vehicles stolen in Germany tripled between 1989 and 1993. The fact that more than 40 per cent are not recovered indicates that large numbers are moved to other countries.

Conclusion

Two factors distinguish the Russian mafia from other organized criminal groups – its violence and its ability (and willingness) to operate abroad. Although all mafia organizations increasingly operate on a world stage, Russian groups appear to have particular advantages in this respect. First, the fact that the Red Army was stationed in many European (and African) countries means that gangs often had contacts abroad, which they were able to exploit when they turned to criminal activities. Second, there are ethnic Russian communities across the world, and – as with the Sicilians in New York or the Chechens in Moscow – organized criminal groups tend to flourish when they come from close-knit and secretive ethnic minorities. While these advantages explain why the Russian mafia has become so dominant in a relatively short space of time, other factors explain its aptitude for business and economic crimes. The Russian mafia has emerged at a time when the international business arena is 'getting smaller' – the great technological advances of the last decade (especially in the field of computing) have created many opportunities for large-scale fraud and crime, particularly for Russians (who are generally exceptionally well educated). Moreover, Russian gangs emerged as capitalist reforms were being introduced in Russia – and they have become the driving force behind the economy. This distinguishes them from the Italian Mafia clans, who, though powerful, have developed like a cancerous growth on the side of an already existing market economy.

Threats to the Foreign Business Community in Moscow

JOSEPH D. SERIO

The collapse of the Soviet Union brought the destruction of the last great empire, opening the gateway to one of the largest untapped markets of the world. Simultaneously, mechanisms holding criminal activity in check disintegrated, creating opportunities for extortion, fraud and embezzlement never before witnessed in the history of mankind. Foreign business people ventured into this environment to 'cash in' on what the Russians call their 'Klondike', the gold rush. Few of these pioneers, however, had an appreciation of *Russkaia deistvitel'nost'*, Russian reality, many consequently falling victim to the numerous and varied pitfalls of conducting business there.

For the first six months of 1996, foreign companies and investors brought their business development nearly to a halt, watching closely as Russia's electorate prepared to decide the fate of Boris Yeltsin and the course of reform in one of the world's most resource-rich countries. Now that the fear of a communist resurgence has been assuaged, the next great opportunity for foreign business to develop the Russian market should be underway. However, the threats which confronted foreign businesses previously still play an important role in determining the success or failure of commercial undertakings. Challenges facing foreign businesses operating in Russia include a bloated and corrupt bureaucracy, an unpredictable tax regime, rapidly developing criminal organizations, unfamiliar business practices, and a host of others. This essay will focus on potential threats to business and personal security.

The first part will present an overview of the obstacles facing business people in acquiring accurate information about the environment in which they will conduct business. In an effort to place the current potential threats in proper perspective, the second section will describe a central theme of *Russkaia deistvitel'nost'* critical to decision making in Russia: primacy of relationships. The next part will discuss selected business threats (extortion, kidnapping and counterfeiting) and personal security threats (assault, car theft and burglary). Particular attention will be given to extortion, the most widely discussed security threat facing foreign companies.[1] The potential dangers enumerated may be greatly reduced through relationships with several institutions and organizations in Russia outlined in the final section of this paper. These include embassies, chambers of commerce, private security firms and the Russian police.

Problems of Information Acquisition

Lack of accurate and detailed information hinders businesses from making well-founded decisions regarding necessary security measures. Obstacles in obtaining sufficient information can be formidable.[2]

First, there is a dearth of substantive information. At first glance, one might question this conclusion, citing the thousands of articles, television programs, news reports and conferences that have been produced regarding crime in Russia. Dramatic changes in the Russian socioeconomic landscape have attracted the attention and aroused the curiosity of scholars, journalists, politicians and business people across the world. Significant portions of material produced, however, rely heavily on information fed from Russian officialdom, divined from anecdotes or borrowed, unconfirmed, from news reports. For example, over the past three years the official number of organized crime groups operating in the Russian Federation as stated by the Russian Ministry of Internal Affairs has been cited by both mass media and researchers *ad nauseam*, shedding little light on the meaning of the figure. How was the figure determined? Which kinds of group does it include? If one considers the environment within which these groups operate, does the figure matter at all? How does this information help or hinder decision making by foreign companies operating in Russia?

The very nature of certain types of information outlets does not allow for adequate coverage of the crime story. Limitations include amount of time allotted (a few days or weeks), space (several columns or a few minutes of broadcast time) and rules against payment of sources of information. The first two limitations can be managed when a media outlet makes a decision to devote time, space and money to the subject. The third limitation is difficult to overcome in Russia where, at present, little happens without money.

Another factor is the need for a certain level of sensation or drama. When discussing a potential project, one television producer said to the author of this article, 'I want grim, grim, grim'. There are times when editors or producers at media outlet headquarters far from Russia make decisions that impair the quality of information transmitted. Changes made by media executives are sometimes dictated by the business of producing information rather than the substance of a story. This is not a problem among foreign media only. The collapse of the Soviet Union deprived most Russian newspapers of state subsidies, forcing them to sink or swim. As the editor of one of the most influential Russian newspapers noted, 'We will print virtually anything about the "mafia" because it sells newspapers'.[3]

Fortunately, the destruction of the Iron Curtain provided an opportunity for a more diverse group of information collectors, not only journalists and diplomats, to scrutinize a society in upheaval. However, this opportunity has encouraged observers who do not have the proper lenses through which to see, resulting in a significant amount of reportage that is out of focus.

Second, lack of access to officials and documentation contributes to inadequacies in reporting on organized crime and security issues. It is important for the business executive to build sufficient networks in political, law enforcement and other circles in order to gain access to information not readily shared with the mass media. Much of this can be done by the executive personally or with the assistance of security consultants, private investigation firms or information agencies.

Third, lack of Russian language knowledge seriously hinders one's ability to avoid the limitations listed above. While many tend to downplay the importance of knowing Russian, citing the assistance of interpreters and availability of information in translation, it is through language ability that the business executive can begin to win the trust of Russian counterparts and gain access to information otherwise unavailable. For the business executive, it is vital to have either a working knowledge of Russian or a trusted associate who is fluent in the language. This is particularly true of small businesses which may not have the resources to hire support staff such as an interpreter or full-time English-speaking manager.

Fourth, lack of contacts and language ability will hinder the business executive in Russia from gaining an adequate understanding of the Russian way of life. Not surprisingly, the best material produced to date about Soviet and Russian society, with an emphasis on crime, corruption and security, has been written by Russian émigrés or by people with strong language ability, long-term visits to Russia and extensive contacts in a wide range of government and social sectors and among rank-and-file citizens. They understand very well the system that existed previously and how it is changing.

Fifth, and related to the above-mentioned points, is the amount of time spent in Russia. Many business people venture into Moscow (which is unlike the rest of Russia in infrastructure development, business opportunities and social trends) for a few days or weeks at a time and frequently make decisions based on minimal or inaccurate information.

Many, coming to Russia for the first time, are unprepared to fulfill their task. After a short time in Russia, they return home and make decisions that inadequately address the issues at hand. This has been particularly evident in the inadequate selection process of business partners or employees (particularly by small companies) who later turn into major security risks.

Sixth, dissemination of unconfirmed or misleading information is perhaps one of the most noticeable results of the preceding five points. Frequently, writers link events and people because of vague or coincidental similarities without exploring the contours of a story or incident. For example, in a June 1994 speech, then Director of the CIA, James Woolsey, wrote, 'Recently, a national parliamentarian who had publicly exposed organized crime leaders was gunned down. This was not an isolated incident. Several city and provincial officials have also been assassinated by organized crime groups'. It is true that Andrei Aizderdzis, a deputy of the parliament who had published a list of approximately 200 criminal leaders, was gunned down (April 1994). However, according to the chief investigator on the case, there was no link between the publication and the murder. Aizderdzis was reportedly murdered for attempting to skim several hundred thousand dollars from a business deal in which he acted as middleman.[4] Contrary to the CIA director's claim, it was an isolated incident. While it may not have been the only incident of its kind, there was no connection between it and the murders of other city and provincial officials.

One reason for the dissemination of unconfirmed or incomplete information is the relatively small pool of contacts in Russia, and the information is passed from journalist to journalist. After some time, the information in circulation becomes stale. Deadlines and limited access make it difficult for journalists to confirm intelligence with the accuracy they would prefer. Because there are relatively few people who read and speak Russian *and* have access to officials and documentation *and* understand the Soviet and Russian systems, the number of sources for more or less accurate information is limited.

Seventh, the rate at which the Russian criminal world is changing and the time it takes properly to research various aspects of the problem means that much of the writing on the subject will be outdated shortly after its publication. Mass media outlets are in a good position to communicate information to a wide audience in a short period of time but, because of the limitations listed above, they are not likely to be able to present a thorough treatment of the subject. The most current information with the depth foreign companies need to make well-informed decisions comes from both Russian and foreign private information agencies and private security firms operating in Russia.

Relationships: A Critical Aspect of *Russkaia Deistvitel'nost'*

Surveys of the foreign business community in Moscow show that, due in large part to lack of accurate information on the nature of the threats facing business people, several basic assumptions have developed.[5] First, it is impossible to conduct business without falling under the control of organized crime groups. Second, virtually all police are corrupt and, therefore, cannot be entrusted with securing one's business. Third, there is no recourse for foreign companies when faced with threats.

Accepting these assumptions to be true can encourage the development of a relationship between a foreign company and criminal group. Several companies, concluding that such a relationship was inevitable, actively sought the assistance of criminal groups for the protection of their businesses. Belief in these assumptions is an indication that the foreign business person has arrived in Russia with little understanding of the nature of the system. A brief explanation of a fundamental aspect of *Russkaia deistvitel'nost'* (Russian reality) may bring greater perspective to conducting business in Russia – the importance of relationships.

Background

Centralized planning helped fulfill Stalin's short-term goal of rapid industrialization and militarization. However, it frequently produced low-quality consumer products and created widespread shortages. With workers under pressure to produce specific quantity, quality control was forsaken. The Soviet satirical magazine, *Krokodil*, illustrated this in a cartoon showing a single, huge nail, with the caption, 'The quota of one million tons was reached'.

In light industry and agriculture, planning did not adequately provide for spare parts; broken machinery sat idle, further damaging production output levels. The distribution system was grossly inadequate. Because priorities were not focused on the domestic consumer economy, there was little incentive to devise a system of efficiently shipping goods to market. The system of roadways was severely underdeveloped, causing damage to vehicles which then sat idle for lack of spare parts. Crops rotted in the fields for want of effective harvest methods and modes of transport. This closed circle continues today and is one of many reasons for minimal production levels and significant imports of foreign goods.

A similar process was at work in the consumer sector. There was little anticipation of consumer demands: when supplies of a product were exhausted, there was little or no stockpile for immediate replenishment, further contributing to shortages. When products appeared on store shelves, they were quickly bought up and the supply depleted. This, in turn, led to long queues and consumer hoarding.

In an effort to meet their quotas or feed their families, enterprises and individuals alike were essentially forced to steal labor, materials, food, goods and equipment from their workplaces and from other enterprises and industrial sectors. The closer one got to product control, the more there was to steal. For example, at a local meat store quality foods would flow out the back door to friends of the manager in exchange for goods and services while less appetizing meats were offered to the public. The net effect of businesses engaging in such (illegal) activities was further intensification of shortages, bottlenecks, waste and low productivity throughout the system. Factory directors and managers of state enterprises developed methods for manipulating the system, diverting raw materials into private workshops on factory grounds to produce goods for the 'black market' while fulfilling (or pretending to fulfill) their quotas for the state. This gave rise to significant underground 'private business'.

State ownership of all property created a lack of responsibility for its maintenance or security – a sense that it was acceptable to steal – since it belonged to everyone and therefore to no one. Economic activity which brought benefit to the individual was illegal since, among other reasons, it necessarily involved the theft of state property. Goods and services illegally diverted from the State were exchanged for other illegally diverted goods and services in vast and complex patterns of bribery, corruption and blackmail. For example, in 1991, a mid-ranking militia officer from Baku was faced with the daunting task of raising 250,000 rubles for his next promotion.[6]

As one observer noted, 'Everyone regarded all this as perfectly normal, day-to-day routine that did not deserve any particular attention. Not only did the locals not condemn the system of merchandise payoffs, they fully approved it, considering it unavoidable, since without it a rank-and-file office worker would find it impossible to live'. From this point of view, little has changed for the better with the collapse of the Soviet Union. Drivers' licenses, university examination grades, access to good office space, promotions, customs clearance, export licenses: everything has its price.

Relationships

The system described above – an oversimplification – created the necessity for people to rely on each other at every level of society for an incredibly wide range of services and favors. From the local doctor who treated gift-bearing patients first and the local butcher who could pass quality meats to a friend in exchange for automotive repair services, to the ranks of the

Communist Party where advancement in one's profession could cost big money, most people had their networks of contacts.

In the Soviet era, millions of cogs in the privileged ranks of the Communist Party machinery maintained their existence through complex relationships held in delicate balance, in part, by a chain of kick-backs, dirtying the hands of the vast majority of those who came in contact with it, from the local level to the pinnacle of power. But even Soviet *nomenklatura* elites, who had access to Western goods, dachas, automobiles, the best universities for their children and other benefits unimaginable to the average Russian, could only live *as part of the system* in accordance with the rules of the game. Deviation from the program resulted in swift justice, Soviet-style: deprivation of all perquisites bestowed by the Party, possible prison term, sometimes execution. The possibility to exist independently, unfettered from one's fellow man, was reserved for people who had no ties: no family, no privileged Party position, no friends in the local meat or milk shop, no dentist or auto mechanic friends. They were destined to survive according to the old Odessa curse: 'May you live on your income'.

It was to this environment that foreign business people came with plans for rapid enrichment. Whether during the cooperative era or that of the joint venture, Gorbachev's *perestroika* or Yeltsin's reform, the results looked the same: the inability of the foreign business person to establish the right relationships in the right way frequently led to failure. After years of 'reform', a direct Western business approach usually does not work in Russia, a place where time and money play roles that differ from those in the West, particularly when considered in an environment built on relationships. For example, foreign companies, especially from the West, frequently complain of the slow pace at which deals with Russians develop, spending hours drinking, feasting and discussing subjects which have no apparent connection to business. For Russians, learning about their business partner is an important element in a deal. Learning about their Russian business partners should be a top priority for foreign companies. It is the single most important task in establishing a business in Russia.

Building the right relationships to create a successful business can take several years. Even then nothing is guaranteed. But they are absolutely essential in order to see the deceptions behind the kind words and vodka toasts; to circumvent the obstacles that abound; to cut through the dense bureaucracy; to avoid criminal organizations. Foreign restaurant owners, retail shop owners, warehouse managers and major corporations come to Russia operating on principles taught in business school and leave empty-handed. Others succeed for several years only to see their key contacts retire, abandon them or, in some cases, killed. Even now, years after the

Soviet Union opened to the outside world for business, major corporations and small businesses alike are leaving empty-handed, failing to have learned the lessons of those companies that preceded them.

While building the right relationships is still critical to any company's success, finding a reliable contact to assist in protecting a business against organized crime groups has become somewhat easier. There are currently several Western security and investigation firms operating in Moscow and in Russia's regions that offer a wide range of protective services. The foreign business person thus has the opportunity to rely on the relationships that foreign security firms have developed over time with both Russian private security firms and Russian law enforcement officials. Preventive measures against organized crime groups can be established and response mechanisms in the event of an incident can be introduced.

Information appearing in the foreign media has led many business people to conclude that almost all police are corrupt and that it is impossible to avoid falling under the control of criminal groups. Most discussions of police corruption, however, do not include an understanding of corruption. What is it? How might it differ from a Western understanding? Are the acts considered 'corruption' by Russian society as a whole? Is it possible for individuals within the system to survive without some level of corrupt behavior?[7] Because the responsiveness of police is frequently based on personal relationships, the question of corruption within the police and how it may impact their performance is rarely raised in Russian daily life. Corruption is a secondary issue. The major issue in resolving problems revolves around the distribution of power and police proximity to it and, of course, a foreign company's ability to access those relationships.

Threats Facing Foreigners Operating in Russia

For purposes of this paper, the threats facing foreigners operating in Russia have been divided into two categories: business threats and threats to personal security.

1. Business threats are those threats initiated for business reasons, frequently but not always by criminal groups, and which directly affect a foreigner's ability to conduct business in Russia. Those threats to be considered below are extortion, kidnapping and counterfeiting.

2. Personal security threats are those threats which are directed at individuals, sometimes but not always by criminal groups, for the purpose of depriving the target of personal property.[8] These threats are assault, car theft and burglary.

It should be noted that threats of a business nature often affect personal security. For example, if a foreign business person is the target of an extortion attempt, it is likely that the victim's personal security and that of his or her family will be compromised. For purposes of this essay, this will be considered a business threat but the personal aspects of these threats will be noted. Personal threats are important in this discussion insofar as they impact on the quality of life of both business people and their families, thus affecting the ability to conduct business.

Business Security

Extortion

One of the classic methods for local gangs to accumulate financial means to expand their criminal activity is extortion. It is by no means a new phenomenon for Russia. During the brief New Economic Policy (NEP) period of limited free enterprise in the 1920s, so-called racketeers became active, targeting small time businessmen. One of the best known extortionists of the era was Misha 'Yaponchik', who was called 'the blood poet, Robin Hood of the Twenties'.

By the end of the 1960s, a new 'Yaponchik', or 'The Jap', appeared on the scene, this time by the name of Vyacheslav Ivankov.[9] A member of Gennady 'Mongol' Kharkov's gang, Ivankov gained a reputation for executing his tasks with particular cruelty and would eventually earn the title 'Grandfather of Soviet Extortion'.[10] During the 1960s and 1970s, Soviet shopkeepers (tsekhoviki) were enriching themselves by passing large amounts of their production output to the black market. The chronic shortage of goods allowed the black market to flourish, creating the means for petty gangs to expand their activities.

One of the most significant events of the perestroika era was passage of the Law on Cooperatives in 1988 which permitted the establishment of private enterprises. In addition to creating opportunities for legitimate business activity, the law unwittingly made possible the dramatic development of extortion by local gangs. Because there was no specific law on organized crime and in many cases the cooperators themselves were in violation of the law, extortionists had little reason to fear the police. In addition, local law enforcement officers were known to act as cover for the developing crime groups as well as unscrupulous cooperators. In time, extortion (and sometimes just the threat of extortion) became much more than a criminal activity in and of itself. Like assault, kidnapping, blackmail and murder, extortion became a business tool to be used in the broader context of a developing economy in a society without a strong rule of law tradition.

There are several sources from which an extortion threat may arise.

Teenage wannabes (khooligani). The wannabes are 17–20 year-olds who pass themselves off as young toughs trying to take advantage of foreigners' well known fear of 'mafia'. They tend to wear regular street clothes (blue jeans, sneakers) or athletic warm-up suits. Wannabes are generally harmless in cases of attempted extortion if the foreigner recognizes them for what they are and takes appropriate measures. This category of extortionist is becoming more rare in Moscow although some cases have been reported over the past two years. For example, an American firm was approached by three wannabes in search of easy money. They presented themselves as members of the Chechen criminal community (*obshchina*), knowing that the Chechens have a reputation for being particularly fierce. The Moscow representative of the firm requested that the aspiring extortionists return after three days since company headquarters would have to decide the issue. The wannabes never returned.

Low level, unsophisticated thugs (shpana). Most *shpana* are not involved in extortion to the same extent as sophisticated organized crime groups. These individuals are frequently part of small, unsophisticated criminal gangs involved in shaking down both foreigners and Russian business people. They frequently approach small businesses in their offices and target foreign tourists in places like inexpensive Russian hotels. (These hotels have been notorious for their criminal activity over the past two decades.) The uniform of the *shpana* is primarily an athletic warm-up suit, their behavior and looks usually rough. Their presence on the streets of Moscow and other major cities is somewhat less evident than a few years ago but should still be regarded as a threat. An American television producer, staying at a Russian hotel with his film crew in late 1995, was accosted in the elevator by two thugs dressed in warm-up suits, and was ordered to bring them 200 US dollars. While they waited in the first floor bar, the producer called his security consultant who instructed the producer to report the incident to the hotel administration. The administration informed the hotel police and gave the guest a different room. There was no further problem. These thugs usually target the easy victims and ignore those who become too troublesome.

Organized crime groups. The most dangerous and threatening extortion attempt comes from sophisticated, practiced criminals. They usually drive foreign cars (Mercedes, BMWs, Jeeps), are well dressed in blazers, turtlenecks or dress shirts, wear jewelry (gold necklaces, bracelets, rings) and frequently carry small leather purses. Moscow groups have developed several typical approaches: Two or three of them will visit the office of a foreign company and inform the company that either

1. It is located on the group's territory and, therefore should pay a monthly 'tax' or

2. Moscow is a very dangerous city and the company should employ the group to protect it.

Once payment is made in the first instance, it is exceedingly difficult and expensive to extricate oneself from the situation. The first payment is symbolic in the sense that it is an admission on the part of the victim that the group is acting as the foreigner's *krysha*, or 'roof', 'protection'. In order to break the relationship, an 'exit' payment must be made by the foreigner. One foreign company paid more than 150,000 US dollars in order to free itself of one of the most powerful Moscow organized crime groups.

Avoiding payment to criminal groups without endangering oneself or business is possible if planned with the assistance of a security consultant and a strong, trustworthy Russian security firm. Because one of the basic pillars of Russian society is relationships, the foreign company should find a foreign (non-Russian) security firm that has long-standing relationships with Russian security firms which have successfully rebuffed overtures by criminal groups. Foreign firms should not search for Russian security firms without the assistance of a non-Russian security firm or other organization (such as an embassy or chamber of commerce).

In the second instance, criminal groups approach foreign firms, offering unsolicited advice about the need to 'protect one's business in the very dangerous Moscow environment'. Naturally, group members then offer their services. These are usually non-threatening situations in the sense that group members are very polite and try to put the business person at ease. In order to persuade the unconvinced, later that night or in the days following, the group might break a window at the office or use some other scare tactic to demonstrate the 'truth' of their warning about dangers in Moscow. It is important to have a relationship with a security company so that when a criminal group does make an approach, the foreign business person can show that he or she is already protected and the services of the group would not be necessary. For example, an American company was visited by three members of an organized crime group offering its 'security services'. The company was given three days to consider the offer after which the group would return. In the three day period, the company found a foreign (non-Russian) security firm that had a relationship with a Russian security firm.

At the second meeting with the crime group, the company's interests were well represented. Members of the group apologized for the misunderstanding, not realizing that the foreign company was already under the protection of the Russian security company.

If a foreign company is using an organized crime group as its *krysha*, as many companies do, this is one more avenue through which crime groups can impact foreign business. At the initial stage, relations between criminal group *kryshas* and their foreign clients are usually good. After some time, any number of things may occur. One of the more popular moves on the part of the *krysha*, starting from about 1992, is to request, and if denied, insist, that the company hire friends or relatives of the group members in key positions such as bookkeepers, managers and so on. Chechen groups have become known for such an approach, requesting that the foreign partner hire a cousin or friend who is a refugee from the war. This happens frequently in the food service industry and retail operations. Foreign companies in these cases tend to be small and have little experience in the environment. Slowly the group will take over the company and eventually force out the foreign partners, who sometimes flee the country fearing for their lives.

Partners, landlord, staff. Russian partners can sometimes be an indirect source of extortion attempts against foreign companies. Joint ventures in Russia are notorious as a mechanism for Russian business people to take advantage of foreign resources, expertise and, most of all, naiveté. Frequently the Russian agenda is very different from that of the foreign partner and, once that agenda has been fulfilled, Russians will walk away from the deal, often leaving the foreigner in debt. When security issues arise, Russian partners will sometimes make their own arrangements without consulting the foreign partner. The result can be two *kryshas* protecting the same establishment. From that point on, there can be an expensive, never-ending battle for control of the business. One foreign company started a business with a partner who was directly involved with a powerful organized crime group. Although the Russian partner agreed to buy out the foreigner, in the end the foreigner lost the business and received no payment. The powerful negative criminal force must be met with an equal or stronger positive force, namely a powerful protector. These can be best found through a variety of organizations (see below).

Landlords can represent a threat to foreign companies operating in Moscow and other Russian cities. There have been numerous cases in Moscow in which foreign individuals and companies have experienced significant complications because of landlords.

On the individual level, foreigners who have located apartments without the recommendations of friends or the assistance of a real estate agency are sometimes forced out when an individual who is willing to pay more appears on the scene. In a society weak in rule of law, there is little recourse in the case of a broken contract, and the Russian will sometimes evict with the threat of force.

On the business level, failure to check the landlord's background and his right to rent the property in question can lead to serious disputes including the involvement of organized crime groups. One foreign company obtained office space on the recommendation of their Russian driver. The company had not checked out the driver or the landlord. After a year of working in the space, the foreigners were approached by an influential criminal group which controlled that particular part of Moscow. The group had good intelligence on the activities of the company not only in Moscow but also in several other Russian cities. The group demanded that payment for occupying an office on its territory come in the form of 20-foot shipping containers of consumer goods that the company was importing. In this case, the foreigners were forced to abandon the site and evacuate family members from the country. Investigation of the situation showed that the landlord was deeply involved in criminal activity on the territory and had been informing the crime group of the foreign company's business activities. Variations on this scenario have happened to numerous foreign companies operating in Moscow.

Some companies have made significant time and financial investments in both personnel and business activities based on *impressions* of openness or even memorable parties around multiple bottles of vodka. For example, a number of companies, attracted to young Russians who have a command of English or good presentation style, have hired them without knowing their last names or home addresses. When these companies report theft, embezzlement or extortion by such employees, it is exceedingly difficult for their embassies, the Russian police or private security companies to investigate for lack of information. When asked about the relationship with their Russian partners or employees, foreign business people often comment about their great friendship, common vision or what 'nice' people they are. As it turns out, in many cases the foreign business people have known their partners or employees for less than a year and, more important, took no steps to confirm, through background investigations, claims partners or employees made in the course of the developing relationship. One company that did check into the background of a 'nice' potential partner found that he had been involved in significant criminal activity, including extortion, since the mid-1980s. A less careful foreign businessman was killed by his partners when he brought 50,000 US dollars in cash to Russia to complete a business deal.

In June 1994, one group decided it would be more time efficient to use a list to target foreign companies operating in Moscow and thus paid a visit to the American Chamber of Commerce. Not surprisingly, the group's request for addresses and telephone numbers of members was met with a flat refusal. In 1993, there were two acknowledged extortion attempts against American businesses. In the first six months of 1994, more than a dozen were reported to the US Embassy.[11] A survey showed that in 1995 the figure was 20 for the entire year.[12] What cannot be known from the figure is the number of foreign business people that initially work with the local organized crime group and, subsequently, get squeezed from their own company. Also unknown is the number of extortion attempts that Russian law enforcement and Russian private security companies handle.

Kidnapping

Kidnapping of foreign business people has yet to become a widespread problem in Russia, although there have been a number of cases over the past five years. It is likely that the number will increase in the coming years.

According to Russian police, the vast majority of kidnap situations are business-related, a typical method used in retrieving debts. Political goals almost never figure into a kidnapping.[13] For example, the daughter of a businessman from a former Soviet republic was kidnapped by the businessman's partner for a ransom of 2,000 US dollars.

While many kidnaps are undertaken to retrieve a debt, kidnap-for-ransom is expected to become more widespread. In April 1992, a foreigner was kidnapped in Moscow and held for a ransom of 15,000 US dollars. The hostage paid part of the sum but fell short by 9,000 US dollars. He called a friend in his home country supposedly to arrange the remaining payment. The friend called Interpol and, as a result, the victim was freed and the criminals detained. Later that year, the representative of a foreign company was held for 10 million dollars. The kidnappers hung the victim from the ceiling and threatened to kill him. When released, the foreigner called the police who arrested the kidnappers and retrieved the money.

In June 1994, the body of a 31-year-old American businessman was discovered four months after he was reported missing. Police believe that the victim went voluntarily with his escorts and that the situation turned into a kidnapping along the way.[14] It is also possible that the victim resisted an extortion attempt and was killed.

Many kidnap situations, whether for ransom or the result of a failed business relationship, end with the victim escaping. A number of foreigners who were held made their escape when their kidnappers fell asleep or got drunk. In most cases, kidnappers are not strangers to their targets.

Counterfeiting/Piracy

A major business threat to manufacturers and distributors in Russia comes in the form of losses due to counterfeit consumer goods. The expense of selling foreign goods on the Russian market, the availability of cheap labor, and the high demand for Western goods at reasonable prices has provided great impetus for those with contacts and access to duplicate name-brand Western goods. In some cases, quality standards are rather high. In any event, the loss to Western companies is hundreds of millions of dollars in areas as diverse as clothing, computer software, candy, sportswear, stationery supplies, and electronics.

The computer industry in the Soviet Union was developed primarily for military purposes, leaving the consumer sector with antiquated systems well into the 1980s. The abacus was, and in many places still is, the primary counting device. In the late 1980s and early 1990s, however, computers became a billion dollar industry, whether traded, smuggled or stolen. During the early years of the cooperative movement and development of joint ventures, the computer was the item requested by Russian partners most often. Frequently, after the machines were received, the joint venture relationship would come to a grinding halt, the Russian side having got what it wanted. The next issue was software. As a Moscow-based computer consultant pointed out, 'Probably a greater proportion of popular PC package software products in use are unpaid for (pirated) copies in Russia than anywhere else in the world. Microsoft Corp. estimates that 98 percent of its products in use in Russia are pirated'.[15] The excitement and long queues for Windows 95 in the United States were largely absent in Moscow where the software package was already widely circulated within days of its US release.

Like the software industry, Hollywood has suffered its share of losses due to counterfeiting. Kevin Costner's *Water World* and Sylvester Stallone's *Cliffhanger!* were being distributed on video cassette through Moscow kiosks prior to their release in US movie theaters. Eric Abraham, producer of *The Life and Extraordinary Adventures of Private Ivan Chonkin*, refused to have his film shown at the Golden Duke film festival in Odessa in October 1994 because of the presence of numerous video cameras in the audience. The loss to the international film industry will likely reach into the billions of dollars and perhaps reduce the attractiveness of the Russian market for Western filmmakers.[16]

Foreign clothing and electronics manufacturers and distributors are feeling the impact of counterfeiting operations which stretch across Russia. Their products can be seen all over Moscow and other cities, in shops, department stores and open-air markets. In many cases, the quality of the goods themselves, as well as labels and packaging, is exceptionally high. These operations are sometimes carried out not by people with criminal records but by those formerly involved in the various industries. They bring experience and contacts, frequently using factories in Asia or within Russia itself to manufacture the goods.

Investigation of counterfeiting cases with the goal of shutting down the operation at the source can be time consuming and expensive since such operations tend to spread across several countries. For example, counterfeited American candy products appearing on the Russian market are frequently shipped from Turkey, Greece, Jordan, and Syria. According to the Russian Ministry of Justice, in 1994 only 16 cases were opened regarding counterfeited products. In 1995, the figure increased by only 2 cases.[17]

Personal Security

A survey of foreign business people showed that nearly all of the respondents disagreed with assessments given in the media regarding the level of personal danger in Moscow.[18] Most responded that with proper levels of awareness, foreigners can avoid most potentially dangerous situations.

Assault

Examination of numerous reports of assault, whether on the street, in hotels or apartments, shows that, in many cases, the victimization could have been avoided. For example, a number of assaults inside foreigners' apartments occurred when the foreigner invited strangers into their homes. Included in this are businessmen who invite prostitutes to their apartments. There have been numerous cases of businessmen being drugged or beaten up by friends of the prostitutes who followed the victim and his escort to the apartment. Similarly, foreign businessmen frequently meet people (men or women) in bars and, after a few drinks and pleasant conversation, leave with them only to be assaulted and robbed.

In 1994–95, there were numerous reports of assault and robbery on Russian trains, frequently on the line between Moscow and St. Petersburg. Victims have been knocked unconscious by drugs slipped into drinks offered by fellow travelers sharing the sleeping compartment.

A headline in a St. Petersburg newspaper read, 'Even a Martial-Arts Pro Isn't Safe in Petersburg', as if to suggest that practically nobody is safe in St. Petersburg. Foreigners are indeed victimized but long-time foreign residents of St. Petersburg and local police believe that their city is no more dangerous than any other, and probably less so. Street crime reported in Moscow differs little from that of any other major city. Travel sections of major newspapers carry stories about foreigners being robbed by gypsies in Spain, police failing to respond to calls for help in Paris, and beatings on the New York subway. Indiscretion or ignorance on the part of foreigners plays as important a role as any other factor in maintaining personal safety.

Auto Theft

The rise of organized crime groups brought with it a dramatic increase in auto theft, one of the most profitable activities. Several hundred thousand cars have been stolen from Europe and the United States and driven or shipped to Russia over the past several years. As one Russian police official noted, 'The profit in car thefts follows only that for drug trafficking and illegal trade of weapons'.[19]

Within Russia, criminal groups attack vehicles on the highways, particularly trucks shipping consumer goods. Frequently they resell both the vehicle and the goods. Russian police officials detained a group of seven highway bandits who were stopping trucks, killing the drivers and selling the trucks in Belarus.[20]

Foreign cars in major Russian cities are attractive targets. One foreigner got out of his car in downtown Moscow to ask two pedestrians for directions. They beat up the driver and stole his car. Although this type of random act can be found in most major cities of the world, foreigners opting to drive a foreign-made vehicle should be aware of the high demand in a country where, during the Soviet era, it could take ten years to get a new car.

Burglary

In 1993–94, news of burglaries among foreigners seemed to be in the press or circulating in the foreign community every day. One of the most common conversations of that period concerned steel doors. Reinforcement of the apartment door of company expatriate employees will help reduce nervousness about being in Russia. Several foreigners have had break-ins at their apartments. One foreign businessman talked for several months about getting a steel door. One night at 3:00am someone tried to break down his apartment door. The attempt was thwarted when the foreigner yelled that he was calling the police.

Another foreign businessman was scheduled to leave Moscow on vacation, although his plans were changed. During the time he should have been away, three men broke into his apartment where he and his wife were sleeping. A fight ensued, and the couple were tied up while the three cleaned out the apartment. There was speculation that an employee of the company was working with the criminals, possibly informing them of the vacation schedule of the businessman and his wife.

Another businessman elected not to put a steel door up at all, reasoning that the neighborhood was generally safe and that such a door would actually attract unwanted attention. The advice of a security consultant in such cases may be useful.

Information Sources

There are several information sources available to foreign business people that can assist at various stages in the development of both business and personal security strategies in Russia.

Embassies

It is generally not an embassy's function to watch after each of its citizens conducting business abroad. In Russia, many embassies do not have the resources or budget to perform what are, in effect, security consulting services. A number of embassies, particularly the US Embassy, have made a concerted effort to assist with security issues when possible. Given the security concerns, the sizable American community (by some estimates, 70,000 in Moscow alone)[21] and the staggering business opportunities, security officials from the US Embassy, along with members of the business community and private security consulting firms, have played an active role in coordinating personal and business security seminars and briefings. They have also assisted Americans in emergency situations or have referred them to trusted and reliable private security firms, both foreign and Russian. Information provided by American Citizen Services and the US Foreign Commercial Section of the Embassy can also be of great value to foreign business people.

Chambers of Commerce

Chambers of Commerce and business clubs are useful channels through which foreign businesses can access information regarding personal and business security. The Security Committee of the American Chamber of Commerce in Moscow has worked closely with the foreign business community and the US Embassy in bringing together security specialists from around the world and amassing a significant amount of information on practical aspects of protecting oneself and one's business in Russia. The Chamber of Commerce is actively developing contacts and expertise in Russia's regions where many believe the significant, long-term business opportunities will present themselves. This expertise is vital from a security point of view as both business and personal security concerns can vary from region to region. The American Chamber of Commerce is the fastest growing

American Chamber anywhere in the world, underscoring the uniqueness of the Russian market as one of the last remaining underdeveloped international markets.

Non-Russian Private Security Companies

It is important for foreign business people to contact, through the organizations mentioned above, non-Russian security companies prior to beginning a relationship with a Russian security firm. There are several reasons for this:

1. Many Russian security firms have been infiltrated or established by criminal elements. An experienced foreign security firm can manage the selection of a Russian security firm;

2. A non-Russian firm can advise a foreign company on the screening of potential employees;

3. Non-Russian security firms frequently work with several Russian security firms, allowing double- and, if necessary, triple-corroboration of information.

Russian Private Security Companies

The significant decrease in law enforcement effectiveness together with the dramatic rise in the number of organized crime groups in Moscow and other cities across Russia created a huge new market in Russian private security firms. By some estimates, 25,000 security firms were set up, employing a total of 600,000–800,000 people. According to one police official, one-sixth of the agencies are outright 'bandit groups' and two-thirds are guilty of tax evasion. Licenses were obtained through bribes. One security company was headed by a former police officer and employed several ex-convicts who kidnapped several businessmen for ransom.[22]

A professional Russian private security company can be important to a foreign company operating in Russia. It can determine who holds the right to rent or sell properties, investigate the backgrounds of potential partners and provide guards for a company's office to ensure against extortion attempts and other threats. It is becoming increasingly common for foreign companies to set up their offices within managed compounds or office buildings. Over the past three years there has been a dramatic increase in Western-style office space with full physical security measures. A foreign company, though, may need to call on a Russian private investigation firm to access information.

Russian Police

Stories of widespread corruption in the Russian police understandably have made foreign companies wary of calling on them in emergency situations. Moreover, operating under the assumption that corruption in the police is synonymous with inability to resolve problems, some foreign business people have actively sought the protection of local organized crime groups, reasoning that their support will be more effective and predictable than that of law enforcement. A direct approach to law enforcement agencies in search of assistance may very well be futile. However, in Russia, the direct approach is rarely used in any aspect of life. Networks of friends and contacts call upon each other daily in order to face life's challenges. So, too, must the foreign business person develop a network of contacts, particularly those in the security field.

NOTES

1. The author would like to thank Ian Brown for his assistance on this paper. While this essay does not cover all threats facing foreigners in Moscow, and Russia in general, it does examine those which are most frequently discussed in the foreign community, reported to foreign embassies and responded to by foreign and Russian private investigation and security firms.
2. There are several sources available which outline the threats to foreigners living in Russia. *Guidelines for Safety and Security in Russia*, by Joseph D. Serio and published by Kroll Associates, is a 40-page document addressing both personal and business security threats. *On Guard*, by Drew Wilson, is a 35-page booklet on personal security threats (St. Petersburg Press). *Understanding Russians: A brief introduction to the psychology of Russian society for the arriving Westerner*, by Matthew Maly, is an 83-page book covering a wide variety of issues including 'The Russian Conception of Law', 'The Mafia', 'The Criminal Superpower'. See also Joseph D. Serio, 'Doing Business Russian-Style', *Chicago Tribune*, 12 July 1996. The Security Committee of the American Chamber of Commerce has sponsored security seminars for the foreign community in Moscow dealing with both personal and business security issues. The United States Department of State publishes pamphlets enumerating general personal and business security concerns in Russia.
3. Personal communication, August 1995.
4. Author interview with Boris Uvarov, the chief investigator of the Aizderdzis case.
5. The author conducted confidential interviews with foreign business people in Moscow regarding their experiences and observations of criminal groups in Moscow.
6. Personal communication, May 1991.
7. A discussion of corruption and the role of law in Russian society will be undertaken in a separate article.
8. The very serious issues of rape and murder are not dealt with in this piece. It must be mentioned, however, that a Crisis Hotline has been established in Moscow, and a campaign is underway to increase awareness of victims' rights issues. Regarding murder, several Westerners have been killed in Russia in the past several years including a Canadian woman in her apartment possibly by a woman she befriended (October 1993); a British consultant was hit and killed instantly by stray bullets in a St. Petersburg hotel (February 1996).
9. Ivankov was arrested by the FBI in New York (June 1995) and convicted a year later of extortion. Contrary to most media reports, Ivankov took his nickname from Misha

'Yaponchik', not from the oriental cast of his eyes.

10. In addition to 'Grandfather of Soviet Extortion', Ivankov was sometimes called 'Father of Soviet Extortion' or 'Father of the Soviet Rackets'. In transcripts of conversations between Ivankov and his criminal colleagues in New York, 'Yaponchik' is often referred to as *Ded*, or Grandfather.

11. Michael Specter, 'US Business and the Russian Mob', *New York Times*, 8 July 1994, p.D1; personal communication.

12. Confidential survey of foreign companies in Moscow conducted by the author.

13. Personal communication, May 1996.

14. Joseph Albright and Marcia Kuntsel, 'Police Find Body of Kidnapped American', *Moscow Times*, 30 June 1994, p.1.

15. Robert Farish, 'New Law to Penalize Computer Pirating', *Moscow Times*, 20 Jan. 1994, p.13.

16. Daisy Sindelar, 'Fear of Piracy Prevents Premiere', *Moscow Times*, 18 Oct. 1994, p.3.

17. Dmitrii Dokuchaev, 'Voina Snikersa s Kikersom' ('War Between Snickers and Kickers'), *Izvestia*, 7 Aug. 1996, Russia On-Line.

18. Confidential survey of foreign companies in Moscow conducted by the author.

19. Petr Iudin, *Moscow Times*, 15 July 1994, p.4.

20. Ibid.

21. Peter Charow, 'Momentous Times', *AmCham News*, Vol.3, No.12 (July–Aug. 1996), p.4.

22. Petr Iudin, 'Okhrannye Firmy Razdrazhaiut MVD' ('Security Firms Irritate the MVD'), *Kapital*, 18 July 1995, p.1.

Recent Trends in Nuclear Smuggling

RENSSELAER LEE

Key Concerns

The illegal trade in nuclear materials that has developed in the wake of the Soviet Union's collapse creates serious problems of interpretation for Western policy makers and analysts. From one perspective, nuclear smuggling appears to be a fragmented, decentralized, chaotic and amateurish business that poses no current strategic dangers to the West. At the same time, this activity arguably carves out new criminal trade channels and increases potential opportunities for proliferation of weapons of mass destruction. These perspectives (which are not mutually exclusive) will be evaluated in this brief paper.

Most observers would argue that nuclear trafficking does not qualify as a particularly successful criminal enterprise. Consider, for example, the quality of materials seized in the former Soviet Union (FSU) and in the West. Most such material possess little or no military significance. The bulk of reported thefts comprise low-grade uranium (containing less than 20 percent uranium-235) and industrial-use materials such as cesium-137, strontium-90 and cobalt-60 which pose environmental hazards but which cannot be used to make nuclear weapons. Diversions of weapons-usable material from Russian nuclear enterprises have occurred (the most important such cases are recorded in Table 1). Yet proliferation significant episodes are still a rarity in the illegal nuclear trade.

Furthermore, authorities in Russia and Central Europe are hard put to identify 'legitimate' buyers of stolen nuclear substances – that is, buyers not linked to undercover police and intelligence operations. (This is true even of known incidents involving weapons-usable materials.) According to the Ministry of Interior (MVD), of 278 radioactive theft episodes recorded in Russia from January 1992 through December 1995 only 8 or less than 3 percent resulted in actual sales and these transactions all occurred among various middlemen and brokers. Similarly, a 1995 report by the *Bundeskriminalamt* to the German parliament notes: 'It has been confirmed that there is no market for illegal acquired nuclear materials in the Federal Republic – allegations that there are potential customers for radioactive materials have not been verified to date.'[1]

TABLE I

IMPORTANT SEIZURES OF NEAR-WEAPONS GRADE MATERIALS IN
RUSSIA AND CENTRAL EUROPE 1992–94

Date	Location	Material Seized	Possible Source
Oct. 1992	Podolsk (Railway terminal)	1.5 kg of uranium 90 % Uranium 235 (U-235)	Luch' Scientific Production Association
Feb. 1994	St.Petersburg	3.05 kg uranium dioxide, 90 % U-235	Elektrostal' Machine Building Plant
May 1994	Tengen–Weichs Baden Wuerttemberg Germany	5.6 g of 99.75 % pure plutonium	Arzamas–16 (Kremlev) weapons design facility
June 1994	Landshut, Bavaria Germany	0.8 g of 87.7 % U-235	Experimental fast reactor, possibly at Obninsk Institute of Physics and Power Engineering (FEI)
Aug. 1994	Munich, Bavaria Germany	560 g of mixed oxide fuel with 363 g of plutonium, 210 g of lithium-6	FEI
Dec. 1994	Prague Czech Republic	2.73 kg of 87.7 % U-235	Experimental fast reactor (chemically the same as Landshut seizures).

Sources: William Potter, 'Significant Cases of Division of Probable FSU-origin HEU and Plutonium,' Monterey Institute of International Studies, May 1995; Lothar Koch, Institute for Transuranium Elements, Karlsruhe; Gennadi Pshakin, FEI; G. B. Bindasov (FSB), Letter to German Ministry of Justice, October 24, 1995; Nikolai D. Bondarev, 'Background Report,' Kurchatov Institute, November 1994; U.S. Senate Permanent Subcommittee on Investigations, 'hearing on Global Proliferation of Weapons of Mass Destruction,' March 22, 1996, See Appendix 3.

Furthermore, important organizations and players in the Russian criminal underworld place a low priority on procuring and brokering radioactive materials. The reason is not gang taboos or patriotic self restraint, but simple economics. Organized crime's core businesses – narcotics, extortion, bank fraud and raw materials smuggling – offer secure profits. Yet it can take weeks or months to find customers for stolen radioactive isotopes, if buyers are to be found at all. This researcher knows of only one case of an organized crime connection to radioactive smuggling. In mid-1993, a *vor v zakone* (thief in law) named 'Poodle' based in the Central Volga region was offered 2.5 kilograms of highly enriched uranium (HEU) and a quantity of tritium by a Volgograd businessman anxious to cancel a debt owed to the gangster's organization. 'Poodle' dispatched several henchmen to the Baltic states and to Central Europe to establish whether or not there was a market for these substances. The response came back negative, and 'Poodle' refused to accept the material in payment. (What happened to the businessman is anybody's guess.)[2]

Finally, nuclear smuggling pathways to date have been fairly predictable. Reflecting the traffic's 'supplier-in-search-of-a-buyer' dynamic, the vast majority of illegally-acquired material exported from the FSU moves westward across the Baltic states and East–Central Europe. Much of this traffic apparently is destined for Germany, still the foremost European entrepot for nuclear contraband. By contrast, in a well-oiled nuclear smuggling system, a large proportion of strategic nuclear materials and components might flow southward and eastward to pariah states such as Iran, Iraq, or North Korea or to Middle Eastern terrorist groups.

The visible face of the nuclear smuggling business, however, obscures some insidious realities. The business is hardly benign; in fact, it is highly unstable and could develop in lethal and unpredictable ways. To underscore the point, the discussion will focus on the following issues:

- economic and security conditions at FSU nuclear enterprises

- effectiveness of smuggling networks

- trafficking in dual use materials

- non-traditional smuggling routes

- recent diversion patterns: submarine fuel thefts

- the threat of nuclear terrorism

- inadequacy of Russian government responses

The Insidious Realities

A first and fundamental problem is that incentives and opportunities to steal are rife in FSU nuclear complexes. Economic hardship creates 'an atmosphere ripe for diversion'.[3] Earnings of most employees of Russian nuclear enterprises fall well below the Russian national average, approximately 150 dollars per month in mid-1996,[4] and delays in payments of salaries are widespread. Employee strikes protesting a lack of pay have been recorded in Russian 'secret cities' housing sensitive nuclear facilities. Physical security is improving in a number of sites – as of May 1996, 37 FSU institutes and enterprises were receiving US assistance to safeguard nuclear materials, 24 of them in Russia. Yet thefts by experienced insiders, especially by insiders working in concert, remain an ever-present threat even at the most secure facilities. At the Kurchatov Institute's (Moscow) Building 116, which boasts relatively up-to-date and stringent security procedures, managers estimate that a combination of only four people could accomplish the successful diversion of weapons-grade uranium from the facility. (Building 116 holds a significant quantity of uranium enriched to 95 percent U-235, enough to make several atomic bombs).[5] Furthermore, an underdeveloped 'culture' of physical protection in Russia, reflected in widespread non-observance of technical norms for handling nuclear materials, diminishes the likely effectiveness of new safeguards.[6] As one US intelligence official observes, 'one wonders what the Russians really do with our advanced security systems after we've installed them and gone home'.

A second point concerns the organization of the illegal nuclear trade. Little evidence exists that a Russian nuclear 'mafia' or transnational criminal organization controls the smuggling of radioactive materials; yet supply chains and mechanisms to transport such materials over long distances and across international boundaries already are in reality in the FSU and in the West. (Figure 1 shows a hypothetical smuggling pathway for nuclear materials.) Networks typically comprise loose assortments of former nuclear workers, small metals traders, opportunistic businessmen and petty smugglers. For instance, the trafficking chain that delivered 363 grams of plutonium – 239 to Munich in August 1994 comprised two former employees of the Obninsk Institute of Physics and Power Engineering an Obninsk businessman, a Moscow chemist, a Colombian medical doctor-turned-broker in military goods and two Spanish entrepreneurs in the construction business. In Russia, this nascent dealer network sometimes is supported by a crew of couriers and guards who transport radioactive material. Fees for these services range from 50 to 400 dollars per day depending on the trafficking route and the commodity in question.[7] Furthermore, nuclear trading channels at times are augmented by the participation of former and active government officials, diplomats, intelligence operatives and other 'responsible' actors. Networks typically have fluid boundaries and tend to coalesce around one or two deals; yet some smuggling configurations or components of them (metals trading firms, for example) might handle nuclear materials on a fairly regular basis.

FIGURE 1

TRAFFICKING PATHWAY FOR NUCLEAR MATERIALS

PLANNING
(employees or former employees
of nuclear enterprises; outside
criminal groups)
|
IMPLEMENTATION
(enterprise insiders: managers,
scientists, equipment operators,
security personnel)
|
INTERIM STORAGE
|
TRANSPORT
|
INTERMEDIATE BUYER* OR BROKER
(small metals traders,
import-export firms)
|
SMUGGLE ABROAD
(couriers, professional smugglers,
transport companies)
|
FOREIGN INTERMEDIATE BUYER
(trading firms, front companies,
specialized distributors)
|
TRANSPORT
|
AGENTS OF END-USER STATES
OR 'SOVEREIGN-FREE' ORGANIZATION
|
DELIVERY TO FINAL DESTINATION

* Might accept materials on consignment only.

Sources: Air Force Institute for National Strategic Studies, 'Conference Proceedings: Combatting Nuclear Smuggling', 5 June 1995 (Dr. Schuller's presentation). Phil Williams and Paul Woessner. 'Nuclear Material Trafficking: An Interim Assessment', Ridgway Viewpoints, nos.95–3, University of Pittsburgh, Pittsburgh, PA, pp.11–13.

A third point is that established organized crime groups in Russia have displayed interest in commercial exports of dual-use isotopes–nonfissile materials which are important in the construction of atomic weapons (hafnium, beryllium and zirconium, for example) but that are also used in civilian industrial manufacture. International markets for such substances are larger and better established than those for radioactive materials (they encompass such diverse client states as South Africa and Japan), and criminal penalties for dual-use trafficking apparently are less stringent. In one well-publicized episode, a 1992–93 transaction resulting in the shipment of 4.4 tons of beryllium from Yekaterinburg to Vilnius, Lithuania reputedly was financed by a Yekaterinburg businessman and political figure (Yuriy Alekseyev) with close ties to the Sverdlovsk criminal underworld.[8] An important Sverdlovsk criminal group based in Nizhny Tagil and Yekaterinburg, the *Sinyaki* (sometimes called the third branch of the Sverdlovsk 'mafia' after Yekaterinburg's Uralmash and Central gangs) reputedly trades actively in strategic metals, including those in the 'dual use' category. *Sinyaki*'s other criminal lines include narcotics, smuggling of body parts and 'abortion material', falsification of documents and computer-generated bank fraud. Ominously, *Sinyaki* appears to be an Islamic-influenced group (the reputed leader is one 'Godfather Timur' who resides in Nizhny Tagil) which maintains close contact with counterpart criminal organizations in the Caucasus, primarily in Chechnya, and the Central Asian States.[9] Also, some observers believe that the largest Chechen gang in Moscow, the *Tsentral'naya* group, trades occasionally in nuclear materials; *Tsentral'naya*'s main businesses are said to encompass extortion, drugs, prostitution, racketeering and illegal petroleum transactions.

Fourth, the perception that the nuclear trade is dominated by bumbling amateurs may obscure important features of the diversion process. Linkages to organized crime are not necessarily the key issue. The archetypal modern nuclear criminal is more likely to be the chief engineer or chief bookkeeper of a nuclear enterprise or the head of an import-export firm than a *vor v zakone*.

Russian customs officials believe that diversion of sensitive materials can occur and, indeed, has occurred through ostensibly legal channels. In one scenario, a legal shipment of a radioactive isotope might be licensed and invoiced as cobalt-60 or cesium-137, but also contain an undisclosed quantity of HEU or plutonium. (Such a diversion scheme would require a foreign partner, perhaps a Western European firm with close ties to Islamic countries). The head of the nuclear contraband section of Russia's State Customs Committee, Nikolai Kravchenko, cites a recent incident in which enterprise managers attempted to ship twice as much radioactive material out of Russia as was recorded on the firm's customs declaration. In this case, still under investigation, the apparent intent of the exporter was to avoid payment of taxes; yet, as Kravchenko notes, 'a mechanism for diversion' clearly exists here.[10] Legal contraband via fraudulent documentation must be considered an important part of the criminal proliferation threat in the former Soviet Union.

An additional problem concerns non-traditional smuggling routes and banking connections. While most stolen nuclear materials still appear to move westward across Eastern Europe and the Baltic states, press reports suggest a growing number of smuggling incidents involving Russia's Southern tier, especially Chechnya, Georgia, Azerbaijan and Kazakhstan. (In this connection an official of the Russian Interior Ministry General Vyacheslav Ogorodnikov reported in October 1994 that unspecified radioactive materials had been seized while en route to Central Asia from Kalmykia in Southern Russia.)[11] Where the material is headed is not always clear from the reports – whether west to Turkey and Central Europe, south to Iran or Iraq or east to Asiatic Communist states. Nevertheless, the Caucasus and Central Asia – traditionally hotbeds of organized crime and narcotics trafficking – are vulnerable areas that could develop into a wide-open transit zone for would-be proliferators. Dismal economic conditions and prospects in the region also contribute to the proliferation threat. Borders are porous and customs checks are perfunctory, according to visitors' reports. No radiation monitoring equipment has been deployed on Russia's borders with Georgia, Azerbaijan and the Central Asian states, and these countries to date lack any equipment of their own to detect nuclear contraband. Also, reports abound that Turkish banks such as the Bank of Northern Cyprus play an important role in the illicit nuclear trade, financing purchases of dual-use and possibly radioactive materials on behalf of clients in the Islamic world.

Russian officials emphasize that there are no cooperative mechanisms within the Commonwealth of Independent States to combat nuclear smuggling (although the states do have agreement or protocols to interdict drugs or weapons trafficking). Hence, there is not much sharing of information on this front. Russian security officers interviewed in March 1996 cite a 1993 case in which representatives of trading companies in Kazakhstan and Uzbekistan went to Russia seeking to buy an array of strategic metals and radioactive substances. Their purchase lists included titanium, germanium, highly enriched uranium, plutonium and californium. The Federal Security Service sought to obtain information about the visitors from counterpart organizations in the Central Asian states but received no response. The prospective buyers visited a variety of metal factories and nuclear sites in Moscow, Central Russia and the Urals but eventually were asked to leave the country.'

A sixth focus of concern is the increased incidence of nuclear theft at submarine bases of the Northern Fleet, where at least six attempted diversions of HEU in the Murmansk–Arkhangelsk area occurred between mid-1993 and early 1996. Targets included uranium fuel storehouses and submarine construction and repair facilities. (The thefts occurred at Rosta and Andreeva Guba near Murmansk and at the Sevmash and Zvezdochka shipyards in Severodvinsk, as Table 2 indicates.) The disease apparently has metastasized to the Pacific Fleet. Approximately 7 kilograms of HEU reportedly were stolen from a base at Sovietskaya Gavan' in January 1996; 2.5 kilograms of this material later materialized on the premises of an import-export firm in the Baltic city of Kalinigrad, some 5,000 miles away. That these different episodes might be linked certainly is within the realm of possibility, at least where the Northern Fleet is concerned. A military prosecutor attached to the Northern Fleet is investigating rumors of a 'Murmansk–St.Petersburg gang' that smuggles nuclear contraband through the Baltic states and that offers Russian naval officers 400,000 dollars to one million dollars for each kilo of highly enriched uranium that they obtain. So far the existence of such a criminal organization has not been confirmed (some observers suggest an elaborate entrapment operation by MVD or FSB officials); but neither can it be entirely ruled out.

Another important factor is the threat of nuclear terrorism. Even if traffic in weapons-grade or weapons-usable materials is successfully contained, widespread availability of toxic radioactive materials such as cesium-137, cobalt-60 and strontium-90 is in itself worrisome. Even ordinary reactor waste can be a weapon in the hands of terrorists. A terrorist might fashion a dispersal device combining conventional explosives with, say, cobalt-60 or plutonium oxide and contaminate a wide area. Certain powdered radioactive substances introduced into a ventilation system of an office building or hospital could create massive fatalities. The question is whether the terrorist group in question can accomplish its aims most effectively with a nuclear device, with conventional explosives, or with chemical or biological weapons. Fortunately, there are few examples of nuclear terrorism to date. Recall, however, that in late 1995 a Chechen military commander Shamil Basayev arranged the burial and the subsequent discovery (by a Russian news team) of a canister of cesium-137 in Moscow's Izmailovsky Park. At the time the Chechen leader threatened to turn Moscow into an 'eternal desert' from radioactive waste. Economic desperation can also lead to terrorist-type episodes. Captain Mikhail Kulik, an investigator for the Northern Fleet prosecutor's office, recounts such a case involving a worker at a repair facility for nuclear submarines. After not being paid for a few months the worker decided to post a notice on the bulletin board of the plant threatening to blow up a workshop containing two reactors. Though he was caught, the incident could be a harbinger of worse things to come.[13]

Finally, some recent reports cast doubt on the effectiveness of Russia's efforts against nuclear crime and proliferation. For instance, a reorganization of the MVD and FSB Economic Crimes Departments in early 1995 reportedly cut the number of officials assigned to nuclear smuggling investigations, redeploying them to conventional organized crime cases – narcotics, contract murder, financial fraud and the like. Nuclear sting operations have been cut back. For example, a network of small front companies set up by the Russian counterintelligence service in Moscow, Yekaterinburg and other cities in 1994 to 'buy' (that is, interdict) radioactive and dual-use metals was largely dismantled in 1995. FSB officials offer the pessimistic assessment that Russian authorities are able to intercept only 30 to 40 percent of materials taken from Russia's nuclear facilities. The rest, the officers assume, are exported, stashed somewhere, or simply discarded.[14]

Some Russian officials obviously view counter-smuggling efforts as a low national priority. The Ministry of Atomic Energy (MINATOM), for example, has openly criticized undercover operations as 'provocations' creating an artificial market for nuclear substances. (By contrast, MINATOM now welcomes US-funded initiatives to increase physical security at Russian nuclear enterprises.) A Federal Security Service official that this researcher interviewed in Moscow called the nuclear smuggling problem 'a kind of hobby for Western journalists and intelligence agents'.[15] This is a discouragingly shallow and short-sighted perspective. Current patterns of nuclear theft and smuggling could simply be setting the stage for more serious proliferation episodes in the future, including major covert exports of fissile material, weapon components and even finished nuclear weapons.

Policy Concerns

Nuclear smuggling remains a low-profile but potentially dangerous threat to international security. Smuggling incidents to date have been minor (most materials offered for sale qualify as radioactive junk, useless for making nuclear weapons.) Yet the record of thefts of weapons-usable materials from Russian facilities is troubling enough and evidence suggests that trafficking networks for such materials continue to advance and proliferate. Collateral threats of nuclear sabotage and terrorism also appear to be increasing. At the same time, the Russian government, facing multi-front challenges from

TABLE 2
SUBMARINE FUEL THEFT

Location	Date	What was Stolen	U-235 Enrichment Level	Perpetrators	Remarks
Andreeva Gulf, Zazimsk Northern Fleet, Fuel Storage site	July 1993	2 fuel rods each weighing 4.5 kilograms (1.8 kg of HEU extracted from one of the rods)	36%	two sailors of radiation safety services	2 officers also accused but case against them dismissed for lack of evidence
Sevmorput Polyarny-Rosta Northern Fleet fuel storage dump	Nov. 1993	3 fuel rods together containing 4.34 kilograms of HEU	appr. 20%	two captains, one lieutenant	material recovered and thieves apprehended six months after theft
Severodvinsk Sevmash (nuclear submarine construction)	July 1994	3.5 kilograms of Uranium Dioxide	20% to 40%	4 local businessmen from Severodvinsk arrested; links to workers in Sevmash plant	trial in progress
Sevmash	Oct. 1994	fuel rods	no info.	no information	perpetrators arrested in Arkhangelsk; not charged

TABLE 2 (continued)

Severodvinsk Zvezdochka (maintenance and repair of nuclear submarines)	July 1995	fuel rods	no info.	contract employees of Northern Fleet	culprits stopped before removing uranium from plant - case under investigation
Zvezdochka	Jan. 1996	fuel rods	no info.	contract employees of Northern Fleet	criminals carried material out of Zvezdochkamash but were arrested in Severodvinsk - case under investigation
Sovietskaya Gavan' Pacific Fleet Fuel Storage and Submarine Repair Facility	Jan. 1996	fuel rods - at least 7 kilograms of HEU, 0.5 kilograms of zirconium, some cesium-137	40% to 60%	3 workers of facility 2 employees of export-import company in Kaliningrad	4.5 kilos seized in Sovietskaya Gavan', 2.5 in Kaliningrad (part of same theft)- case under investigation

Sources: Williams Potter, 'Significant Cases of Diversion of Probable FSU-Origin HEU and Plutonium, 'Monterey Institute International Studies, May 1995, Interviews with investigate journalists, Moscow, March 1996.

established organized crime groups, accords relatively low priority to combating nuclear crime. Russia's export control system, while elaborate and procedurally stringent, contains significant loopholes – as noted, legal contraband in nuclear materials and components is emerging as a major concern. Also, bureaucratic disputes (especially opposition by MINATOM to tighter controls on nuclear-related exports) undermine the effectiveness of the system.

Such considerations should guide policy. To date, the US–Russian dialogue on counterproliferation policy has been dominated by participants in the Department of Energy's Lab-to-Lab program. The focus is on stopping nuclear trafficking at the source, that is in facilities that house sensitive nuclear materials. So far, US programs have done much less to strengthen interdiction of nuclear contraband in the FSU. In Fiscal Year 1996 approximately 20 million dollars were allocated for this purpose compared to more than 80 million dollars for safeguards at enterprises and institutes. However, bureaucratic delays and conflicts have slowed implementation of counter-smuggling efforts, especially in Russia. A focal point of conflict is a provision in the Nunn–Lugar (Cooperative Threat Reduction) legislation that requires US inspections and audits of equipment purchased with funds allocated under that law. Russian customs' refusal to accept such audits precludes deployment of US radioactive sensors at customs posts in Russia (Russian sovereignty concerns on this issue perhaps are understandable). Yet the proliferation of crime groups in Russia and other FSU states requires US and Russian policy makers to plan for the contingency that parts of the nuclear arsenal might escape into criminal channels. At this point, the ability of FSU law enforcement, security and customs organizations to counter nuclear smuggling becomes the main line of defense against international nuclear proliferation. Devising and implementing comprehensive programs of assistance to these front-line organizations hence must play a larger role in US counterproliferation policy *vis-à-vis* Russia and other post-Communist states.

NOTES

1. Helmut Loelhiffel, 'Only an Undercover Policeman Wanted Plutonium', *Frankfurter Rundschau*, June 13, 1995, p. 4.
2. Moscow Investigative journalist. Interview with FSB officials, Moscow, March 1996 (hereafter FSB interview).
3. US Senate, Permanent Subcommittee on Investigation *Hearing on Global Proliferation of Weapons of Mass Destruction*, March 22, 1996, p.30.
4. Average salaries for engineers and equipment operators of the Kurchatov Institute and at the Obninsk Institute for Physics and Power Engineering were 100 to 120 dollars as of early-mid

1996. Author's interviews, Kurchatov Institute, May 1996, Obninsk Institute, March 1996.

5. Author's interview. The Kurchatov Institute, Moscow, May 1996. Michael Gordon 'Russia Struggles in Long Race to Prevent an Atomic Threat,' *New York Times*, April 20, 1996, p.A1.

6. William Potter 'Nuclear Smuggling in the Former Soviet Union,' Testimony prepared for the Permanent Subcommittee on Investigations, US Senate Committee on Governmental Affairs, March 13, 1996.

7. Author's interview with Moscow investigative journalist. Moscow, May 1996.

8. Tim Zimmermann and Alan Coopermann 'The Russian Connection,' *US News and World Report*, Oct. 23, 1995, pp.57–67.

9. Interview with a senior executive of Atompromkomploks, a major Yekaterinburg holding company with close ties to MINATOM. Washington, D.C., June 1996.

10. Author's interviews with Nikolai Kravchenko, Moscow, May 1996. Washington (John Sopko's Office) June 1996.

11. Phil Williams and Paul Woessner, *Nuclear Materials Trafficking: An Interim Assessment.* Ridgway Viewpoints, no.98–3, 1995, Appendix 2, p.13.

12. FSB interview.

13. Mikhail Kulik, 'Andreeva Guba Raskryto Yeshcho Odno Yadernoye Khishcheniye,' *Yaderny Kontrol,* no.11, Nov. 1995, p.5.

14. FSB interview.

15. Authors' interview with FSB official, Moscow, June 1996.

Post-Soviet Organized Crime:
A New Form of Authoritarianism

LOUISE I. SHELLEY

The collapse of the socialist system in Eastern Europe and the Soviet Union has been hailed as the end of authoritarianism. With the demise of Communism, analysts concluded that citizens could no longer be denied access to information, restricted in their mobility, or compelled to obey by a powerful central state.

The pronouncements on the end of authoritarianism may have been premature. With the declining importance of the nation-state at the end of the twentieth century, the state is no longer the pre-eminent determinant of international politics or individual lives. But diminishing state sovereignty does not necessarily mean the disappearance of authoritarianism[1].

Post-Soviet organized crime represents a new form of non-state based authoritarianism. Citizens still live in fear but are now intimidated by non-state actors in the form of organized crime groups. The coercive apparatus of the state (the KGB and MVD) has been privatized to organized crime. Unlike Soviet authoritarianism which was focused on citizens within its borders or sphere of influence, the international reach of post-Soviet organized crime groups causes them to intimidate individuals and the media outside the confines of the Newly Independent States.

One Russian who served as a witness in an American legal proceeding concerning an alleged Russian organized crime figure commented:

> In Russia today, it is the same terror system of the old days, just with different people ... My grandfather was a general who was discredited and killed by Stalin in 1937, so I know. Now it's not the communists, it's the mafia, But everyone in Russia is extremely afraid of them, and they have all the power. They don't even have to say they will kill you. You just know it.[2]

Traditional authoritarianism was based on the state's ability to force compliance, intimidate its citizenry and limit free elections and expression. Under communism, citizens were also limited in their economic and labor rights. The traditional authoritarian state, limited by national boundaries, could only fully control its citizens within the nation-state or the empire.

The organs of state control functioned within the country; rarely could or would the state reach outside its borders to control or punish its members who sought autonomy from the authoritarian state. While KGB operatives worked overseas in emigre communities and Trotsky was killed in Mexico, the force of Soviet repression was confined primarily within its borders.

Traditional Soviet authoritarianism was state-based and differs in many respects from the new authoritarianism of post-Soviet organized crime. But both traditional and non-state based authoritarianism affect all aspects of society including economic relations, political structures, legal institutions, citizen–state relations and human rights. The non-state authoritarianism has evolved from the old existing structures contributing to its current form. (See Table 1).

Traditional authoritarianism is based on total state control. The authoritarianism of organized crime represents abnegation of the state's obligations to its citizenry and reflects its inability to protect them from threats against their life, livelihood, or economic security. Organized crime is such a threat because the government is weak and simultaneously compromised by the corrupting influence of crime groups. Government structures fail to protect their citizens because they are collusive and complicit in the organized crime activity.

The authoritarianism of post-Soviet organized crime manifests itself in the following ways:

1. Domination of economy and ruling structures

2. Intimidation of citizenry

3. Privatization of state coercion

4. Intimidation of the press and journalists domestically and internationally

5. Privatization of state resources to organized crime

6. Subversion of emergent civil society

The New Authoritarianism

The Ruling Structures

Traditional theories of authoritarianism were based on the concept of the nation-state or the empire. Centralized governmental control was exercised by a monarchy, a military government or a communist system. Often there was a hegemonic political party or a dictator ruling the state. The Soviet period was characterized by both the personal dictatorship of Stalin and the

TABLE 1

SOVIET AUTHORITARIANISM VS. AUTHORITARIANISM OF
POST-SOVIET ORGANIZED CRIME

	Soviet Authoritarianism	Authoritarianism of Post-Soviet Organized Crime
Ruling	1. Based on concept of Soviet state	1. Not state based: predicated on demise of nation state or complicit with compromised governmental
	2.Centralized governmental control through communist system	2. Decline of centralized control; replacement by regional leaders beholden to or complicit with organized crime
	3. Controlled elections	3. Infiltration of organized crime into state structures undermines democracy and results in impotent state. Presidential, executive and legislative branches unable and unwilling to protect citizens' interests.
State Relation to its Citizens	1. Subordination of citizens' interests to the state and Communist Party	1. Corruption of state institutions undermines integrity of government
	2. Compulsion of the citizen by state legal system	2. Abnegation of state's obligations to its citizens
	3. Citizens often mobilized for state's objectives	3. State cannot protect its citizens or residents from global reach of organize crime groups
	4. State limited civil society and denied human rights	4. Subversion of emergent civil society
	5. State provided public services	

TABLE 1 (Continued)

Ideological control	1. Control by Soviet state over film, art, mass media and scholarship through Glavlit (censorship authority) and criminal law	1. Intimidation of journalists, domestically and internationally 2. Acquisition of mass media to circumscribe news coverage 3. Lawsuits against foreign media who seek to disclose organized crime activity 4. Intimidation of scholars
Economy	1. Under communist system, state ownership or control of economy 2. State domination of labor force or labor unions 3. Disorganized areas not immune from organized crime 4. Use of economic levers to control other states 5. Strategic economic alliances with other authoritarian states 6. Government guarantees business transactions	1. Organized crime groups control large sectors of economy at home base; invest transnationally 2. Create new monopolies 3. Exploit privatization process of state economies to gain control of key industries 4. Intimidation of labor force and cooptation of labor unions 5. Strategic alliances with crime groups for economic objectives 6. Organized crime guarantees business transactions in absence of state protections

TABLE 1 (Continued)

Legal System	1. Legal system serves interests of state or controlling Party elite rather than welfare of citizenry	1. Weakened state legal system serves interests of organized crime rather than state or citizens
	2. State maintains monopoly on forces of coercion and deployment of violence	2. Privatization of forces of state coercion to organized crime.
	3. Absence of independent judiciary and executions	3. Corruption by organized crime undermines law enforcement, judiciary in successor states and in foreign countries.
	4. Extensive reliance on penal institutions and executions	4. State penal institutions are rendered ineffective because of domination by organized crime groups
	5. State-sponsored violence remains unpunished	5. Violence perpetrated by organized crime remains unprosecuted and unpunished by the state
		6. Exploitation of weaknesses in legal structure.
		7. Intimidation now central feature of contract enforcement

subsequent dominance of the powerful Communist Party under different Party Secretaries. In the USSR there were no free elections and elections were controlled by the Communist Party to ensure desired results.

The USSR epitomized the modern authoritarian state, mobilizing its population and using its highly developed control apparatus to ensure compliance from the citizenry.[3] The military, law enforcement, the judiciary and the penal system were important in guaranteeing compliance with state objectives.[4] The Soviet state collapsed in 1991 because it was no longer able to maintain centralized control over its empire. The failure of Soviet power does not mean the end of authoritarianism. Authoritarianism can exist without the state, an idea recognized by enlightenment thinkers.

While their analysis was based on man in a primitive state, their conclusions also apply to the contemporary period beyond the nation-state.

With the breakdown of state institutions, citizens do not enjoy legal protection for their life or their property.

Organized crime groups arise to provide the protection that the state cannot provide as was the case of Sicily in the nineteenth century.[5] But in the successor states of the USSR, the collapse of existing state institutions has transferred individuals from the state to the private control apparatus. While previous analysts have focused on primitive societies which gave rise to some organized crime groups,[6] in the USSR collapsing state structures contributed to the growth of organized crime.

The new authoritarianism of post-Soviet organized crime is a distinct phenomenon blending the privatized elements of the state control apparatus with existing organized crime groups. It replaces the state at the same time that it is collusive with the decaying state institutions.

Infiltration of Government

Transnational organized crime is able to assert control at all governmental levels by infiltrating governmental structures. This undermines existing democracy and results in an impotent state. Once this infiltration has occurred, presidential, executive and legislative branches of government are unable or unwilling to protect citizens' interests.

The impact of organized crime on the development of the state is particularly pernicious in the successor countries of the former Soviet Union that are presently in fundamental transition. Organized crime, by undermining the electoral process, is shaping the development of the future legal system and the norms which will govern daily life and the operation of the economy. The penetration of organized crime into the state exists from the municipal up to the federal level as organized crime groups have financed the election of candidates and members of the newly elected Russian parliament as well as those of other CIS states.[7] Candidates, once elected, acquire parliamentary immunity.

The criminalized banking sector has financed different political campaigns as an insurance against post-election clean-up of the banking sector by the president or the parliament. Their presence within legitimate state institutions undermines political stability because their goals are to further the crime group's interest (illicit profits), not the interests of the populace at large.

In the Soviet successor states, corrupt officials and organized crime groups have ample opportunities to infiltrate and exploit the weaknesses of state structures. These compromised states cannot combat organized crime nor can they protect citizens from its power. Citizens who have resided in traditional authoritarian states still live in fear. But now the source of their fear is different. It stems not from the state but from organized crime groups which have managed to privatize or coopt the coercive capacity of the state.

The State's Relation to Its Citizens

Under the authoritarianism of the Soviet Union, citizen interests were subordinated to the state and its ruling elite. Citizens were compelled by a legal system that did not uphold the rule of law but was a primary form of intimidation for the citizenry. Citizens were mobilized, particularly in the Stalin period, often through governmental propaganda.

Civil society was eliminated by state control of religious bodies and the prohibition of any independent clubs, sports activities or charities. The absence of any legitimate independent economic activity denied citizens the financial resources to initiate or run any activities. In this way the state prevented individual initiative.

State paternalism existed as the government provided for social and individual welfare, denying a role to civil society that might challenge its hegemonic control. Human rights were routinely denied because citizens did not have labor rights, mobility, access to a free media or the right to individual expression.

The Soviet system has collapsed. Both the coercive and the social welfare mechanisms of the state have deteriorated along with the central state. Instead, they have been supplanted by the force and highly limited protection of post-Soviet organized crime.

Democracy Undermined by Transnational Organized Crime

The global reach of transnational post-Soviet organized crime groups is especially pernicious because it denies residents of even democratic countries the protection they expect from the state. With the ability to travel internationally, many former citizens of the USSR have emigrated. Others travel or work overseas, often in Western Europe, Israel and the United States. Even when they obtain the legitimate right to residence and work in their new country, they often cannot escape the intimidation of the long arm of organized crime.

Post-Soviet organized crime groups intimidate Russian athletes and businessmen in Europe, Canada and the United States. Individuals abroad who fail to make their pay-offs have been killed by hit men specially sent from Russia to execute their crimes. Prostitutes in Western Europe are compelled to stay in prostitution because enforcers from the former Soviet Union threaten them and their families.

Legitimate businessmen who emigrated from the USSR in the 1970s and 1980s to Germany and the United States are now being extorted by organized crime groups; law enforcers are often unable to protect these businessmen from the intimidation. These emigrants from an authoritarian state are still living in fear because the democracy in which they live is unable to protect them.

Civil Society

Organized crime thrives in an environment in which there is limited civil society. As Robert Putnam has pointed out in his recent book *Making Democracy Work: Civic Traditions in Modern Italy*, Southern Italy lacked the civil society that had developed over centuries in Northern Italy.[9] Consequently, Southern Italy provided fertile ground for the development of organized crime.

A traditional authoritarian state like the Soviet Union, as previously discussed, limited civil society because such a society could undermine state control. Likewise the organized crime groups which have assumed much of the state's authority view civil society as a threat to their existence. Organized crime groups, therefore, undermine and coopt civil society.

Civil society has seemingly flourished since the collapse of the USSR. Yet recent research reveals that Russians believe that civil society is dominated by organized crime. Their assessment of this phenomenon is not misplaced. Many criminalized companies which, having illegally privatized state resources, now support sports teams and other performance groups as a way of currying favor. Heads of crime groups have sponsored sports clubs. The significant role that the criminalized banking sector has assumed in the development of 'civil society' has prevented the emergence of truly autonomous groups.[10] Many charity funds have been used to launder money. The recent indictment in New York of individuals who embezzled from the Chernobyl victims' fund raises serious questions about the propriety of the management of this Russian charity.[11]

There are no self-sustaining anti-mafia groups of any importance in the former USSR even though citizens recognize the pervasiveness of organized crime as one of the most serious problems facing their society. Citizens working against organized crime have had to curtail their activities following threats. Others have lacked the financial resources to support such activities. Potential activists are deterred by the risk with little prospect of success. They sense their impotence in a society where crime groups and clans dominate the economy and the political structure.

Citizens who confront organized crime groups still live in fear. Hit men are used to silence those who threaten the monopolies of organized crime or challenge their dominance in the banking sector or disclose their activities in the mass media. Law enforcement is incapable of protecting citizens or even legal personnel who stand up to organized crime.

Ideological Control

The Soviet state maintained strict ideological controls.[12] This resulted in central state control over film, art, mass media, and scholarship. The legal system and the state bureaucracy were used to maintain this control. Censorship boards controlled expression and errant writers and scholars were prosecuted or even eliminated by the Stalinist legal system.[13]

Post-Soviet organized crime groups also achieve ideological control. Like the authoritarian state, they seek to suppress all challenges to their economic and political power. Disclosure of organized crime activity is an essential first step to combatting the phenomenon.[14] Suppression of information about their activities is of paramount importance to leading crime groups.

Suppression of Information

In Russia, organized crime groups seeking to shape the future development of their economy acquire newspapers and television stations to restrict citizen access to objective economic coverage. Russian journalists and regional newspapers which attempt to confront organized crime are subjected to the strong arm techniques of organized crime. Journalists are resisting the purchase of newspapers by the criminalized banking sector because it is subverting newspaper coverage. Nevertheless, newspapers and magazines unable to stay viable without injections of cash are often selling out to banks. This is particularly affecting financial and banking reporting on television and in print.[15]

The significant financial resources of Russian organized crime are limiting press freedoms abroad by using intimidating law suits to stifle revelations in European and American newspapers. The *Wall Street Journal* was willing to assume the legal costs that followed the publication of an article revealing the significant role of former KGB personnel in a Russian bank. The suit against the *Journal* was dropped by the Russian side after it had spent millions of dollars in legal fees. Several western newspapers have failed to publish articles that disclose the activities of Russian organized crime groups because they fear the costly suits that will follow.[16]

Intimidation of scholars of organized crime is rare but not unknown. Olga Kristanovskaya, a Russian researcher received threats after publishing her sociological research on the criminalized banking sector.[17] The journal, *Sociological Research,* subsequently was forced to issue a disclaimer.

The Economy

In the USSR, the state had control over the entire economy creating a state monopoly of trade and production. A compliant labor force was assured through cooption, domination or control of labor unions.[18] Strategic economic alliances were made with other authoritarian states through such trade organizations as COMECON.

Despite state control and domination of the economy, a shadow economy existed on a mass scale in the USSR. This economy prevailed in consumer areas not in strategic military areas or the corporate sector of paramount interest to the state. Therefore, even in an authoritarian state, disorganized areas of the economy were not immune from an organized or parallel economy.[19] These shadow economies often laid the seeds for the future development of organized crime activity after the collapse of the Soviet state.

The Soviet court system, although denying individual liberties, upheld the financial interests of the state. Under the communist system, in the absence of private property, the role of government in the protection of transactions was less important than in a capitalist system with competing business interests.[20] Nonetheless, the state-controlled court and arbitration system ensured predictability and stability.

In the post-Soviet states there is no effective legal framework to protect the property rights of the new owners or to guarantee the security of businesses. Trade and business relations continue among entrepreneurs in the successor states. But with the breakdown of the USSR, there are no functioning legal mechanisms to ensure the repayment of debts or the resolution of financial conflicts between businessmen in Russia and Ukraine or Ukraine and Kazakhstan.

In the absence of courts with effective enforcement mechanisms, organized crime, as in Sicily in the past century, becomes the protector of private property and the guarantor of contracts.[21] Businessmen in the successor states hire enforcers from organized crime to settle their disputes within their countries and across the NIS. The intimidation once associated solely with Soviet criminal justice is now a central feature of the contract enforcement of the growing civil sector.

Organized Crime and Control of Markets

Contemporary global markets prevent the extent of control that states once enjoyed over their national economies. Yet organized crime groups attempt to replicate the controls of an authoritarian state. Within the former USSR, organized crime groups are replicating the monopolistic controls over the economy that existed in the Soviet period. Organized crime groups are monopolizing many sectors of the economy including consumer goods, construction and much of banking. They are consolidating their wealth through privatizing the huge resources of the state to themselves and their associates. Organized crime groups, according to investigations of the MVD, now control 40,000 businesses representing a significant share of existing capital.

Investment: National and International

Transnational crime groups have acquired billions of dollars in the last few decades. Highly speculative estimates of the extent of the illicit global economy range up to 1 trillion dollars. Soviet organized crime figures have entered into this global illegal economy since the collapse of the former USSR. Russian governmental authorities estimate that at least $50 billion has been exported from Russia and a significant share of this money is illicit.

With this newly acquired and highly unregulated wealth, crime groups have been able to acquire key sectors of their national economy. In Colombia, organized crime groups have acquired significant urban real estate and large ranch areas.[22] In Italy, crime groups own significant real estate holdings, resorts and increasingly have purchased large sectors of burgeoning light industry.[23] In Russia, possibly the most extreme case, organized crime groups have acquired or dominate a very significant share of the total economy including the banking sector, joint ventures and the highly lucrative export sector of natural resources.[24]

With such significant assets at home, mature transnational organized crime groups diversify their portfolios investing very significantly overseas.[5] While this same investment approach is pursued by legitimate multi-national corporations,[26] transnational organized crime groups do not necessarily globalize their portfolios because they are shrewd investors. In the Soviet successor states, the export of capital and the purchase of real estate and businesses abroad reflects the insecurity of domestic financial institutions and of private property.[27] Not surprisingly criminal groups are already noticeable players in lucrative real estate markets in the South of France, Cyprus, Israel and England.

Intimidation of Businessmen and the Labor Force

Private property, according to John Locke, is to be the citizens' bastion against state authoritarianism. But in the Soviet successor states, organized crime and the financial oligarchy have already acquired property on such a mass scale that citizens do not possess the property they need to be autonomous actors.

With organized crime's acquisition of businesses, citizens of the former Soviet Union have moved from one kind of control to another. The labor force once controlled by the state or state-dominated trade unions is instead subject to the intimidation of organized crime which now operates as a major employer. Individuals cannot initiate businesses because organized crime intimidates all its potential competitors.

Exploitation of Privatization

State ownership or domination of the Soviet economy has been exchanged for control of the economy by organized crime groups which have a monopoly on existing capital. The much heralded process of privatization of state resources in many successor states is proving a growth industry for organized crime groups. These groups presently have the large capital resources necessary to acquire significant shares of the denationalized economy. Because transnational crime groups thrive in transitional or weakened states, the Soviet successor states have no effective safeguards against the criminalization of the privatization process. Furthermore, organized crime control of, and collusion with, legislators prevents the institutionalization of effective safeguards.

Citizens of the former Soviet states have acquired almost no resources from privatization. Instead, almost all property has been transferred to organized crime groups, former members of the Communist Party elite and corrupt members of the law enforcement and security apparatus. These groups now have the financial resources to execute their illicit activities both domestically and internationally.[28]

Strategic Alliances

Strategic alliances are being formed by post-Soviet organized crime groups with many groups abroad, This is not the pax mafiosa enunciated by Claire Sterling but it expands the reach and capabilities of post-Soviet organized crime.[29] The cooperation among the organized crime groups from different regions of the former Soviet Union with foreign crime groups enhances drug trafficking capacities, permits the smuggling of nuclear materials, and the trafficking in human beings. Geographic proximity explains the ties among Asian organized crime groups and criminals in the Soviet Far East.[30] All of these crimes reduce individual civil liberties and increase the authoritarian threat of organized crime.

The alliances are not explained solely by proximity because African crime groups have links with groups in Russia and Ukraine and Colombian groups have worked with their counterparts in these countries as well.[31] In these cases the criminals are exploiting the weaknesses of the international legal system which permit them to forge alliances unimpeded by the laws or enforcers of their respective societies.

The Legal System

Authoritarian societies depend on the their legal systems and their institutions of social control for the maintenance of their power. In the USSR, the state did not respect the rule of law. Instead, the legal system served state interests and the controlling Party elite. Citizen needs and interests were subordinated to those of the Communist Party and the Soviet state.

The state maintained the monopoly on the forces of coercion. There was no room for private police or security until the end of the Soviet period. The state relied on violence as an instrument of control. Random and calculated violence ensured a submissive population, particularly after the mass killings and the imprisonments of the Soviet period. Arrests in the middle of the night characterized nearly three decades of the Soviet period. These state-sponsored acts of violence remain unpunished because there is no accountability of the law enforcers to legal norms.

The independence of the judiciary, a key enlightenment idea, did not exist because the interests of the state were paramount. Legal institutions were highly repressive with reliance on severe and lengthy punishments. Executions were frequently used against both common and political offenders.

Weakened State Institutions

With the collapse of the USSR, existing state institutions were weakened and subject to manipulation by individual interests. Organized crime through bribes and coercion corrupted the already weakened legal institutions. In many of the former socialist countries low-paid police are bribed by or collusive in organized crime activity.[32] Strategic bribes to judicial personnel preclude effective action against organized crime personnel.

The successor states with limited traditions of the rule of law have legal institutions highly susceptible to infiltration by organized crime. They are unable to protect the interests of their citizens in this transitional period.

Privatization of Law Enforcement

Privatization of law enforcement in the socialist context has not meant the same as in western countries. Rather than representing a new form of policing, privatization merely continued the worst of Soviet policing practices while freeing private police forces from legislative and institutional controls.[33] The approximately 800,000 individuals working in security bodies comprised of former law enforcement, security and military personnel do not just protect businesses but intimidate honest citizens and business competitors. Many of them exist just as fronts to collect protection money from businessmen. They institutionalize organized crime violence. The significant role of organized crime in private policing is not confined to the former USSR; Poland and to a lesser degree other Eastern European countries face the same problem. With this massive presence, organized crime becomes a pervasive threat that touches the many aspects of daily life.

International Reach

The threat of post-Soviet organized crime groups is not just domestic. With their global reach, transnational crime groups also undermine the administration of justice in foreign countries. Law enforcers in different European countries have been bribed by crime groups from Eastern Europe and the successor states to ignore alien smuggling, drug trafficking or prostitution rings. The failure to enforce money laundering legislation by compromised regulators is particularly pernicious to the regulation of international financial markets.[34]

The international mobility of the members of post-Soviet organized crime and their access to huge sums of money impedes apprehension and punishment. Criminals exploit the inconsistencies in the international legal system by wiring money through many countries, thereby impeding investigations of their financial activities. They avoid capture by travelling to countries that do not have extradition treaties with the country in which their crime was committed.[35]

Penal Institutions Rendered Ineffective

Even when the courts in the Soviet successor states manage to convict and incarcerate members of their organized crime groups, their efforts often prove ineffective because the resources of the criminals permit them to bribe even top correctional officials. In Russia, transnational crime groups operate unimpeded from penal institutions even recruiting new members for their operations.[36] Detention facilities are presently so horrible that organized crime members threatened with an investigation will pay huge sums to avoid confinement. Therefore, even the most coercive actions of the government cannot protect citizens from the threat of organized crime.

Unpunished Violence

Legal institutions permit the most serious of organized crime offenders to perpetuate their activity with impunity. Perhaps the most visible sign of state impotence is that the violence perpetrated by organized crime remains unprosecuted and unpunished by the state. Almost none of the hundreds of contract killings perpetrated by organized crime groups throughout Russia have been solved.[37] The same problem exists in many of the Soviet successor states. Furthermore, contract killings by Russian crime groups in the United States and Western Europe often remain unsolved.[38]

Conclusion

Post-Soviet organized crime represents a new form of authoritarianism. While Soviet authoritarianism was based on a strong and highly coercive centralized state, the authoritarianism of organized crime groups is based on the weak and collusive governments of the successor states. By penetrating and influencing the already weak government structures, organized crime groups are undermining the states' responsibilities to their citizens.

The authoritarian threat posed by post-Soviet organized crime is not presently as dangerous as that of traditional authoritarian states. Citizens of the Soviet successor states cannot be sealed within the closed borders of a traditional authoritarian state like the Soviet Union nor subject to its comprehensive controls. But the increasing wealth and power of post-Soviet organized crime groups have the potential seriously to impede the transition to democracy.

Citizens cannot enjoy their new freedom because the collapse of the social safety net and of economic institutions has left many citizens in a weaker position than previously. The state can still exercise coercion, albeit less than before, but citizens also face the threat of organized crime. The collusion of corrupt state institutions with crime groups makes many individuals vulnerable to intimidation.

Individuals who live in fear of organized crime may welcome authoritarian controls and the enhancement of state power in the name of fighting organized crime. Therefore, organized crime represents a double threat. Post-Soviet organized crime groups intimidate individuals, promote violence, corrupt governmental structures, limit free markets, circumscribe expression and undermine the rule of law. At the same time, the comprehensive measures needed to combat the phenomenon may lead to a serious reduction in civil liberties.

The weak and collusive governments of most of the Soviet successor states are unable and/or unwilling to address the post-Soviet organized crime problem. The coordinated international effort needed to combat post-Soviet organized crime does not presently exist. In its absence, this crime may grow nearly unimpeded in the coming decades. The present passivity against the growing power and entrenchment of post-Soviet organized crime may usher in a new form of authoritarianism with very severe long-term consequences for the citizens of the Former Soviet Union – and indeed for the rest of the world.

NOTES

1. For a discussion of state sovereignty see, for example, Michael P. Fowler and Julie M. Bunck, *Law, Power and the Sovereign State* (University Park: Penn State University Press, 1995), Raymond Vernon, *Sovereignty at Bay: The Multinational Spread of US Enterprises* (New York: Basic Books, 1971).
2. Pamela Constable, 'From Russia with Chutzpah,' *Washington Post,* 18 Aug. 1996, p.F4.
3. Amos Perlmutter, *Modern Authoritarianism* (New Haven, Conn.: Yale University Press, 1981).
4. Hannah Arendt, *Totalitarianism* (San Diego, New York, London:Harcourt Brace, 1976), Adam Podgorecki and Vittorio Olgiati (eds.), *Totalitarianism and Post-Totalitarian Law* (Aldershot, UK: Dartmouth, 1996).
5. Diego Gambetta, *The Sicilian Mafia* (Cambridge:Harvard University Press, 1993).
6. E.J. Hobsbawm, *Primitive Rebels* (New York: Praeger, 1959).
7. 'Duma Adopts Anticorruption Bills,' *FBIS Daily Report,* 16 May 1994, p.32; A. Uglanov, 'Prestupnost' i vlast',' *Argumenty i Fakty,* No.27 (July 1994), pp.1–2.
8. Interviews with American law enforcement and BKA (German National Police) in Weisbaden, Germany, Aug. 1993.
9. Robert Putnam, Robert Leonardi and Raffaella Nanetti, *Making Democracy Work: Civic Traditions in Modern Italy* (Princeton, Princeton University Press, 1993).
10. Igor Baranovsky, 'To Jail in America from Russia–With Love,' *Moscow News,* No. 26, 25 June 1993, p.13; Paul Khlebnikov, Joe Stalin's Heirs,' *Forbes,* 27 Sept. 1993, p.131.
11. The indictment was issued in March of 1996.
12. According to Juan Linz, ideological control differentiates totalitarian and authoritarian regimes, see Juan Linz, 'Totalitarian and Authoritarian Regimes,' in F. Greenstein and N. Polsby Reading (eds.), *Handbook of Political Science* (Mass: Addison-Wesley, 1975), Vol.3, *Macropolitical Theory,* pp.175–412.
13. See various contributors in Carl J. Friedrich, *Totalitarianism* (New York: Universal Library, 1964).
14. Interview with Jonathan Winer, Deputy Assistant Secretary of State, Bureau of International Narcotics and Law Enforcement Affairs, US Department of State on 1 Dec. 1995.
15. Elizabeth Tucker, 'The Russian Media's Time of Troubles,' *Demokratizatsiya,* Vol.4, No.3 (Summer 1996), pp.443–460.
16. Author interview with Michael Waller who wrote the article for the *Wall Street Journal European edition* and was subsequently a party to this legal suit, March 1996, Washington, DC.
17. 'Mafia's Growing Power Detailed by Sociologist,' *Current Digest of the Soviet Press,* Vol. XLVII, No.38, Oct. 18, 1995, pp.1–3.
18. Leonard Bertram Shapiro and Joseph Godson (eds.), *The Soviet Worker: From Lenin to Andropov* 2nd ed. (New York: St. Martin's Press, 1984).
19. See for example Maria Los, *Communist Ideology,Law and Crime: A Comparative View of the USSR and Poland* (London: Macmillan, 1988); K.M.Simis, *USSR: The Corrupt Society* (New York: Simon and Schuster, 1982).
20. For a discussion of the importance of the legal system in guaranteeing transactions see Gambetta. In the absence of these guarantees, organized crime can flourish.
21. Gambetta, pp.251–256.
22. Francisco E. Thoumi, *Political Economy and Illegal Drugs in Colombia* (Boulder: Lynne Rienner, 1995).
23. 'Mafia Money Laundering Practices Explained, Italian Federation of Public Enterprises' reprinted in *Trends in Organized Crime* Vol.1, No.4 (Summer 1996), pp.96–102.
24. Timur Sinuraja, 'Internationalization of Organized Economic Crime: The Russian Federation Case,' *European Journal on Criminal Policy and Research,* Vol.3, No.4 (1995), pp.34–53.
25. Thoumi; Ernesto U. Savona (ed.) *Mafia Issues Analyses and Proposals for Combatting the Mafia Today* (Milan: International Scientific and Professional Advisory Council of the United Nations Crime Prevention and Criminal Justice Programme [ISPAC], 1993).

26. Raymond Vernon, *Sovereignty at Bay: The Multinational Spread of US Enterprises* (New York: Basic Books), 1971.

27. Sinuraja.

28. Louise I. Shelley, 'Privatization and Crime:The Post-Soviet Experience,' *Journal of Contemporary Criminal Justice*, Vol.II, No.4 (Dece. 1995), pp.248–254.

29. Claire Sterling, *Thieves' World: The Threat of the New Global Network of Organized Crime* (New York: Simon and Schuster, 1994).

30. A.G. Korchagin, V.A. Nomokonov and V.I. Shul'ga, op.cit., pp.68–95; Observatoire Géopolitique des drogues, *Géopolitiques des drogues 1995* (Paris, 1995), pp.59–60; conference on organized crime in Irkutsk sponsored by the organized crime study center of the law faculty of Irkutsk State University, 30 May 1996.

31. Observatoire Géopolitique des drogues, *Géopolitiques des drogues 1995*.

32. Louise I. Shelley, *Policing Soviet Society: The Evolution of State Control* (London: Routledge,1996), pp.173–176.

33. The head of the Russian State Duma Committee on Security, Viktor Iliukhin, estimates that there are now approximately 800,000 individuals working in private security forces many of them controlled by organized crime. July 1994 interview with Viktor Iliukhin, Moscow.

34. Margaret E. Beare, 'Money Laundering: A Preferred Law Enforcement Target for the 1990s,' in Jay Albanese (ed.), *Contemporary Issues in Organized Crime* (Monsey: New York Criminal Justice Press, 1995).

35. The present federal indictment of a lawyer for Colombian drug traffickers suggests that he was hired by the Cali cartel because he had written the extradition legislation with Colombia while a high level US Justice Department official. See Meredith K. Wadman, 'Cocaine and Abbell,' *Washington City Paper*, 3 Nov. 1995, pp.17–32..

36. V.I. Seliverstov, 'Nekotorye voprosy preduprezhdeniia organizovannoi prestupnoi deiatel'nosti v mestakh lisheniia svobody,' *Aktual'nye problemy teorii i praktiki borby s organizovannoi prestupnost'iu v Rossii* (Moscow: Institute MVD Russia), pp.41–46.

37. For a discussion of recent conference sponsored by the Ministry of Interior on contract killings see 'MVD nazyvaet avtorov zakaznykh ubiistv', *Interfaks–AIF*, 3–9 June 1996, pp.1, 29.

38. For a full discussion of the transnational crime activities of post-Soviet organized crime see George J. Weise, Commissioner, US Customs Service, Statement before Committee on Governmental Affairs, Senate Permanent Subcommittee on Investigations, Hearings on Russian Organized Crime in the United States, 15 May 1996.

Russian Emigré Crime in the United States: Organized Crime or Crime that is Organized?

JAMES FINCKENAUER and ELIN WARING[1]

In recent years there has been a tremendous amount of media, scholarly and law enforcement attention to organized crime involving émigrés from the former Soviet Union (henceforth, Russian émigrés).[2] The Federal Bureau of Investigation, for example, has reflected this concern by issuing reports and establishing a field office in Moscow. Newspaper and magazine headlines trumpet the presence of 'Russian godfathers', and publications have begun to appear in criminological and legal journals.[3] The law enforcement and media attention has mostly occurred in cities and states where there is a concentrated population of Russian émigrés, such as New York City, Philadelphia, and parts of Florida and California.[4]

Despite this increasing attention, there has been little systematic research into the nature of the criminal activities of Russian émigrés in the United States or into how they are organized. As a result, we know relatively little about such issues as:

1. the nature of the organization of Russian émigré 'organized crime'

2. the nature of the harm caused by Russian crime networks

3. the areas of potential development of other types of harm by these networks in the United States.

In fact, there has been little evaluation of whether the use of the term organized crime to describe the criminal activities of Russian émigrés is appropriate. Our purpose here is to begin to address these issues.

Conceptual Framework

The assessment that follows is premised upon a number of assumptions. Three of these assumptions are critical in furnishing the prism through which we will view Russian émigré crime. The first is that criminal organization can be usefully examined both in terms of its structure and in terms of the activities in which it engages. The second is that criminal organization is not synonymous with organized crime. The third assumption is that the nature and extent of harm caused is an essential dimension for characterizing a criminal organization.

Structural approaches have proven particularly useful for the study of traditional organized crime, that is, the *Cosa Nostra*. *Cosa Nostra* maintains continuing hierarchical structures (crime families) which are supported by crime and other ancillary activities and that have a division of labor. When criminal activities extend over time, and when the same individuals are engaging in multiple criminal ventures (as is true for the *Cosa Nostra*), a high degree of interpersonal trust among the co-offenders is demanded. For the *Cosa Nostra*, the code of *omerta* acts to guarantee and enforce this trust. Absent the interpersonal trust that derives from ethnic bonds, rituals, long-standing relationships, being 'men of honor', and the insurance of *omerta*, criminal organization will differ from that of the *Cosa Nostra*. Instead, it is expected that structures which either incorporate market elements or, over time, those which more closely resemble licit 'upperworld' organizations will dominate.[5] In the latter forms, coordination of criminal activities would be focused on short-term criminal ventures and would not incorporate a great deal of repeated-partnering of the same offenders. Instead, *ad hoc* teams come together for specific criminal ventures, forming opportunistic partnerships. This short-term network structure resembles what McIntosh called the 'project type' of criminal organization.[6] Organizational structure is created on an as-needed basis to enable the co-offenders to carry out particular crimes. The criminal opportunities come first, and the organizational arrangements needed to take advantage of these opportunities follow.

There can be organized crimes without there being organized crime. Crime that is organized is characterized by the coordinated activity of a number of actors. A criminal venture may be highly complex and require intricate and sophisticated arrangements, sometime including links between the licit and the illicit spheres.[7] Crime that is organized may also operate for long periods of time, as in the case of monopolization of licit areas of the economy and long-term frauds.[8] Once a venture is completed, however, the organized structure created to carry it out may dissolve. In contrast, organized crime structures continue to exist outside of the specific criminal undertaking or criminal opportunity. Organized crime involves coordination of a number of separate criminal activities in different areas of criminal endeavor, whereas crime that is organized is usually focused on a single area. This contrast is in many ways parallel to that between the ongoing bureaucratic structure of large corporations and the structure of teams which come together for particular projects, such as the production of motion pictures.[9]

Organized crime is characterized by three types of harm: criminal monopoly, violence and corruption. Other forms of criminal organization may involve one or two of these harms, but organized crime is distinctive in engaging in all three and in using each of the three to reinforce the other two. Just as a desire for market monopoly exists in the licit marketplace, it also exists in the illicit marketplace. Monopolization represents total control of a market. Criminal monopolies are attained by eliminating competition. Criminal organizations attain monopoly control through the threat and use of violence and through corruption of the legal and political systems.

Violence as a type of harm committed by organized crime may have both a specific instrumental purpose, as in the case of creating and maintaining criminal monopolies, and a more general intent to create an atmosphere of fear and intimidation. Ultimately, force and violence facilitate community control and undermine the legal system because people are unwilling to report crimes, to be witnesses, or to serve on juries. This type of intimidation is more generalized than that which may exist between an individual victim and an individual victimizer.

Like violence, corruption is instrumental in providing organized crime with insurance against arrest, prosecution, and conviction for crimes. Corruption also facilitates monopoly control by enlisting the authorities in the elimination of criminal competitors. Corruption harms the very integrity of the legal and political systems. Law enforcement becomes distorted, and the rule of law is undermined. The supreme harm is in the minds of citizens who lose respect for the legitimacy of the system and who, as a result, fail to support what they come to believe are corrupted processes.

These assumptions about the structure of organized crime and the nature of the harms it causes will guide our examination of Russian émigré crime in New York, New Jersey, and Pennsylvania. We will first describe the types of crime in which Russian émigrés have been implicated and then examine the extent to which these activities fit definitions and understandings of organized crime.

The Data

In 1992, in response to what was perceived as a growing problem, the New York State Organized Crime Task Force, the New York State Commission of Investigation, the Pennsylvania Crime Commission, and the New Jersey State Commission of Investigation agreed to form the Tri-State Joint Soviet-émigré Organized Crime Project (hereafter TSP). The purpose of the project was 'to identify the nature and extent of Russian-émigré crime within the tri-state region ... in order to assist law enforcement in its ongoing effort to combat the threat of organized crime'.[10] Through a cooperative agreement with the TSP, we were able to examine the law enforcement and other (mainly news media) records assembled by the project team.[11] This enabled us to get a wide view of the types of offending by Russian émigrés who had come to the attention of these agencies. The source materials included 404 separate documents with a variety of formats and lengths. Although this, of course, reflects numerous biases, such as the willingness of other agencies with knowledge of criminal activities of Russian émigrés to cooperate with the project, and the problem of criminal activities that never come to the attention of law enforcement agencies, the project staff made great efforts to collect information from as wide a variety of sources as possible.

Although we are continuing to subject our data to a variety of analyses, a great deal about the nature of the crimes committed by these networks has already been learned by reviewing the crime descriptions in these documents. Following the operational definition used by the TSP, by Russian émigrés we mean individuals in the United States who were born in the region formerly known as the Soviet Union, and their children. These definition includes not only Russians, but others with a variety of ethnic identities including Armenian, Chechen, Ukrainian, Azeri, and Jewish.

Russian Emigré Crime in the Tri-State Region

The most common type of crime disclosed in the TSP investigation is fraud. Although the fuel tax evasion cases are the largest and best known cases of this type, other forms of fraud also appear to be common, and the range of types is quite broad.[12] Many involve typical confidence schemes, and, in these cases, the victims are generally members of the Russian émigré community. For example, there have been several incidents of jewelry switching in which an inexpensive piece is substituted for the real one, while the offender pretends to inspect the item.

More sophisticated frauds are similar to those found elsewhere. A number of incidents involve Medicaid fraud. In these cases, bills for services are submitted when the named services were never provided or were actually non-medical in nature. The services not provided range from medical examinations to the purchase of medical equipment. Another scheme involved the use of ambulettes for transportation that were then billed as medical, and the operation of a prostitution ring through a home health attendant service.

An automobile insurance ring which staged accidents in order to receive insurance payments was operated by Russian émigrés in Pennsylvania. It submitted over 1 million dollars in phony claims in the early 1990s. Here again, the involvement of actors in the legitimate economy – the leader was the owner of a medical clinic and at least one of the doctors employed at the clinic was involved in the scheme – are an essential part of the organization of the crimes. The organization of this scheme is not very different from that used by other insurance scam teams.

Counterfeiting, like fraud, is an area of non-violent criminal activity in which some Russian émigrés have been active. There are numerous incidents involving the production of counterfeit credit cards, and there appears to be a well-established market for such cards that are then used to make purchases to be sold on the stolen goods market. The operation of this ongoing market indicates that this type of offense also involves some level of organization, although individuals who purchase the cards may operate on their own. Counterfeiting of checks, Immigration and Naturalization Service documents, passports, and other documents is another area of activity involving a number of separate individuals who organize the market and supply others with their products.

Russian émigrés are also involved in drug and drug paraphernalia markets. These cases generally involve established networks of individuals and include the importation and street level sales of drugs. There are instances involving cooperation with people from other ethnic backgrounds; most notably there is some evidence of cooperation of Russian émigrés with Colombian drug cartels. There is evidence that former Republics of the Soviet Union are being used as transshipment points for drug importation to the United States.[13] Other Russian émigrés have been charged with the operation of factories producing crack vials in New Jersey and Pennsylvania.

Smuggling incidents involving Russian émigrés range from aluminum to weapons to currency to drugs. There are a number of cases of apparent money laundering involving large cash transactions just below the size that would require the filing of a Currency Transaction Report. Drug marketing, smuggling and money laundering are all activities frequently associated with traditional organized crime. As in the case of stolen goods and counterfeit documents, these are areas in which crime networks composed of individuals from the former Soviet Union are providing illegal goods and services through an organized market.

Russian émigrés have shown both a willingness and a capacity to use violence, including murder, extortion, and assaults. Enforcers work in the extortion of businesses in Brighton Beach, Brooklyn. These specialists work for whomever pays them, and there seems to be little evidence of monopoly control of extortion by any clearly defined group.[14] There are sometimes fights over extortion victims, and those victims who refuse to pay are beaten.

There have been more than 65 murders and attempted murders involving Russians and Russian émigrés since 1981 that have indicia of organized crime. A number of them occurred in the tri-state area, and many remain unsolved or unprosecuted. The murders and attempts that have occurred so far seem, however, to be neither systematic nor designed to protect a criminal enterprise. Instead, they appear to have been motivated mainly by greed or personal vendetta. In some instances one homicide seemed to trigger a long series of murders and attempted murders. In most cases, the offender apparently was paying the victim back for some offense. Russian émigré violence is not random; care seems to be exercised in the choice of victims, avoiding harm to innocent bystanders. The threat of violence is clearly used to intimidate others in the émigré community. In the case of homicides, witnesses have refused to come forward or to cooperate with the police. As has been true in US drug markets involving other criminal groups, Russian émigré violence is also believed to be an aspect of the unregulated competition that exists in their criminal ventures.

Other forms of violence or threatened violence are also common. Kidnapping is one example. Extortion of businesses in exchange for protection is also practiced by Russian émigré criminals. To some extent this may represent the continuation of a practice that operated in the former Soviet Union that allowed legal and illegal businesses to operate without disruption by either the state or criminals. One form of extortion in Russia involves persons called 'roofs'. These extortionists offer protection and security to businessmen and their associates. In return, 'roofs' receive a share of the business profits. The term 'roof' is also used by Russian émigrés in this country. It is not yet known, however, whether the term is being used to describe the US extension of Russian-based criminal organizations, or whether it has simply been appropriated to distinguish a hierarchy among Russian émigré crime groups. Several substantial cases of extortion have been prosecuted in the tri-state region, including the case against Vyacheslav Ivankov, who is charged, in part, with murder in the course of an attempted extortion of two Russian émigré businessmen.

Across a wide variety of types of offenses, these schemes require extensive coordination between actors and infiltration of legitimate areas of the economy. The organization of these offenses is responsive to the specific nature of the criminal opportunity, for example, the need to mimic the operation of legitimate businesses, rather than any existing criminal organization. The crime networks described in the TSP documents are formed by criminal entrepreneurs in response to specific settings rather than by existing structures either continuously operating in a field or branching into a new area.

Of the types of harm that are traditionally associated with the operation of organized crime – violence, monopoly and corruption – the one most clearly evident in these data is violence. The violence is used mainly to intimidate the public, potential competitors, and those who might be seen as disloyal. In this respect, the crime networks described here resemble traditional organized crime. There is, however, no indication that Russian émigrés have established any criminal monopolies; rather the offenses take place in a variety of areas and do not represent the total domination of any markets. Further, at this stage Russian émigré criminals do not appear to be using systematic corruption in order to protect their enterprises in the United States.

Criminal Organization

Licit organizations are shaped by their environments, the actors which inhabit them, the technologies which they use, and the nature of the activities in which they engage.[15] In a comparable way, criminal organizations are shaped by the culture and institutional patterns of criminal organizations in the places of origin of their members, as well as by the nature of criminal opportunities and the institutional patterns of criminal organization in the new location. Thus, Russian émigré criminal organization in the United States is influenced by the institutionalized practices of criminal organization in the former Soviet Union, the nature of the criminal opportunities available in the contemporary United States, and the operation of preexisting organized crime activity in specific markets and locations. We will review the nature of each of these influences and how they have affected the organization of Russian émigré crime.

Influences from the Former Soviet Union

The most obvious influence from the former Soviet Union is the set of cultural practices known as 'conniving and surviving.'As described by Rosner, the particular focus of Soviets on illegal ways of obtaining legal goods and services may be transplanted to the United States.[16] The use of bribery, black markets, and other schemes to survive in Soviet society is well documented.[17] Rosner and others have argued that the attitudes towards everyday fraud and corruption can be expected to be directly transplanted to the United States. In the former Soviet Union organized crime and its accompaniments – corruption, the shadow economy, and the black market – first flourished because of the peculiarities of the Soviet economy and politics. Both the economy and the politics have changed dramatically in recent years, but those patterns had a strong influence on those who have emigrated.

Because of the unique confluence of circumstances and characteristics, the USSR in many ways produced a people uniquely socialized to facilitate their involvement (both as clients and victims) in organized crime. Rosner concluded:

> The new Russian immigrant [to the United States] arrived on these shores already steeped in a criminal system ... and with certain skills already in place. It is the conclusion of this study that these immigrants did not change their behavior to ascend the American social ladder. Rather, they continued patterns of behavior that were ingrained after a lifetime in a social system where extralegal values were stressed .... [18]

Rosner divided Soviet émigrés into survivors and connivers, then further subdivided them into necessary criminals, criminals, and system beaters.[19] Necessary criminals were those who were forced by circumstances in the USSR into criminal behavior there. System beaters were those who violate US law in dealing with bureaucratic agencies here. Ex-Soviets have arrived here steeped in criminal methods and values, and undoubtedly some have used these to continue their criminality and even to become sophisticated, organized criminals.

All the émigrés from the former Soviet Union share a common heritage. It includes the state-run, centrally-planned Soviet command economy which produced product shortages as well as widespread bribery and thievery. No area of life in the Soviet Union was exempt from pervasive, universal corruption. Scarce goods and services which were unavailable through normal channels could usually be gotten through *blat* (connections) or *na levo* (on the left). An illegal second or shadow economy arose to operate in tandem with the official economy.

The notorious Soviet black market was a component of the shadow economy. It marketed a wide variety of products from Western consumer items to stolen goods, drugs, and bootleg liquor and cigarettes. Because goods were priced much higher on the black market, there was also incentive to siphon off goods from the official market for sale on the black market. There is considerable evidence that this practice has not ended with the collapse of the Soviet Union, but, rather, it has expanded. The nature of the goods being marketed has become much more sophisticated, and the consumer market itself has become much more international. The amount of money involved is much greater. The range of illegal goods being marketed today through multi-national links includes antiques, drugs, stolen cars, weapons (including nuclear weapons materials), metals, etc. It has been projected that organized crime in the former USSR may quickly move into such areas as video piracy, crack refining, and computer crime.[20]

The *perestroika* reforms of the late 1980s, and the demise of the USSR itself in 1991, followed by the economic problems of the past several years have all fed an enormous growth of new forms of organized crime in Russia. It is under these conditions that some of the traditional activities of Western organized crime (mostly unknown in the old Soviet Union), such as drug trafficking and prostitution, but especially extortion of new companies, businesses, and restaurants, have become among the more prevalent forms of current criminal enterprises in Moscow and other Russian cities.

The old Soviet political and socioeconomic system bred illegality and corruption on a scale matched by few countries.[21] Simis described the pervasiveness of Soviet corruption and its links to the shadow economy:

> Underground enterprise is a positive tumor of corruption. Like a drop of water, it reflects the whole world of Soviet improbity. Just as the human body cannot live without air; underground enterprise could not survive except for the fact that the Soviet state and society alike are rotten with corruption from the top to bottom.[22]

Although the partocracy of the Communist Party which engendered this kind of corruption is gone, there is every indication that so far at least the crime and corruption have only gotten worse.[23]

Criminal Patterns from the Former Soviet Union

Beyond these cultural explanations, however, lie institutional ones. Those Russian émigrés who are criminally active in the United States will follow patterns and structures similar to those that they are familiar with from their places of origin. This allows us to look at how crime is organized, instead of why people have certain attitudes towards crime and the police, or differing propensities to commit crime. Existing analyses of types of offenders in the former Soviet Union identify four major categories, each of which may have a place among Russian émigrés in the United States. They are professional criminals, criminal entrepreneurs, 'thieves in authority' and the *vory v zakone* or 'thieves in law'. There is some evidence of the operation of each of these types among Russian émigrés in the United States.

Ordinary professional criminals are those who make their living through criminal activity and who specialize in particular crime types.[24] Often, they know each other and either worked with each other or were in jail together in the Soviet Union. These criminal types are of varying levels of criminal sophistication. One of the predominant criminal professions, for example, is pickpocket. There are many examples of professional criminals from the former Soviet Union who are involved in crime in the United States, although in some instances they branched into new areas. For example, David Schuster, who was involved in one of the bootleg gasoline scams in New Jersey, was known as a professional pickpocket back home.

The young entrepreneurs see crime as the easy route to riches.[25] These are young people – in their late 'teens, twenties and thirties – who were not criminals before the collapse of the Soviet Union, but who did of necessity have experience in the black market and the shadow economy. Some are students or graduates of higher education; others were in the military. None has attractive job prospects in the legitimate sector. They are a pool for recruitment by criminal organizations in Russia, or they operate with their own small networks. Unlike that of the professionals, their criminal behavior is not very well entrenched. They are first generation criminals, and their crimes are most often crimes of opportunity.

The 'thieves in authority' (*avtoritety*), labeled comrade criminals by Handelman, emerged largely during the last decades of the Soviet Union, especially during the Brezhnev period. Some were part of the *nomenklatura* of the Communist Party or were Soviet bureaucrats. Some were deputy directors, former administrators of factories or other business enterprises, or ran cooperatives during the Gorbachev era. Some were members of the national security and military establishments. Whatever their specific background, nearly all of them are well educated; they often had international connections before the collapse. Vaksberg called this group the Soviet Mafia.[26] As Handelman points out, these 'gangster-bureaucrats' operate at the intersection of crime, capitalism, and government in the former Soviet Union.[27] They have the knowledge, the experience, the sophistication, and the contacts, to run international banking schemes and major commodities deals. They are also the ones best suited to deal in black market nuclear materials. For these reasons, they have the greatest potential for future harm.

Reputed members of the *vory v zakone* have been said to be the closest thing the ex-Soviets have to being a 'made guy' in the *Cosa Nostra*, and the top members are portrayed as godfather-like figures. The *vory* are the most criminally sophisticated of the professional criminals. Their roots are generally traced to the Soviet prison system, particularly the Stalinist *gulag* of the 1930s. They are characterized by a complete commitment to the criminal life. Following their own laws and rules, they reject any involvement with or obligation to the legitimate world. The *vory* have a relatively non-hierarchical structure, with a low differentiation among the members, and an elite that is considered the first among equals.[28] Afanasyev reports an estimated 600 *vory* in the former Soviet Union, with approximately 200 of them in Russia itself.[29] He says there is a Moscow-based 'politburo'of 10 to 15 *vory* who govern the criminal world through their representatives. Ivankov, arrested with much attention in New York, is believed to be one of the Russian *vory*, and perhaps even among the top leadership group.[30] The FBI estimates that there have been four other *vory v zakone* in the United States at one time or another.[31]

The *vory* share a number of characteristics with other criminal organizations and subcultures, including a set of rules and a code of behavior, nicknames, a slang, and the ability to eject members from the association. They also have a system for mediating and resolving disputes. Whether there is any enforcement mechanism to back-up these resolutions is not clear.

Some challenge the importance of the *vory* both now and as a future threat in the United States.[32] It is alleged that the traditional initiation into the *vory* has been corrupted by the selling of the title of *vor*. If this is so it could mean that there will be increasing difficulty with maintaining internal discipline. The criminal expertise of the *vory* revolves around common crimes like theft, robbery, and extortion. The complex crimes of commodities scams, international banking, dealing in strategic metals, and international money laundering are beyond the scope of criminal expertise for most of them. They may be the most criminally sophisticated at present, but this may change over the long term. Afanasyev and others believe that although the *vory* still dominate the traditional criminal world, especially in prison, the so-called comrade criminals and gangster bureaucrats, with their intertwined links to the government, are growing in dominance of the social, economic, and political structures of the former Soviet Union.[33] Except for money laundering opportunities, the former USSR itself is right now the more ripe location for criminal activities of the comrade criminals, but when that is no longer the case – perhaps 10 or 15 years from now – we can look for them to shift their sights to the United States and elsewhere.

Influence of the Four Types in the United States

Of the four major forms of criminal organizations, the *vory v zakone* may constitute the greatest potential criminal threat currently presented by Russian émigrés in the United States. Whether this threat develops into a reality depends upon a number of contingencies including the presence of a sufficient number of *vory* in the United States, how closely they are linked to the Moscow-based crime leaders, and how successfully they can organize and control the multitude of criminal ventures in which ex-Soviets who are not *vory* are involved in the United States. The potential for harm from the *vory* will depend on how well some semblance of internal discipline can be maintained outside the prison walls where their roots lie. This control will be complicated by the fact that criminal activity is now taking place thousands of miles away from Moscow.

The comrade criminals also pose a potential threat to the United States in the sense that they can interfere with business, trade in dangerous weapons and materials, and interfere with the ability of US authorities to control crime. The threat of Russian émigré criminals seeking to use corruption and collusion to undermine United States law enforcement and other government agencies through the recreation of the comrade criminal status is, as of now, more of a potential than an actual harm. There have been allegations and rumors about police payoffs, for example, but so far no hard evidence has been offered and no corruption cases have been brought. Although they have the knowledge and the money, Russian émigrés do not now have the political contacts and the power to influence the legal and political processes in the United States. However, given that the individuals involved in criminal activity here are products of a system that is used to buying politicians and government officials, and in which corruption is a way of life, it would be naive to believe that American officials cannot be corrupted by these same individuals. At the same time, the pervasive corruption that has been acknowledged to exist throughout governments in the former Soviet republics creates problems for American law enforcement in collaborating with their counterparts in those countries. Thus, for example, attempting to find out whether a suspect now in the United States has a criminal history or is currently under investigation is complicated when there is a substantial risk that the target will be informed about the inquiry. The Immigration and Naturalization Service indicates that it is often impossible to find out if a visa applicant has a criminal background. In these and other ways corruption in the former USSR facilitates Russian émigré crime in the United States.

Although the *vory v zakone* and the comrade criminals may pose the greatest hypothetical threat to the United States, current criminal activity among Russian émigrés much more often takes the form of either professional criminal activity or entrepreneurial crime. Professional criminals carry out confidence schemes, low level thefts, and use of counterfeit credit cards. Entrepreneurial offenders take advantage of specific opportunities, such as those for insurance frauds, tax schemes, long term frauds, and cooperation with other crime groups. At this point there has been no substantial evidence that these activities are operated primarily by individuals with connections to the *vory v zakone* or comrade criminals in the former Soviet Union.

The Influence of Criminal Opportunities in the United States

Criminal organization usually is structured in a way that is thought to be effective for achieving the illegal aims of the organizers. At the same time, the expansion of opportunities for defrauding of government programs, and the ability to take advantage of credit systems that are much more widespread than they were in the past means that organizational forms that are effective in these types of environments may emerge. The frauds of various types, counterfeiting, and marketing of stolen goods that are most frequently found in the TSP files are, regardless of ethnicity, generally committed by small networks of individuals, some of whom may be specialists.[34] In the case of low-level confidence games, this team structure allows the offenders to gain the trust of the victims but to retain the ability to disappear after the deception is revealed. In order to defraud social welfare programs, offenders have to pose as legitimate actors in the system, such as pharmacists, patients, and ambulette companies. It would be very difficult for a single actor to create this appearance successfully. Instead, a network of actors can serve to create the appearance of legitimacy. However, once the scheme is over there is no need or benefit for the exact same set of actors to continue to cooperate. Therefore, a project-oriented network structure is likely to emerge as a consequence of the types of crime being committed.

The Influence of Existing US Patterns of Criminal Organization

DiMaggio and Powell call the tendency for organizations operating in the same areas of endeavor to resemble each other isomorphism.[35] They suggest that three types of forces – mimetic, coercive and normative – operate to create isomorphism. Mimetic isomorphism occurs when one structure is deliberately constructed as an imitation of another. Coercive pressures operate when one organization is forced by another to adopt a particular structure or element of structure, for example by requiring that such a structure be present in order for an organization to receive a resource. Normative pressures operate when individuals in an area of endeavor, who may move from organization to organization, come to expect or prefer a given set of structural arrangements. All of these pressures for similarity to other crime networks may operate on Russian émigré crime networks.

Some authorities have compared the organized crime among Russian émigrés to the American *Cosa Nostra* structure as described by Cressey [36] and others. For example, agents of the Federal Bureau of Investigation have stated that there are between three and five Russian émigré organized crime families in the New York area,[37] and investigators occasionally informally comment that some émigrés try to imitate the 'mob style.' Cooperation between Russian émigrés and individuals associated with the Colombo crime family members in the bootleg gas tax evasion scheme would also seemingly lead to the operation of institutional processes influencing the Russian émigrés to adopt an organizational structure similar to all or part of that of the Colombo family. The reported ties of Russian émigrés to other hierarchical organized crime structures would also seem to support this.[38] Other existing forms of criminal organization, such as those in other communities of recently arrived immigrants, may also be influential if they are seen as successful.[39] The cooperation of Russian émigré criminals with the Cali cartel may, therefore, lead them to adopt a similar structure. Because of the actual nature of the crimes in which Russian émigrés have been involved, it is perhaps more likely that they are influenced by the criminal organization of other groups involved in similar crimes. For example, the auto insurance scheme and some of the Medicaid reimbursement schemes are similar to those operated by other groups.

Actual Russian Emigré Criminal Organization in the United States

Russian émigré criminals operating in the United States have been described by some law enforcement authorities and by some in the media as being structured much like the *Cosa Nostra*. When Vyacheslav Ivankov was arrested in June, 1995, he was labeled the 'capo di tutti capos' of Russian émigré crime in the United States.[40] His arrest was taken as proof of a centralized Russian émigré criminal organization, along the lines of the *Cosa Nostra*.

Another view is that Russian émigré crime networks have no defined organizational structures or hierarchies that look anything like the *Cosa Nostra*.[41] Instead of being organized, according to this view, they operate mostly as individual specialists. As such, they have very fluid groups that occasionally come together to commit a crime. They do not have rigidly authoritarian and hierarchical structures, and the people involved do not answer to anybody in particular.

It is our assessment that neither of these positions is accurate. Our preliminary analyses of the TSP information indicate that there are large ongoing networks of individuals identified by law enforcement as involved or suspected of criminal activities who are directly or indirectly connected to each other. However, there is no evidence of a complex hierarchy or set of hierarchies. Instead, *ad hoc* teams of specialists are mustered for specific criminal ventures in an opportunistic manner. They may move across ventures, and sometimes work on the basis of referrals, vouching for each other. They often create flexible, project-oriented structures, to enable them to carry out particular crimes. In this they do not differ greatly from current trends in licit organizations, where there are indications of a decrease in the amount and degree of hierarchy, increasing reliance on strategic partnerships and task groups, and growing reliance on third party service providers.[42]

The predominant structure is one in which individuals who knew each other in the former Soviet Union, or who know people who know each other, collaborate for some particular criminal opportunity. The backgrounds of these individuals vary, but overall, the non-*vory* professional criminals and the opportunists who currently dominate Russian émigré crime here typically mistrust each other. There are few references to loyalty based on shared ethnicity or culture, despite the fact that some of the players knew each other prior to emigration. With the exception of the gas tax scheme and rare other exceptions, however, Russian émigré criminals seem to associate mainly with each other both criminally and socially.

The use of this type of flexible structure by Russian émigré criminals in the United States is a product of a number of forces. Perhaps most important, it represents a continuation of the patterns and practices that were institutionalized in the former Soviet Union. In particular it reflects the dominance of professional criminals and the young entrepreneurial offenders, rather than the *vory v zakone* or the comrade criminals. Second, it is well-suited to the types of offending in which these criminals are involved. This most often requires team work, flexibility, and the ability to mimic the operation of a legitimate actor or organization. Fraud and confidence schemes, and also certain violent crimes are particularly suited to this type of structure, while control of the gambling in a given area or other similar activities seem not to be. Should any of these situations change, however, for example if the *vory* emerge as important long-term actors in the United States, or if the nature of the crimes in which they are involved should shift, this could all change.

NOTES

1. The writing of this paper was supported by grant No.93–1–CX–0019 from the National Institute of Justice. The views expressed in this paper are those of the authors and may not reflect those of the US Department of Justice, the National Institute of Justice, the Tri-State Soviet-émigré Organized Crime Project or any of its members or cooperating agencies. Emmanual Barthe and Paul T. Haskell provided assistance with the collection and organization of these data. Don Sobocienski of the New York State Organized Crime Task Force provided a number of important insights.

2. We use this general characterization for simplicity's sake, recognizing the distinction between émigrés and immigrants, and also that many émigrés to the United States from the former Soviet Union are not Russians. Virtually all of the émigrés speak Russian.

3. For example, Scott Anderson 'Looking For Mr. Yaponchik', *Harper's*, Dec. 1995, pp.40–51; Traci Anne Attanasio, 'How Russian Organized Crime Took Root in the US', *Organized Crime Digest*, Vol.15, No.19, 12 Oct. 1994, p.1; Robert I. Friedman, 'The Organizatsiya', *New York*, 7 Nov. 1994, pp.50–58; Selwyn Raab, 'New Group of Russian Gangs Gains Foothold in Brooklyn', *The New York Times*, 23 Aug. 1994, p.1; Lydia S. Rosner, 'The Sexy Russian Mafia', *Criminal Organizations*, Vol.10 No.1 (1995); *The Times* (Trenton), 'New Comrades of Crime', *The Times*, 14 Aug. 1995, p.A1.

4. California Department of Justice *Russian Organized Crime: California's Newest Threat* (Sacramento, CA: 1995); authors's interviews with DEA and INS officials, Miami, FL, June 1995.

5. Walter W. Powell, 'Neither Hierarchies nor Markets', *Research in Organizational Behavior* in Barry Shaw and L.L. Cummings (eds.), Vol.12 (Greenwich: JAI Press, 1990), pp. 295–336; Oliver Williamson, *Markets and Hierarchies: Analysis and Antitrust Implications* (New York: The Free Press, 1975).

6. Mary McIntosh, *The Organization of Crime* (London: Macmillan, 1975).

7. See, for example, David Weisburd, Stanton Wheeler, Elin Waring and Nancy Bode, *Crimes of the Middle Classes* (New Haven: Yale University Press, 1991).

8. Ibid.

9. Wayne E. Baker and Robert R. Faulkner 'Role as Resource in the Hollywood Film Industry', *American Journal of Sociology*, Vol.97 (1991), pp.279–309.

10. The Tri-State Joint Soviet-Emigré Organized Crime Project, *An Analysis of Russian-Emigré Crime in the Tri-State Region* (New York, NY: New York State Commission of Investigation, 1996), p.1. See below.

11. We had complete access to investigative reports, memos, information from other agencies and other investigative materials collected by the TSP. However, we did not have access to grand jury transcripts, the identities of confidential informants, and other similar materials.

12. Alan A. Block, 'Racketeering in Fuels: Tax Scamming by Organized Crime', in Alan A. Block (ed.), *Space, Time, and Organized Crime* (2nd ed.) (New Brunswick, NJ:Transaction Books, 1994); Richter H. Moore, Jr., 'Motor Fuel Tax Fraud and Organized Crime: The Russian and the Italian–American Mafia', in Jay Albanese (ed.), *Contemporary Issues in Organized Crime* (Monsey, NY: Criminal Justice Press, 1995), pp.189–200.

13. Louis Freeh, Testimony before the Senate Permanent Subcommittee on Investigation, 25 May 1994, 100 Russell Senate Office Building, Washington, DC.

14. The Tri-State Joint Soviet-Emigré Organized Crime Project, op. cit., p.33.

15. Howard Aldrich, *Organizations and Environments* (Englewood Cliffs: Prentice-Hall, 1979); Paul DiMaggio and Walter W. Powell, 'The Iron Cage Revisited: Institutional Isomorphism and Collective Rationality in Organizational Fields', *American Sociological Review*, Vol.48 (1983), pp.147–160; Richard Scott, *Institutions and Organizations* (Thousand Oaks, CA: Sage Publications, 1995).

16. Lydia S. Rosner, *The Soviet Way of Crime: Beating the System in the Soviet Union and the USA* (South Hadley, MA: Bergin and Garvey Publishers, 1986) .

17. Konstantin M.Simis, *USSR: The Corrupt Society* (New York: Simon and Schuster, 1982).

18. Rosner, op. cit., 132–133.

19. Ibid.

20. Mark Galeotti, 'Organized Crime in Moscow and Russian National Security', *Low Intensity Conflict and Law Enforcement*, Vol.1, No.3 (Winter 1992).

21. Simis, op. cit.

22. Ibid., p.179.

23. See Steven Handelman, *Comrade Criminal* (New Haven: Yale University Press, 1995); Claire Sterling, *Thieves' World* (New York: Simon and Schuster, 1994).

24. Marshall Clinard, and Richard Quinney, *Criminal Behavior Systems: A Typology* (New York:

Holt, Rinehart and Winston, 1967).
25. Handelman, op. cit.
26. Arkady Vaksberg, *The Soviet Mafia* (New York: St. Martins Press, 1991).
27. Handelman, op. cit.
28. Vyacheslav Afanasyev, 'Organized Crime and Society', *Demokratizatsiya,* Vol.II (Summer 1994), pp.426–441.
29. The FBI has reported that there are 279 *vory* in Russia. James Moody, 'Remarks', Fifth Annual Economic Crime Investigation Conference, New York, NY, Sponsored by Utica College of Syracuse University (Oct. 1994).
30. Friedman, 1994, op. cit.
31. Moody, 1994, op. cit.
32. Afanasyev, op. cit.
33. Handelman, op. cit.
34. Elin J. Waring, *Co-Offending in White Collar Crime: A Network Approach* (Ann Arbor, Michigan: University Microfilms International, 1993).
35. DiMaggio and Powell, op. cit.
36. Donald Cressey, *Criminal Organization: Its Elementary Forms* (New York: Harper and Row, 1972).
37. John Stafford, 'Remarks', First International Law Enforcement Sharing Conference on Russian Organized Crime, 19–23 Sept. 1994.
38. Nathan M. Adams, 'Menace of the Russian Mafia', *Reader's Digest* (Aug. 1992), pp.33–40; Robert I. Friedman, 'Brighton Beach Goodfellas', *Vanity Fair* (Jan. 1993), pp.26–41.
39. William Kleinknecht, *The New Ethnic Mobs* (New York: The Free Press, 1996).
40. *The Times* (Trenton), op.cit.
41. Lydia S. Rosner 'The Sexy Russian Mafia', *Criminal Organizations,* Vol.10 No.1 (1995); Roy Surrett, 'Remarks', First International Law Enforcement Sharing Conference on Russian Organized Crime, 19–23 Sept. 1994.
42. Walter W. Powell and Laurel Smith–Doerr, 'Networks and Economic Life', in Neil Smelser and Richard Swedborg (ed.), *The Handbook of Economic Sociology* (Princeton: Princeton University Press, 1994).

On the Origins of Fuel Racketeering: The Americans and the 'Russians' in New York

ALAN A. BLOCK

In the last several years public attention on organized crime in the United States has increasingly focused on criminals from the former Soviet Union and various Eastern European states. There has been a blizzard of news stories over the past decade on the theme 'the Russian mob is active in America' and numerous journal articles on organized crime in the former Soviet Union.[1] This new orientation is also an important priority for government. On May 15, 1996, the US Senate's Permanent Subcommittee on Investigations (PSI) held a five-part hearing on 'Russian Organized Crime in the United States.' Testifying on 'The Big Picture' was the US Customs Commissioner, a Deputy Assistant Director of the FBI, the Director of Criminal Investigations of the IRS, and Igor Nikolayevich Kozhevnikov, the Russian Deputy Minister of the Interior. The second and third sections concerned Russian connections to US Italian/American organized crime. The final two parts featured testimony from a Russian criminal, from police detectives from New York and Los Angeles, and an undercover officer from 'another [US] city.'[2]

A briefing paper prepared by the Los Angeles Police Department's Organized Crime Intelligence unit for the PSI pointed out that the new face of 'Russian Organized Crime in the US' was one consequence of a more lenient emigration policy toward Soviet Jews in the 1970s. Over the course of that decade and the next about 200,000 Soviet citizens came to the United States.[3] The majority of them settled in the metropolitan area of New York City. The next largest concentration was in the greater Los Angeles area.

The crimes committed by racketeers known by the generic term Russians (which includes individuals born anywhere in the former Soviet Union and its former Eastern and Central European satellites) run the gamut from extortion and narcotics smuggling through various frauds. During the course of the past sixteen years, however, their major mark has been made in fuel racketeering. According to California authorities, 'fuel tax fraud is probably the most lucrative criminal activity in the State.'[4] The loss of revenue from excise fuel taxes in California is estimated to be about a million dollars a day, with one half going to Russian organized crime groups.

While this crime is obviously booming in California, its origins lie in New York. I will therefore explain how this racket (perhaps more accurate to call them rackets) began and evolved in New York, who the principals were, how the 'Russians' got involved, what happened to all the original players, the structure of the racket, and the public corruption that helped sustain it. Though I call it a racket, this type of criminal activity is becoming known as 'enterprise crime.'[5] Analyses centered on enterprises, whether the enterprise is international drug smuggling or money laundering for tax evasion or beating quotas on the importation of automobiles, removes the activity from the overheated world of criminal exotica in which organized crimes are typically explained by some form or other of 'mafiology'. Fuel racketeering in its purest sense is one expression of the rather mundane desire for people not to pay taxes, and the sometimes extraordinary lengths they will go to avoid them. I should also point out that there is nothing intrinsically ethnic about this racket. The wholesale and retail fuel industry in New York, and doubtlessly Los Angeles too, has been and will continue to reflect the panorama of migration to the United States. Anyone who is fraudulently minded and can develop the right connections can take part.

The Early Days

Before the first Russian émigré landed at Kennedy airport in the 1970s, the fuel industry, composed of refineries, re-refineries, terminals, haulers, wholesalers, and retailers, was ripe with fraud. Price-fixing by gas station owners was standard as was cross-hauling, delivering unbranded fuel to branded stations such as Mobil and Exxon. The stealing of state and federal excise taxes, which is what became known as fuel racketeering, was done at the retail level. Excise taxes, as mandated by New York law, had to be ponied up by the retailers. To avoid paying, retailers manipulated gas pump registers in order to under-report gallons sold. They also purchased smuggled fuel which allowed station owners and/or managers to sell fuel that was outside any accounting or reporting system.

Fuel industry knaves engaged in a wide variety of other crimes including selling gas, diesel, and heating oil (which is chemically the same as diesel) adulterated with liquid toxic waste. One of New York's prime locations for toxic blending in the 1970s was the decaying Mattituck terminal on the north shore of Long Island owned by New York Governor Hugh Carey's brother Martin. This racket was endemic in the waste oil business and continued on through the following decade.[6] For instance, in 1982,

Maryland state environmental investigators found the highly toxic chemical PCB in fuel tanks at a large truck stop, and in 1984, the Attorney General of New Jersey, Irwin Kimmelman, announced the indictment of several individuals and five corporations on charges that they mixed 'toxic, ignitable and corrosive hazardous wastes' with an oil blend and sold the product as fuel oil throughout New England and the Middle Atlantic states. There were several interrelated reasons why this became a booming criminal enterprise.[7] The first was a dramatic drop in re-refined oil prices coupled with a rise in cleaning costs because of new environmental regulations. Re-refineries went bankrupt. At the same time, the price of heating oil increased more than ten times. Thus, in this new era, many dealers did not even bother to clean out anything but the big rocks, as one of the nation's largest waste oil dealers put it, before loading it on tankers. Waste oil cost dealers anywhere from zero to twenty cents, and sold for between 80 and 95 cents a gallon as heating oil.[8] Dealers made extremely profitable arrangements with large volume purchasers in New York City which happened to have the highest fuel oil prices in the nation.[9] Back in 1984, a regional trade association of fuel oil dealers estimated that at least ten percent of marketed oil in New York was contaminated with toxic wastes; this meant over 300 million gallons a year.

Fuel fraudsters also vastly over-reported the sale of home heating oil to government subsidized housing even when they were not lacing it with toxics. The housing owners and/or managers in turn took a large cut for their part. Indeed, wherever government subsidized fuel purchases, cheating was rampant. Fraudsters with terminals and blending plants also changed low-grade fuel called raffinate by spiking it with butane in order to raise the octane level. This brew had to be moved rapidly because the butane rather swiftly evaporated. This was common practice. Some New York fuel racketeers even had a blending plant in Channelview, Texas, just south of Houston, for this specialty.

Until the 1980s, the ownership of New York area fuel terminals was in the hands of established firms, though this did not mean they were uncooperative when it came to frauds. But having to kick back money to terminal owners appeared to some budding racketeers as an unnecessary expense. In the 1980s, several important terminals were bought by the fuel racketeers in an attempt to garner more profit.

Before that took place, many retailers on Long Island worked with the northeast's largest fuel terminal, Northville Industries, which had a pipeline fortuitously built under the Long Island Expressway.[10] At some point in the 1970s, Northville had to divest its retail gas operation, called Vantage Petroleum, because of potential legal problems. They sold (using the term quite loosely) their gas stations to Lawrence Iorizzo who became one of the most important retailers on Long Island. His position was enhanced by exclusive gas station contracts from New York State for several major parkways which, Iorizzo has stated, were secured through bribes paid to New York State's Governor whose brother, the toxic Martin Carey, had become Iorizzo's partner. The purchase of Vantage supposedly cost Iorizzo at least one million dollars, though most of that figure came from a credit line established by Northville for Iorizzo. In addition, Iorizzo had to 'kick back' one half cent per gallon to Northville's credit manager who thus was known to insiders as 'half a cent Farrell'. Several other Northville key employees worked hand in glove with fuel racketeers. These included the Chief Financial Officer and the company's Treasurer.[11]

In the early 1980s, Northville was scrutinized by detectives from Suffolk County, Long Island, and the New York State Organized Crime Task Force. Their interests were piqued by Northville's relationship to a somewhat mysterious 'organized crime figure named Salvatore "Sam" Albicocco'.[12] Suffolk County police intelligence sources reported that Albicocco had enormous political leverage palling around with leaders of the New York State Assembly, the Executives of several Long Island counties, congressmen, a slew of judges, and various business leaders. In all, Albicocco was thought to either own or have a strong financial interest in about 37 companies of which ten, including Northville, were in the fuel business. What initially brought Albicocco to attention was his control over gravel used in just about every major New York construction job.[13] At that time, organized criminals had a virtual stranglehold on construction throughout the Metropolitan area.[14] Though Northville eventually was listed as a target of federal prosecutors working exclusively on gas tax crimes, nothing ever materialized. It is Iorizzo's opinion that no prosecutor would touch Northville because of its political connections in both Albany and Washington, DC.[15]

A Year of Change

In the summer of 1982, the State of New York changed its method of collecting fuel excise taxes.[16] Beginning in September of that year, the responsibility for paying the excise tax was moved from the retailers to the fuel wholesalers. The tax was due from the wholesaler when it sold its product to a retailer thus allowing un-taxed trading between registered wholesalers.[17] Former prosecutor Ray Jermyn has described the result in this way: 'New York went from 6,000 little thieves to 600 big ones'. The change reoriented tax fraud in the fuel industry. The so-called 'daisy-chain' was born.

Credit for this invention was attributed to George Kryssing, whose idea it was 'to burn the Federal and State taxes on the gasoline' by using a series of fictitious transfers among wholesale firms in which the last one was supposed to be untraceable. For example, a company known as Pilot International which had both a federal and state tax registration number was sold by Kryssing to other fuel racketeers for $250,000 in cash. The name was changed from Pilot to Northbrook Associates which became what the racketeers called the 'burn' company. From late 1982 through 1984, Northbrook sold about $150 million worth of fuel a month. The federal and state taxes owed by Northbrook were approximately $30 to $40 million a month.[18]

It was not enough simply to create companies from whole cloth, however. The 'burn' company, as in the example above, had to have a tax registration number. For several years this was easily accomplished. But eventually New York authorities began to take a closer look at the firms. This caused a new market to emerge. Anyone with a legally registered company had a property worth hundreds of thousands of dollars. Fuel racketeers scoured the state for willing sellers. From small distributors who serviced rural communities to older established firms attracted by lots of quick cash, the market took shape. The demand was very heavy for the life of a 'burn' company was relatively short, often only months long. Over time they resembled classic 'bust out' operations.

In the beginning the most sophisticated racketeers created bearer-share Panamanian companies, such as Northbrook, either to secure their own registration numbers or to use to buy licenses from companies that had them. In Panama, Hungarian-born Steve Samos did the necessary paper work through his firm Inter Credit Trust. Samos also incorporated companies for drug smugglers. The profits from tax cheating were moved to Europe, most to Vienna's Creditanstalt-Bankverein which was handily just across the street from the Hilton Hotel.

The primary architect of these foreign arrangements was Iorizzo. He was introduced to both Panama and Vienna by a sophisticated conman, Eric D'Antin, who claimed to be the Duke of Alba. D'Antin connected Iorizzo to a former president of Panama who received a huge payoff to allow the process to go forward. As far as Vienna was concerned, the way was smoothed by D'Antin's wife who really was a descendant of the Hapsburg monarchy. Iorizzo was a most innovative man. He took his most important Panamanian company, Houston Holdings, to Vienna. The new company was called Houston Warenhandelsgesellschaft M.B.H., and was set up by a crooked Austrian lawyer. Iorizzo and his partners intended to start a 'chain of gas stations,' and to distribute 'petro chemicals throughout Austria,' and finally had plans for 'a closed circuit TV system'.[19]

The year 1982 was also significant, for it brought new players into the fuel racket. Again, Iorizzo was the catalyst. In the preceding year there had been an attempted strong-arm takeover of Vantage engineered by an Oklahoma oil fraudster and one of his employees, Andy Gazzara, who came from Long Island. To counter this move, Iorizzo turned to a renowned gangster, John 'Sonny' Franzese. In return for his help, Iorizzo took his son, Michael into the business. Along with Michael came members of his crew of organized criminals. By 1982, Iorizzo and his people were working for Michael and his people.

The Alliance

It was this new syndicate which formed an alliance with the so-called Russian mob; actually the new allies represented a partnership between David Bogatin from the Soviet Union and Michael Markowitz from Romania, which he left at the age of thirteen for Israel where he worked as a teacher and engineer. In 1979, the family Markowitz emigrated to the United States. The most important broker of this marriage was Marvin Kramer, a Brooklyn attorney with a reputation for gritty personal injury litigation.

Markowitz had come to Kramer, who was also Kryssing's attorney, for what he said was advice on financing a gasoline operation.[20] It was a serendipitous visit. Kramer had, living in his office, a more-or-less petty crook from Brooklyn, Philip Moskowitz, who had accumulated about a dozen arrests and several convictions since 1947.[21] Down on his luck, Moskowitz worked as a sometime process server for Kramer, though Kramer gave him the title 'paralegal'. Though down at heel, Moskowitz was courting a sister-in-law of Michael Franzese's brother (they later married.) What made this significant was that Moskowitz suggested that Franzese could help. When Markowitz left Kramer's office that day, a meeting had been set with Franzese and several of his henchmen. That meeting held at Kramer's office was attended by Franzese, Kryssing, and several of Franzese's gunmen including a fellow named Vinnie Corroza whose mother, oddly enough, worked for Markowitz as a bookkeeper. A second meeting was held at David Bogatin's office on Long Island with the usual suspects and Iorizzo.

Markowitz had become involved in the gas business in a very small way in 1981. In March of that year he left a firm where he worked as a design engineer to develop a taxi cab meter that he had invented. It was a marvelous design which he discussed with a friend, Efraim Shurka, a Russian émigré who owned a cab and a gas station. They became partners in this venture and in return Shurka offered Markowitz a partnership in the gas station.[22] Jay Turoff, the corrupt New York City Taxi Commissioner, wanted 50 percent of the meter business, promising a Commission rule requiring the meter to be installed in all licensed cabs. Markowitz turned him down.

He next answered a newspaper advertisement placed by an old-timer in the fuel industry, Joe Skolnik, who offered a kind of course on the industry.[23] Markowitz enrolled and soon he and Skolnik became partners. They bought their fuel from the M & Q (Manhattan and Queens) terminal. In the summer of 1982, before the new tax collection law took effect, they decided to become fuel importers. Their idea was to bring in fuel barges to M & Q and another terminal called General. They needed a New York State distributor's license and so turned to Markowitz's accountant for help. They formed Shoppers Marketing Incorporated (SMI) and, being clever, used a front for the business. Skolnik provided SMI's president and only shareholder, Szpila Toduesz, a Polish immigrant, who worked as a gas station attendant at one of Skolnik's stations.[24] This arrangement lasted only a few months, Markowitz recounted. Once they became confident that they knew what they were doing, their names appeared on SMI corporate records as the President and Secretary respectively. They did not change the stock ownership, however, for that would have required obtaining a new license. This took place in November 1982. Two months after that, Markowitz wanted to dump SMI and form another company. Instead, Skolnik offered Markowitz a share in Gas Stop, a company Skolnik had owned for about 20 years. Markowitz took the offer. Attorney Marvin Kramer got them their distributor's license.

There was no point in having two companies, they thought, and looked for a buyer for SMI. Around this time, January 1983, Markowitz met Leo Persits, who was renting a car wash at a gas station, but had, a bit earlier, owned a Mobil station in Manhattan. Persits came to New York in 1975 from the once fabled city of Tashkent, the capital of the Soviet Republic of Uzbekistan. He was one of the important 'Russian' gangsters from the now notorious Brighton Beach section of Brooklyn, home to the largest Russian émigré population in the United States. Persits primarily worked with Marat Balagula, once called the Russian 'Godfather.'

Persits helped broker the SMI deal by bringing David Bogatin into the picture. Bogatin decided to do the deal but wanted Markowitz to stick around and help him run SMI. In effect, Bogatin became a partner for $100,000 which was split equally between Markowitz and Skolnik after $20,000 was taken off the top for Persits' finder's fee. Skolnik's lawyer, David Hellenberg, worked out the paper transfer reflecting a change in ownership from Toduesz to Mieczyslaw Szczepkowski, who was Bogatin's and Persits' Polish front man, and like his counterpart, a gas-station attendant. They set up a 'daisy chain' which left SMI and the alcoholic Szczepkowski with the tax liability while the money went to a company called Lesez cobbled together earlier by Bogatin. Skimming the New York tax, the operation made a considerable amount of money for Markowitz and Bogatin, and somewhat less for Skolnik and Persits.

The SMI operation under the care of Markowitz and Bogatin did not last very long. In the late spring of 1983, tax investigators came around looking for Szczepkowski. This would never do, and he was sent packing back to Poland. To solve the tax problem they also paid 100,000 dollars to Markowitz's accountant, who passed it to an attorney 'who could straighten everything out [with the tax department]'.[25] Apparently it worked. With this 'daisy-chain' disrupted, Markowitz went to Marvin Kramer and subsequently found himself in the world of Michael Franzese and Larry Iorizzo.

When Markowitz and Bogatin joined this world, the split on profits from tax evasion was 75 percent for Franzese and his associates and 25 percent for them. The difference was supposedly for political connections and mob muscle. Franzese was a member of the Colombo crime syndicate and that was more than enough to inspire respect in most of the 'un-mobbed' enterprise criminals. During the next year or so, this entire enterprise reportedly stole around a billion dollars. Franzese's cut was somewhere between $200 and $300 million. The two key operators were Iorizzo, who handled the real books and records, and Bogatin, in charge of the 'Russian's' contribution.

The Time of Troubles

Of course it could not last. First of all, the racketeers stole from one another. Franzese cheated his bosses in the Colombo mob out of millions; one of his prime gunmen stole from Franzese; Markowitz was stealing from Bogatin, so Bogatin has said; Iorizzo accused Bogatin of holding out on the Alliance and, in fact, so testified in Florida; and Iorizzo, it has been said by Bogatin, was cheating everyone. There was also constant turmoil from all the other fuel racketeers – Russians, Turks, Americans, Greeks – who were in competition with this particular alliance. Grievance meetings, sit-downs, threats, beatings, and shootings all took place. Prosecutors in New York and Florida were closing in. The fuel racketeers had expanded to Florida in the winter of 1982–83 and within months Florida authorities were deep into their investigation.They rounded them all up far faster than did New York.

Iorizzo had first talked with New York and federal authorities in 1980 about fuel-related crimes including tax cheating, after he and Martin Carey had a falling out. Nothing of any consequence happened, however. Almost three years later a special Organized Crime Strike Force began a serious inquiry codenamed 'Sludge.' The impetus for this came from a completely unexpected encounter between an FBI agent who was an avid fisherman and an oil slick oozing from a Long Island north shore terminal. The agent was very angry and became the stimulus for the Long Island investigation which began even though the US Attorney in the Eastern District, which covers Brooklyn, Queens, and Long Island, was uninterested. Despite this important roadblock, two Grand Juries were empaneled. The first, known as the Martin Carey Grand Jury, although Carey was not bothered at all, concentrated on 'organized crime's infiltration and control of the gasoline and fuel oil industry', while the second pressed against Michael Franzese and his crew for labor racketeering, Small Business Administration fraud, fraudulent bankruptcies at auto dealerships, counterfeit bonds and credit card scams, loansharking, and so on.[26] Naturally, there was considerable overlap in the investigations which reported to the Justice Department in Washington, not the Eastern District's US Attorney. Iorizzo was the first to fall. He was convicted in the spring of 1984 but fled to Panama with a phony passport in the name of Salvatore Michael Carlino just before sentencing. He was tracked down and finally seized by Panamanians who put him on a plane to the United States. He immediately became a cooperating witness.

In what must have been his first official interrogation, Iorizzo told about several Franzese-inspired 'rip-offs' of two petroleum firms, the dumping of hazardous wastes into the underground storage tanks of an abandoned gas station, the purchase and distribution of weapons, the work done by a private investigative firm operated by two former New York cops in the service of the criminals, the 'daisy-chain' using Pilot and Northbrook, and how Shelly Fishman, an accountant working for Markowitz, created false financial statements. Two months later, Iorizzo continued the Fishman story telling that Fishman knew corrupt bankers eager to make loans for payoffs. Iorizzo spoke about a corrupt banker, David Goldberg, who worked for Gotham Savings Bank and then Union Chelsea Bank. Goldberg was paid 1,000 dollars a week by Lev Persits for one loan, he said. Fishman also worked at the Oceanside Terminal, a fuel 'bootlegger's' paradise, bought from British Petroleum by Markowitz, Bogatin, Skolnick, and secretly Franzese in the summer of 1983. The deal was done by attorney Marvin Kramer.[27]

Iorizzo was a gold mine of information, and after serving a little time was placed into the Witness Protection Program, but got bounced in 1987.

He could not stay away from fuel racketeering and was convicted in spring 1996 in a federal trial in Dallas. Iorizzo is currently serving a fifteen year sentence.[28]

Michael Franzese was also convicted for a variety of frauds including fuel tax evasion. He was supposed to pay 14 million dollars in restitution but has been able to avoid repaying anything of consequence. Franzese had several hooks into the Federal Parole Board and for a while was able to continue his favorite pastime, movie making, while serving his short sentence in Southern California. He also testified in several organized crime trials though not always to the satisfaction of prosecutors.

Michael Markowitz was indicted and became a cooperating witness. Within days of his first 'debriefing', the word was out that he was talking. Franzese's men decided to murder him but failed in two or three botched attempts. He was finally murdered by Israeli gunmen working on a contract from yet another of his accountants, Joe Reisch, who had been very busy stealing from Markowitz and romancing Markowitz's wife. The accountant and the shooters went to Israel where US law finally caught up with them. They were tried and convicted in Israel on US charges. Persits was shot on November 17, 1987, and is partially paralyzed. And poor Phillip Moskowitz, who was quite ill with cancer, was nonetheless beaten and garrotted to death.

The law also took down David Bogatin. He plead guilty to tax frauds but before sentencing traveled to Vienna where he was detained by the Austrian authorities while they investigated him for currency and counterfeiting violations. He was unable to leave Vienna, forced to stay at the Hilton until his case was resolved. Long before his own indictment, Bogatin had begun to move outside the Iorizzo/Franzese orbit thinking the Iorizzo conviction was ominous. Though he did travel to Panama while Iorizzo was a fugitive there, he had also quietly and somewhat tentatively teamed up with a fuel racketeering syndicate run by Marat Balagula. This decision was also likely driven by his search for another fuel supplier somewhat more dependable than the Iorizzo/Franzese crowd.

The Balagula Assembly

Balagula came to the United States from Odessa in 1976 and sprinted to the top of the émigré underworld in Brighton Beach. About a year after he entered the United States he had a chain of fourteen gas stations. In November 1983, he formed a fuel distributorship called Mallard with Lev Naum, originally from Kiev, Efram Nezhinski , and Carlos Orsini. His other primary fuel corporation was Energy Makers of America. One way that the latter company got product without paying taxes was to buy it from the R & R Cab Corporation, which was owned by Russians Boris and Benjamin Nayfield, notorious organized crime figures. R & R had started out as a taxi company but soon transformed itself into a sham oil company.[29] The Nayfields had once been the bodyguards for Evsei Agron, the most notorious Russian organized crime figure in New York until he was gunned down, no doubt either by them or with their cooperation. The Nayfields were also involved in a shoot-out at the Platenum Energy Company in Brooklyn in the spring of 1986. Dead on the spot was Ilia Zeltzer, another émigré criminal who had been arrested by the Secret Service for credit card fraud the year before. Boris Nayfield was shot in the hand. Michael Vax, yet another Russian organized criminal, was wounded. Benjamin Nayfield was at the scene of the shooting but was not injured. A police search of the office uncovered records of R & R Cab and two pistols hidden above a drop ceiling.[30]

Boris Nayfield was an international criminal long suspected by the Belgian police as being both a jewel thief and counterfeiter. He palled around with Efim Laskin, a Russian émigré in Germany whose criminal record in the West began in 1974 with an 'illegal entry' into Switzerland, then moved to theft in Munich, counterfeiting in Greece, importing weapons and explosives in Italy, and a conviction in Munich for counterfeiting US currency. This takes us only to 1981. In subsequent years he was believed to have become a world class heroin smuggler. He raised the money for the enterprise by stealing gold jewelry which was melted into ingots in Poland and then smuggled through India to Thailand. One of his key associates in this complex trade was a diplomat from Sierra Leone who was arrested in India with 20 kilos of gold ingots. Another associate of Laskin was Lev Persits. Laskin, Persits, and two others were stopped at The Netherlands/German border in June 1985. The four men were carrying around 360,000 dollars worth of Deutsche Marks. They said they were on their way to a casino in Ostende, Belgium.[31] In 1995, Boris Nayfield, who had fled the United States were he was wanted for trafficking in narcotics, was captured in Italy.

Balagula finally got caught in a credit card scam in Philadelphia. He went on the lam chased by a Secret Service agent, Henry Bibb. For about four years, Bibb tracked him around the world. Balagula had impeccable criminal connections in Berlin where he spent some time, and in the West African nation of Sierra Leone and the South African bantustan Bophuthatswana. The latter two were run by a mysterious Russian/Israeli gangster and KGB spy, Shabtai Kalmanovitch, who was also wanted in the United States for a bank fraud in North Carolina. Not everyone thought

Kalmanovitch was a bad guy. New York Congressman Benjamin Gilman (now the majority leader of the House Banking Committee), for example, wrote to the court in North Carolina lauding Kalmanovitch's character. Nevertheless, Kalmanovitch was indeed a major league crook.

He took over Sierra Leone, which had had a fairly large Russian Jewish community since the days when the country had aligned itself with the Soviet Union. Oddly enough, there was also a resident Palestinian community which used the country for a bit of R and R. With the collapse of Communism, Sierra Leone had lost its tiny place in the great power struggle. All that was really left were diamonds, Sierra Leone's most profitable natural resource. And Kalmanovitch and his cronies looted them with abandon. Kalmanovitch's relationship with Balagula was leavened through his association to some other strange bedfellows who were close to the Hasidic community in New York's Rockland County, the heart of Gilman's district. Rabbi Ron Greenwald was one, Bill Davidson another. Davidson's wife was Balagula's secretary. They all worked fuel scams along with Arthur Tarricone of Tarricone Oil Co., in Yonkers. One scheme dreamed up by Kalmanovitch and Balagula was to import gas to Sierra Leone. Tarricone financed the deal 'against a 500,000 dollars personal guarantee' put up by Balagula and one of his associates. 'The gasoline was then brokered through the Spanish office of Marc Rich – the billionaire American commodities trader wanted in the US on tax evasion and fraud charges – by Greenwald, who was an agent for Rich in New York'.[32]

For crooks like Kalmanovitch and Balagula, Bophuthatswana was like Coney Island used to be for kids – extremely poor but lots of fun. The South African government handsomely funded the regime, which had not the slightest idea what to do with either the money or their patch of sorry sovereignty. Kalmanovitch, however, knew precisely what to do with the money. He never went back to the United States, but did go to Israel where he had in the past lived and cultivated numerous politicians. On his last trip, however, the Israelis nabbed him for being a KGB spy, selling Israeli secrets to the Syrians through his Soviet handlers. For such a serious crime he received a fairly light sentence. Informed speculation in Israel holds that his arrest really stemmed from US pressure on Israel to do something about Kalmanovitch's selling of US high technology to Eastern Bloc nations. When released from prison, he returned to Russia where he has the reputation of being a major mobster. Balagula, on the other hand, was finally taken by Bibb and brought back to the United States. He was sentenced for the credit card fraud and then tried and convicted for gas racketeering in New York. He has a long way to go before he sees the outside world.

Bogatin's Extraordinary Odyssey

Over a year after he was detained by the Austrians, Bogatin's case was dismissed. He now faced an interesting dilemma – whether to return to New York for sentencing or try to put the past behind him.[33] He was in constant contact with New York authorities, who actually were allowed to visit him in Austria, but he thought it was better to stay in Europe while his attorney negotiated over such issues as restitution and time to be served. He first learned that Markowitz was cooperating with the government after his Austrian problem was resolved. During the course of two interviews with him in 1995, he had very unkind things to say about his former partner, believing that he had stolen a great deal of his money and had likely set him up for the authorities in New York. Bogatin also discounted the significance of the Alliance with Franzese and Iorizzo, stating that Markowitz was 'scared of the Italians because they were pushing him,' but that he was not. He was also particularly upset with Iorizzo because the deal at the heart of the Alliance was stealing New York State taxes, not the federal tax. Markowitz and Bogatin turned over tens of millions of dollars to Iorizzo which were supposed to be paid to the government. Instead, Iorizzo stole it. In retaliation, Bogatin told the authorities, when they came to Vienna, precisely where Iorizzo had hidden approximately half a billion dollars in various currencies. However, he added that 'the government wouldn't touch it because Iorizzo was its star witness'.

Following his Viennese sojourn, Bogatin moved to Poland and started a candy business. It apparently did well and helped bankroll his next move, which was into banking. In December 1990, Bogatin got his banking license and on March 1, 1991, opened the First Commercial bank of Lublin which soon had branches in fourteen Polish cities. His plan was to expand his banking operation into Belarus. He also had joined forces with the ubiquitous Marc Rich on a proposal to rebuild the Polish port city of Gdansk. And then, according to Bogatin, the President of Poland wanted a piece of his action. Nobel Prize winner Lech Walensa thought it appropriate to pressure Bogatin into sharing First Commercial. Bogatin disagreed. Walensa came up with a counter offer. Bogatin could have a piece of Poland's illicit weapons trade with Iraq and Libya if he opened the bank to Walensa. Confirmation that such a trade was going on can be found in a *Time Magazine* account published February 20, 1995. The report states that the CIA was still protecting 'dubious characters out of cold war loyalty'.[34] In particular, *Time* noted that law enforcement agencies were angered in November 1993 'when the CIA intervened to have charges dismissed against Heiko Luikenga, a German shipping agent, and two Polish arms dealers, Thaduesa Koperwas and Zbigniew Tarka. The Poles worked with Cenzin, Poland's state arms-trading company. The charges that were dropped were based on a 35 million dollar sale of weapons to Iraq in 1992 that violated the UN embargo. The CIA favor was in return for past covert arms shipments to the US military of advanced Soviet weapons, and for weapons which the CIA smuggled to the Afghan rebels. Luikenga, the middle-man in these arms swaps, delivered tons of weapons to Pakistan, Egypt and naval stations in San Francisco and Virginia.

Bogatin refused the offer and quite suddenly Warsaw's leading newspaper published an exposé of David Bogatin, a 'Russian mafia' figure wanted in the United States, who was running Poland's newest and hottest bank. The Polish authorities then arrested Bogatin and asked the United States if it would like to extradite him. The United States agreed and back went Bogatin. He was sentenced to a term at Attica prison.

On the Issue of Public Corruption

It is quite impossible that the massive tax evasion in the New York Metropolitan Area was accomplished without official corruption. In fact, this conclusion was reached in the winter of 1986 by the head of the New York State Senate Crime and Corrections Committee who reasoned that corruption in the State Tax department was at least partially responsible. In a memorandum to the State Senate's Majority Leader, Warren M. Anderson, he wrote the following: 'A former high official in a New York City law enforcement agency has told committee staff that City investigators uncovered a "pad" run by State Tax investigators headed by ... the then Director of the Special Investigations Bureau. The "bag man" for the pad was alleged to be the Tax Department's Inspector General'.[35]

Though this memorandum went out under the name of State Senator Christopher J. Mega, he did not write it. In fact, Mega wanted as little to do with investigating state corruption as possible. The actual author was the Committee's counsel, Jeremiah McKenna, who had been involved in investigating gas tax racketeering since 1981. For years McKenna had gathered material from Suffolk County detectives as well as from the work of the Committee's own sleuths. In 1987 McKenna planned to hold a hearing on the fuel tax racket and bootleg cigarettes. He arranged to contact Iorizzo who was in the Witness Protection Program. Iorizzo agreed to testify. And then a series of bizarre events unfolded.

In the early autumn of 1987, the well known writer Nicholas Pileggi wrote a story for *New York Magazine* vilifying people who, as he put it, floated vicious rumors that New York Governor Mario Cuomo was connected to organized crime.[36] Cuomo was in the midst of a flirtation with running for the Democrat nomination for the presidency, and had complained to *The New York Times* about 'an organized campaign of slander against him'. Pileggi wrote that there was no substance to the rumors, which had been around for years. Among the rumor mongers were so-called 'political gadflies and adversaries of the governor who breezily pass out misinformation'. One of them was described as a 'veteran, conservative legislative aide who has long been a source for the press on organized-crime matters'.[37]

Pileggi remarked that one of the rumors passed on by the aide concerned campaign contributions to Cuomo from mobsters, particularly racketeers involved in gasoline tax frauds. Pileggi wanted proof and in an interview with the aide he was given a copy of a congressional transcript in which convicted fuel racketeer Lawrence Iorizzo testified before the Oversight Subcommittee of the House Ways and Means Committee in the summer of 1986. (Pileggi wrongly identified the date as 1985.)[38] The substance of Iorizzo's testimony concerning Cuomo was that he had made contributions to Cuomo's gubernatorial campaign at the behest of Michael Franzese.

Pileggi did not try to contact Iorizzo nor do any independent investigation. Instead, he interviewed Mario Cuomo's son, Andrew, who had run his father's two gubernatorial campaigns. Andrew Cuomo said that he first became aware of the supposed Franzese contribution when NBC News called him late in 1985. He checked the campaigns' 'computerized contribution list' of 16,000 names and there was no Franzese. NBC called him again, he told Pileggi, and mentioned Iorizzo. Another review turned up nothing. A third call from NBC suggested some corporate contributors and this time Cuomo located five 1,000 dollars checks from the following: 'The Northbrook Assets, Inc., Lesez Petroleum Corporation, Houston Holdings, Inc., Future Positions Corporation, and CMC Corporation, all of Long Island'. These firms, law enforcement officials told Pileggi, were sham corporations created to steal fuel taxes. Pileggi added that the checks found by Andrew Cuomo were for 'tickets to a fund-raising dinner for Governor Cuomo held November 26, 1984, at the Sheraton Centre'.

Andrew Cuomo said to Pileggi that the staff had no way to review all the contributions it received, and that when 'we found out what happened, we tried to send the money back, but it turned out the companies were already out of business. We sent the money to charity'. Nonetheless, NBC News ran the story of the five mob corporations on December 4, 1985. The source was Iorizzo. Quoting Andrew Cuomo, Pileggi wrote: 'It was unfair, it was wrong, but there it was on national television'.

Although Pileggi framed his story as an investigation into whether or not the rumors about Cuomo had any basis in fact, that was not his real agenda. Pileggi never probed the key issue of whether or not racketeers, in particular Iorizzo, had contributed to Cuomo's 1982 campaign. In his story he talked about rumors surrounding Cuomo's 1983 campaign and permitted, perhaps encouraged, Andrew Cuomo to deflect the issue of mob contributions to the last week of November 1984. No one who read the story either knew or noticed that before that time Iorizzo had been tried and convicted of fuel tax violations, fled the United States for Panama, and remained there for about four months until captured through the efforts of Octavio Pena, a private investigator. He was shipped back to the United States, and become a cooperating witness with the Organized Crime Strike Force's investigation into motor fuel tax evasion. He did not write checks in November 1984 for a Cuomo fund-raising dinner, and a competent investigator would have known that to start with. But that was not the point. The agenda was to catch McKenna.

The political fallout from Pileggi's story was almost immediate. Cuomo workers claimed they knew McKenna was the legislative aide, and 'pressed reporters to investigate and expose him'.[39] By November 23, 1987, Mega identified McKenna as the source and dramatically repudiated him. The forthright Mega said the following: 'Any statements which were attributable to Mr. McKenna were false, unauthorized and made without my knowledge'. He then demanded that McKenna prepare a report on the Pileggi allegations.

One week later McKenna gave Mega a long memo in response. McKenna noted that Pileggi had come to him asking 'if we could direct him toward any sources or documents for substantiation of the leads *he* was pursuing. None of the leads mentioned by Mr. Pileggi originated with us'.[40] Concerning Iorizzo, he pointed out that Pileggi came to him after the NBC story ran asking if he could point him toward the source. McKenna did, telling him about Iorizzo's congressional testimony.

What interested the Committee about Iorizzo, McKenna wrote, was his testimony 'that Martin Carey had funneled the profits from the sale of toxic contaminated gasoline into the gubernatorial campaign of 1978'. In addition, Iorizzo had testified before a Florida court that the Governor's brother and Michael Franzese had been business associates, and that Martin had been stealing the excise tax on gasoline and running the money into Governor Carey's campaign.

McKenna also reminded Mega that he had given him a detailed memo on December 6, 1985, (the one commented on above) about the gas tax racket and corruption, which went out with Mega's name on it. He had also written to Iorizzo with Mega's permission.through the Department of

Justice asking him to testify before the Committee in an Executive Session. Iorizzo, as noted above, had agreed in August 1987. One month later, Iorizzo called McKenna and told him that 'he would try to coordinate his appearance before the Committee with his appearance to testify in a federal trial in New York'. During the conversation, Iorizzo was asked if he knew the amount of stolen fuel tax money that went into the 1978 gubernatorial campaign. Iorizzo answered two million dollars.

However correct McKenna was about this affair, however unfair Pileggi had been, whatever sordid little conspiracy had been created to prevent the Committee from questioning Iorizzo about the gas tax racket and political corruption, this memo was McKenna's swan song. Mega was not interested in anything but his resignation, which came soon after, and a judgeship, which he eventually received, some say, as a reward for dumping McKenna.

There is no doubt that Iorizzo sent checks to the Cuomo campaign, and there is no doubt that he has claimed in interviews that he also supplied 'bags of cash' that were intended for Cuomo. But there is no proof that Cuomo either received them or did anything for them. However, there is another source, who posits another route for the gas tax racketeers to Cuomo. Attorney Robert Eisenberg, who once worked as an associate of Marvin Kramer, and then became a sort of 'consiglierie' for Marat Balagula, has said that the route supposedly went through Brooklyn Surrogate Court Judge, Bernard Bloom, who was both corrupt and close to Cuomo.[41] Eisenberg gave the following information.[42] When the State of New York seized a barge on its way to Balagula's Energy Makers of America, Balagula asked some of his contacts how he might handle the situation. He was told to contact Bloom's clerk. He did and the clerk said that campaign contributions to Cuomo would make the current problem disappear. Balagula paid the clerk about 50,000 dollars in cash. Eisenberg remarked that afterwards the case was dropped and that other law enforcement pressures were also eased for several months. Like the Iorizzo statements, there is, of course, no proof that Balagula's money went into Cuomo's pocket. But, as the McKenna case illustrates, no one really bothered to look. And maybe that was because there was a certain danger to one's public career in pursuing that line.

Reflection

Fuel racketeering was endemic because of the ways in which the different parts of the industry were structured and regulated. Cross-hauling, selling unbranded gasoline to branded stations was, and probably still is, to almost everyone's advantage. Motor fuels are all the same, it is only advertising that misleads the public. The wholesale price for unbranded fuel is cheaper than branded products and thus the profit margins are higher than they would be otherwise. Mixing toxic waste with motor fuel at fuel terminals, which were almost never inspected, dramatically increased profits for all those who bought and moved the fuel to the consumers. The blenders' motto, as one of the Carey's put it, was 'if it burns, sell it'. Concerning tax evasion, one wonders why anyone wonders why it became commonplace. Under-reporting sales was easy enough to do, particularly in what was a primarily cash business in the late 1970s and early 1980s, thus reducing on paper any taxes owed. Long Island's fuel fraudsters delivered so much 'smelly' cash to the fraudulently run Extebank, that tellers complained they could hardly breathe.[43] The tax differential at the state level was also remarkable for leading to evasion. As an anonymous memorialist wrote, on December 1, 1982, to New York law enforcement, 'Basically there are two popular methods of avoiding NYS sales tax; first is by physically transporting gasoline from out of state in to state, and reporting the sale out of state; second, a more sophisticated game of inside paperwork with dummy corporations may exist today'. The writer then went on to note the tax 'economics' between New York and New Jersey. Both states, he noted, require the same excise taxes – 4 cents federal and 8 cents at the state level. However, New York's sales tax on gasoline sold on Long Island was about '.085 dollars per gallon'; New Jersey had none. Certain distributors were sensibly buying product in New Jersey, trucking it to New York, and if they reported their sales at all, reporting only a New Jersey transaction. When the figures are worked out, he wrote, the distributor's margin of profit per gallon was .079 dollars per gallon in New Jersey and .024 dollars in New York. The gas trucks were flowing over the bridges linking the two states. The mystery writer was correct, of course, and the situation was far worse than even he reported. Other states had quite massive differentials between both excise and sales tax. Some time ago, for example, the State of Georgia dramatically dropped its fuel tax knowing the 'bootleggers' would beat a path to their terminals. Neighboring states were not pleased.

When one couples the taxing structure and the other factors mentioned with a state taxing department that was both lax and corrupt, with law enforcement that took a terribly long time to get enthused, with a phalanx of corrupt attorneys, accountants, and bank officers eager to help those criminally inclined, with the possibility of payoffs to high state officials, the sociology of fuel racketeering becomes clear. And add to this the fact that the racketeers were also so internationally minded, working with Panamanian 'bearer' share corporations and tax havens such as Austria, first and foremost, but also Switzerland and the Cayman Islands. All this shows that the overall success of fuel racketeering was assured no matter how many individual tax fraudsters were eventually taken down. One final point. Fuel is smuggled into the United States from foreign ports on what is reported to be a regular basis. The Customs Service is supposed to collect a tariff on these shipments, but if what the racketeers have said is true, this is not routinely done. As one smuggler said, 'no one is really watching'.

NOTES

1. See, for example, the new journal *Demokratizatsiya: The Journal of Post-Soviet Democratization*, Vol.II, No.3, which features eight articles on Organized Crime by scholars such as Louise Shelley, Rensselaer W. Lee, III, and J. Michael Waller.
2. US Senate, Committee on Governmental Affairs, Permanent Subcommittee on Investigations, 'Russian Organized Crime in the United States', 15 May, 1996.
3. Ibid., untitled paper prepared by the Los Angeles Police Department's Organized Crime Intelligence Division, p.1.
4. Ibid., p.7.
5. See R. T. Naylor, *The Theory and Practice of Enterprise Crime: Public Perceptions and Legislative Responses*, prepared for the Ministry of Justice and the Solicitor-General of Canada, 7 June 1996.
6. For a full account of what follows, see Alan A. Block and Tom Bernard, 'Crime in the Waste Oil Industry', *Deviant Behavior* (1988).
7. See, Dennis W. Brinkman, 'Used Oil: Resource or Pollutant', *Technology Review*, Vol.88, (1988), pp.46 – 51, and his 'Re-refining vs. Burning: How Do You Decide', in *Used Oil: The Hidden Asset* (Washington, DC: Association of Petroleum Re-refiners, 1982), pp.226 – 232, and James A. McBain, 'Industry Experience in North America', in the same publication, pp.30 – 32; and L.Y. Hess, *Reprocessing and Disposal of Waste Petroleum Oils* (Park Ridge, NY: Noyes Data Corporation 1979).
8. New York State Senate Select Committee on Crime, Its Causes, Control and Effect on Society, 'In the Matter of a Public Hearing on the Subject of Toxic Wastes', 30 April 1984, p.33.
9. Ibid., p.128.
10. The first record this author has been able to find concerning Northville's desire for a pipeline goes back to 1962. At that time, Northville Industries (then Northville Dock Corporation) wanted to acquire a right-of-way along the Long Island Railroad track for a pipeline 'for the transportation of fuel oil, and possibly gas, in connection with Northville's storage, terminal and docking facility at Riverhead, Long Island'. See 41 N.Y. 2d 455; 362 N.E. 2d 558; and 393 N.Y.S. 2d 925.
11. Author's interview with a private detective hired by Northville to investigate cost overruns on its Panama pipeline project. The detective stated unequivocally that Northville's credit manager (Farrell), CFO, and Treasurer were on the pad of fuel racketeers.
12. New York State Senate Select Committee on Crime, 'Memorandum, Re: Organized Crime- Long Island', April 22, 1982, p.1.
13. Ibid., pp.4 – 5.
14. See New York State Organized Crime Task Force, *Corruption and Racketeering in the New York City Construction Industry: Final Report* (New York: New York University Press, 1990).
15. Beginning on 9 Dec. 1993, this author had numerous long interviews with Iorizzo. The Northville discussion took place on 9 Oct. 1994, at the Marriot Hotel at Newark airport.
16. See *Laws of New York*, 'Sales Tax-Sale of Automotive Fuel by Distributor, Chapter 469,

approved and effective 7 July 1982.

17. Ibid., Title 20, Taxation and Finance, Chapter 111, Miscellaneous Taxes, part 410.7 'Sales between registered distributors'.

18. Federal Bureau of Investigation, Special Agents Michael O'Brien and Edward Krayewski, 'Memorandum of Interview, In Re: Joseph Aracri, George Kryssing, John Papandon, Anthony Zummo, Federal Courthouse, Atlanta, Georgia, 6 April 1988, pp.1 – 5.

19. This information can be found in a series of letters from Houston Holdings, Inc., European H.Q., Hilton Centre, to Dr. Erhard C.J. Weber, A – 1030 Vien, Hilton, Am Stradtpark, 16.Stock, Nr. 1630 – 1638. The correspondence in my possession begins in December 1982 and ends on 16 Sept. 1983.

20. State of New York Department of Law, Office of Attorney General Robert Abrams, 'Memorandum, Re: Day 6, 1 Oct. 1986', 4 Dec. 1986, p.2. This is one of a series of 'debriefings' of Michael Markowitz who became a cooperating witness in the fuel tax investigations (hereafter 'Markowitz Debriefings'.)

21. Moskowitz's FBI number was 4 779 976, and his arrest record was obtained from the Federal Bureau of Investigation's Identification Division.

22. National Center on Institutions and Alternatives (NCIA), Northeast Regional Office, to the Honorable Eugene H. Nickerson, United States District Court Judge, United States District Courthouse, Eastern District of New York, 'Re: United States v. Michael Markowitz 87 CR 671 (EHN), 15 April 1988, p.4. This is from a proposed 'sentencing memorandum' worked up by the NCIA following Markowitz's conviction.

23. 'Markowitz Debriefings', Day 3, 19 Sept. 1986, p.1.

24. Ibid., p.2.

25. Ibid., p.7.

26. County Court, State of New York, Suffolk County, 'In the Matter of Lawrence S. Iorizzo, a Government Witness in People vs. Louis Fenza, Indictment 1701 – 84, Affidavit of Raymond M. Jermyn, Jr., Assistant District Attorney, 27 Feb. 1985, pp.2 – 3.

27. See Suffolk County District Attorney's Office, Complaint Report, Supplementary Report, Serial No. 83 – 0104 – 21, 3 Oct. 1984, pp.1 – 6; and Serial No. 84 – 0400 – 13, 10 Dec. 1984, pp.1 – 4, both filed with the Suffolk County Court and appended to the Jermyn Affidavit.

28. See US Department of Justice, 'Former Organized Crime Figure Sentenced in Million Dollar Fuel Tax Fraud Scheme', Press Release, 7 June 1996.

29. New York State Department of Taxation and Finance, Bureau of Tax Investigations, 'Investigation Report, Y & F Enterprises Ltd.', Complaint Number MF 85 – 928, date of complaint 3/28/85. p.1.

30. City of New York, Police Department, Unit Supervisor, Organized Crime Monitoring Unit. to Commander, Criminal Section 'Subject: Three Soviet Emigrés Shot – One DOA – Within the Confines of the 61st Precinct (OCMU #19 – 86)', 27 May 1986.

31. This information comes from a New York Police Department Investigation of Alexander Kapusta, who changed his name to Alexander Shkolnik ,and was involved with a credit-card ring that moved stolen US cards to Germany, and was with Persits and Laskin when they were stopped by border police. The NYPD material was translated into German and then re-translated into English.

32. Robert I. Friedman, 'Did a Mystery Tycoon Double-Cross Israel', Washington Post, May 8, 1988, p.B1.

33. The following material was gathered in two interviews with Bogatin at Attica prison in New York. The first was on 27 Jan. 1995; the second on 10 Feb. 1995.

34. Time Magazine, Feb. 20, 1995.

35. New York State Senator Christopher J. Mega, the New York State Senate Crime & Corrections Committee, 'Memo to Senator Warren M. Anderson, Re: Sales Tax Fraud Investigation', 21 Jan. 1986.

36. Nicholas Pileggi, 'Cuomo and Those Rumors', New York, Vol.20, No.43, 2 Nov. 1987, pp.44 – 51.

37. Ibid., p.48.

38. Ibid., p.51. To locate the actual hearing see US House of Representatives Committee on Ways and Means, Subcommittee on Oversight, *Hearing: Compliance With Federal Gasoline Excise Tax Provisions*, 99th Congress, Second Session, July 15, 1986.
39. Jeffrey Schmalz, 'Senator Apologizes on Cuomo Rumors', *The New York Times*, 2 Dec. 1987, p.B3.
40. New York State Senate Crime & Correction Committee, 'Memo to Senator Christopher J. Mega, from Jeremiah B. McKenna', 30 Nov. 1987, p.1.
41. Reporter Jack Newfield has recently written about Bloom saying 'Colossal arrogance and ethical indiscretion have characterized Bernard Bloom's 18 years as Brooklyn's Surrogate Court Judge.... When Bloom first ran for surrogate in 1978 – opposed by the Bar Association – he defiantly declared, "I am the product of the Democratic machine and proud of it. I will give patronage to all of my friends who are qualified. And if they are from the political parties, all the better",' Jack Newfield, 'Bully threatened to kill a cop and lied under oath', *New York Post,* 1 March 1995.
42. Extensive taped interviews with Eisenberg were done by reporter Jim Rosenthal. He has most kindly given me a copy of the transcript.
43. On Extebank see United States District Court, Eastern District of New York, United States of America – against – Extebank, *Information*, CR 87 – 00472.

DOCUMENTATION

An Analysis of Russian Emigré Crime in the Tri-State Region

NEW YORK STATE
ORGANIZED CRIME TASK FORCE

NEW YORK STATE
COMMISSION OF INVESTIGATION

NEW JERSEY STATE
COMMISSION OF INVESTIGATION

JUNE 1996

New York State Organized Crime Task Force

GEORGE E. PATAKI, Governor; DENNIS C. VACCO, Attorney General
ERIC SEIDEL, Deputy Attorney General – In Charge

New York State Commission of Investigation

STEPHEN L. WEINER, Chairman; EARL W. BRYDGES, JR.; THOMAS
J. CULHANE; JOSEPH S. DOMINELLI; SALVATORE R. MARTOCHE;
WILLIAM F. PASSANNANTE, Commissioners

New Jersey State Commission of Investigation

LESLIE Z. CELENTANO, Chair; LOUIS H. MILLER, JUSTIN J. DINTINO
M. KAREN THOMPSON, Commissioners

THE TRI-STATE JOINT SOVIET-EMIGRE ORGANIZED CRIME PROJECT

The Tri-State Joint Soviet-émigré[1] Organized Crime Project (the 'Project') commenced on March 1, 1992, as a two-year joint intelligence and investigative/prosecutive effort by the New York State Organized Crime Task Force, the New York State Commission of Investigation, the New Jersey State Commission of Investigation and the Pennsylvania Crime Commission.[2] The goal of this effort was to identify the nature and extent of Russian-émigré crime within the tri-state region of New York, New Jersey and Pennsylvania in order to assist law enforcement in its ongoing effort to combat the threat of organized crime. In furtherance of this goal, the Project set out to gather and analyze intelligence information about Russian-émigré crime within the area through research, investigative effort and the creation of an informational database.

The participating agencies assigned a total of six to eight investigators, supported by attorneys and analysts, to the Project staff. Staff members were responsible for gathering information and intelligence within their respective jurisdictions and for initiating investigations whenever warranted. Project staff met on a bi-monthly basis to report on investigative results, discuss and exchange ideas, and plan future investigative strategies. To assist the Project staff, a police officer on loan from the Belarus Ministry of Internal Affairs was hired for a two-year period to develop informants within local Russian communities and serve as a liaison with law enforcement agencies in the former Soviet Union. In addition, the officer assisted the Project by regularly reviewing local Russian newspapers, providing insight on Russian customs and traditions, and assisting in the pronunciation and spelling of Russian words and names.[3] The Project was further augmented by a grant provided by the National Institute of Justice to a Rutgers University, School of Criminal Justice, research team. Members of this research team took part in Project meetings and assisted Project staff by analyzing the Project's database of accumulated information regarding Russian-émigré crime.

Fueled by a growing perception within the law enforcement community that Russian-émigré crime has become a more serious problem in the United States since the collapse of the Soviet Union and the expansion of the European Common Market, the Project directed its efforts at identifying the nature and dimensions of Russian-émigré crime in the tri-state area. Project staff sought to:

1. Determine the extent to which Russian-émigré crime is organized,

2. Ascertain whether any type of structure exists within the Russian-émigré criminal community,

3. Identify the methods and techniques Russian émigrés use to carry out their criminal activities, and

4. Define the relationships maintained with other criminal groups operating in the United States or abroad.

As part of their efforts, Project staff conducted extensive interviews with various law enforcement personnel involved in the investigation and prosecution of Russian-émigré crime and reviewed records pertaining to the arrests and prosecutions of Russian-émigré criminals. The staff also gathered and reviewed public information concerning Russian-émigré crime, including government publications, public hearing records, and newspaper and magazine articles, and conducted interviews with academicians, journalists, authors, businessmen and residents of the region's predominantly Russian communities. Conventional law enforcement techniques, such as surveillance, informant development and telephone toll analysis, were also employed to gather information about Russian émigrés known to be, or suspected of being, engaged in crime.

Additional information was developed by the Rutgers University research team which, in collaboration with Project staff, conducted a nationwide survey of law enforcement agencies to determine what experience, if any, law enforcement across the country was having with Russian-émigré crime. The response to this survey, which is described in greater detail in Appendix C, was overwhelming. The research team received nearly five hundred survey responses from various federal, state, county and municipal agencies. Many respondents indicated their agencies had at least some contact with Russian-émigré criminals and nearly half of those considered Russian-émigré crime to be a major law enforcement problem in their area. Based on this information, Project staff concluded that Russian-émigré crime in this country is more widespread than originally suspected.

In gathering the information described above, the Project was forced to overcome several problems. For example, it is widely recognized within the law enforcement community that informant development within any immigrant community is extremely difficult.[4] Having lived in a society ruled by an oppressive government, Russian émigrés tend to be inherently distrustful of government and, generally, are more reluctant than most other émigré groups to speak with or seek assistance from law enforcement.[5] Thus, voluntary cooperation from the Russian-émigré community is frequently minimal.

Moreover, opportunities to obtain information from Russian émigrés are further hampered by the lack of Russian speaking police officers. Most law enforcement agents investigating Russian-émigré crime do not speak Russian and are unfamiliar with the peculiarities of the language, such as the use of the Cyrillic alphabet, the feminization of surnames, and the inversion of birth dates. This often results in inaccurate recording of biographic data. In addition, interviews of Russians who are suspects, witnesses, or victims of crime often require the use of translators with varying skill levels. Information obtained from these persons, which might otherwise provide insight into the workings of Russian-émigré criminal enterprises, is, therefore, often limited or obscured.

Furthermore, Russian émigrés tend to be highly educated. Those who engage in crime are very resourceful and sophisticated in their methods of operation.[6] They often carry false identification documents or use variations of the spelling of their names to conceal past criminal histories and/or facilitate present criminal conduct. These tactics, coupled with a transitory lifestyle, make identification and apprehension of Russian-émigré criminals an arduous task.[7]

Notwithstanding these difficulties, Project staff constructed a computerized database to store information regarding Russian-émigré crime. The database, which represents an accumulation of all information obtained by the Project, presently contains the names of over four thousand persons and businesses. These names have been periodically reviewed to eliminate duplicates caused by the problems described above.

Analysis of the information in the database has permitted Project staff to identify relationships among criminals within the various Russian-émigré communities in the tri-state area as well as between Russian criminals operating in different communities. For instance, telephone toll records obtained and analyzed by Project staff revealed a high level of communication between Russian-émigré criminals in Brighton Beach, Brooklyn, and northeast Philadelphia, Pennsylvania. The database has also been an invaluable aid to numerous law enforcement agencies in their investigations of Russian-émigré crime. To date, the Project has taken part in or assisted more than thirty-five international, federal, state, county and local investigations of Russian émigrés. Several of these have resulted in the indictment and conviction of Russian-émigré criminals.[8]

The Project's success in assisting these other agencies can also be attributed, in part, to the liaison developed between Project staff and law enforcement agencies in the new Commonwealth of Independent States (the 'CIS'). This unique relationship has enabled the Project to obtain information which otherwise would have been unavailable. The Project intends to continue to maintain the database and provide assistance to law enforcement agencies investigating Russian-émigré crime by making the information in the database available upon request.

RUSSIAN-EMIGRE CRIME IN THE TRI-STATE AREA

During the first two decades of the twentieth century, more than two and one-half million Russians entered the United States along with millions of other European immigrants.[9] This first large wave of Russian immigration slowed dramatically, however, after the 1917 Bolshevik Revolution. Since then, the rate of Russian immigration into the United States has depended largely upon the political relationship between the two countries. When the United States and Soviet Union were allied against Germany during World War II, many Russians were able to leave the Soviet Union. During the Cold War period immediately following the conclusion of the war, however, Russian emigration was again stifled as Soviet leaders closed the 'Iron Curtain' and permitted few people to leave that country.

Russian emigration remained at a low level until the early 1970s when the Soviet government liberalized its emigration policy and permitted certain citizens to leave the country. The first wave of émigrés consisted mainly of Soviet Jews fleeing religious persecution, most of whom emigrated to Israel or the United States After that, the number of Russians permitted to emigrate rose steadily as the Soviet Union, nearing its collapse, began to ease travel and emigration restrictions.

The tri-state region of New York, New Jersey and Pennsylvania has long been one of the top areas in the United States for the relocation of Russian émigrés. In New York City, Russian émigrés settled predominantly in Brighton Beach, the oldest and most prominent Russian community in the United States A long-time, working-class Jewish community located near Coney Island in the southern part of Brooklyn, Brighton Beach is currently home to about 30,000 Russian émigrés.[10] Philadelphia's Russian community is located in the northeast section of the city near Bustleton Avenue.

By the mid-1980s, as the Russian communities in New York and Philadelphia were starting to become crowded, Russian émigrés began to move out of the cities and into the surrounding areas. From New York, they moved eastward into Nassau and Suffolk Counties on Long Island, and westward into Essex, Bergen, Middlesex and Monmouth Counties in New Jersey.[11] At the same time, Russian émigrés began to populate several counties outside Philadelphia, including Bucks and Montgomery Counties in Pennsylvania, and Camden and Burlington Counties in New Jersey.[12] Simultaneously, law enforcement agents began to see increasing evidence of Russian-émigré crime within these communities. The specific nature and seriousness of this criminal activity and the degree to which it might be organized were, at the time, largely unknown.

Prior to the mid-1980s, few law enforcement agencies in the tri-state region had taken notice of the growing problem of Russian-émigré crime. The scant information then available in records maintained by these agencies reflected the lack of any serious dedication to the problem. Agencies which sought to attack the problem could barely afford to assign more than one detective to the task of tracking Russian-émigré criminals. Those assigned often often provided with little assistance while facing formidable investigative roadblocks similar to those encountered by Project staff.

Much of the information available at that time concerned the number and size of local Russian organized crime groups. Various federal agencies reported that twelve Russian-émigré crime groups, with an estimated membership of between 400–500 persons, were operating in New York City, while the New York Police Department listed about 500 Russian émigrés as being suspected of criminal activities.[13] At the same time, the Philadelphia Police Department had identified about fifty Russian-émigré criminals,[14] many of whom traveled regularly between New York City and Philadelphia.[15]

Similarly, Russian-émigré crime in the United States attracted little academic attention. Prior to 1992, there had been only one serious study of Russian-émigré crime in the United States. In 1986, Lydia Rosner, a professor at the John Jay College of Criminal Justice in New York City, published a book about Russian-émigré crime based upon a four-year study of crime in Brighton Beach.[16] In her book, Rosner stated that a 'vast amount of at least informally organized crime' existed in Brighton Beach.[17] She attributed this crime to networks of interconnected criminals acting in conjunction with each other.[18] Rosner did not, however, attempt to determine whether the crime she had uncovered was part of a structured network of national or international criminal activities, or whether it was being controlled by persons in the United States or the Soviet Union.

As Russian-émigré crime increased, law enforcement agencies in the tri-state region and across the nation realized they needed to evaluate this growing problem. Although the criminal activities attributed to Russian émigrés included such common predatory street crimes as burglary, robbery, theft, arson, prostitution and low-level narcotics trafficking, they also included murder and a number of more complex and sophisticated crimes. Russian-émigré criminals were linked to forgery, counterfeiting, tax and insurance fraud, confidence schemes and sophisticated extortions. Some forged ties with members of *La Cosa Nostra*. Russian-émigré criminals were associated in various ways with the Colombo, Gambino, Genovese and Lucchese families in New York and New Jersey.[19]

The relatively few United States law enforcement agencies that had concerned themselves with this issue offered varying explanations for the emergence of Russian-émigré criminal activity. One was that Soviet officials had intentionally released criminals from its prisons and commingled them with Jewish-émigrés permitted to leave the Soviet Union in the mid-1970s.[20] Another was that members of organized crime groups in Odessa, Ukraine, had smuggled themselves out of the country by assuming the identities of Soviet-Jews who were either dead or in jail.[21] Still another explanation offered was that the Soviet intelligence agency, the KGB, allowed the criminals to emigrate so as to undermine legitimate Russian communities in other countries and make them unattractive to Soviet citizens.[22] For several reasons, all of these explanations proved inadequate. First, each assumes that Russian-émigré crime in the United States is largely a product of a professional criminal class that has imported its criminal ways onto our shores. Several of the criminals known to have operated in Brighton Beach during the 1980s and 1990s, such as Evsei Agron, Marat Balagula, Emil Puzyretski and Boris Nayfeld, provide support for this assertion as they were, in fact, products of the Soviet prison system. Nevertheless, the actual number of known Russian-émigré criminals who entered the United States in the 1970s and 1980s, either with or without the consent of Soviet officials, was relatively small and, in general, their crimes have been very localized.[23] No matter how aggressive or vicious they may be individually, they have neither the critical mass nor the criminal sophistication to create a major local or regional threat, much less a national or international one.

Second, none of the explanations take into account the effect which the collapse of the Soviet Union has had in the United States. History has shown that the growth of organized crime in any community is invariably linked to the recent migration into that community by ethnic groups having weak ties to the dominant political culture.[24] During the years immediately prior to, and even more so after the collapse of the Soviet Union, the number of persons permitted to emigrate to the United States from former Soviet republics increased dramatically. For example, in 1992, 129,500 non-immigrant visas were issued to persons from Russia, Belarus and Ukraine. In 1988, just four years earlier, only 3,000 such visas were issued.[25]

Currently, about 350,000 Russian émigrés reside in the United States,[26] as compared to about 75,000 just ten years ago.[27] Much of this growing population is concentrated in a few cities like New York and Philadelphia.

In addition, it has been estimated that a large number of Russian émigrés have over-stayed their visitors' visas and are living illegally in the United States.[28] Thus, the rise in crime in Russian-émigré communities is more likely attributable to the increased numbers of Russians living in this country than to a small number of violent criminals.

Finally, the proponents of these explanations fail to recognize and understand the peculiarities of the societal environment of the Soviet Union. As is true in all societies, people are conditioned by the moral, social and economic environment in which they live. Soviet citizens were reared by a government which, although unable to adequately provide basic necessities for its people, lavishly rewarded high-ranking and loyal members of its dominant political party. Thus, to survive, many Soviet citizens were forced to find ways to 'beat the system' without getting caught.[29] Actions such as bribing an official to do a favor, paying a premium to obtain desired goods, or buying necessities from black market salesmen became common practices accepted by the general population as necessary for survival. Consequently, many Russian émigrés are well-schooled in this type of behavior.

Lydia Rosner observed that 'immigration from the Soviet Union brought to America's shores many people for whom crime [is] but ordinary behavior.'[30] According to Rosner, some Russian émigrés are criminals who, out of necessity, manipulate the system in order to survive. They do not consider themselves to be criminals, even though they regularly break the law. Others are professional criminals, those already pointed to as the core of Russian crime in the United States. Both types know very well how to skirt the bureaucracy and adapt governmental services for private gain. This is not to suggest that all Russian émigrés either came to the United States for the purpose of committing crimes or became criminals after arriving. It does suggest, however, that the potential crime problem should not be considered as being limited to the professional criminals.

Crime in general, and organized crime in particular, have traditionally provided routes of upward mobility for immigrants in the United States.[31] Immigrants who turned to crime often did so out of frustration at being blocked from other avenues for advancement. Russian émigrés differ considerably, however, from prior immigrant groups in their ability to take advantage of both legitimate and illegitimate routes to success.[32] Unlike the farmers and unskilled laborers who comprised the majority of earlier immigrations to this country, Russian émigrés are generally urban in origin, well-educated, and industrially and technologically skilled.[33] Despite a language barrier, they have marketable skills and have not been closed off from the legitimate ladders of upward mobility.

In sum, Russian-émigré crime in the United States did not grow out of the same cultural alienation and economic disparity experienced by other immigrant groups. Russian-émigré criminals did not begin their criminal careers as members of adolescent street gangs in ethnic ghettos, as did many Irish, Italian, Jewish, African-American, Latino, and, more recently, Chinese and Vietnamese criminals. Instead, they engage in a variety of frauds, scams and swindles because those are the kinds of crimes that most closely build upon their previous experience in the former Soviet Union. Unlike their ethnic predecessors in crime, Russian émigrés do not have to go through any developmental or learning process to break into the criminal world in this country. They are able to begin operating almost immediately upon their arrival.

THE NATURE OF RUSSIAN-EMIGRE CRIME

One of the central challenges facing the Project was gaining an understanding of the underlying nature of the types of crimes committed by Russian émigrés. Analysis of the information gathered by Project staff reveals that Russian émigrés are involved in a broad variety of crimes ranging from simple theft to sophisticated fraud to murder. Some of these crimes are being committed by individual criminals while others bear some indicia of organized criminal activity. As illustrated by the examples set forth below, Russian-émigré crimes often involve extensive planning within varying networks of individuals.

Crimes of Deception

Project staff found that the most common types of crime being committed by Russian émigrés are those which involve some form of deception.[34] Many of these crimes, such as jewelry switching, are simple scams perpetrated by low-level, street criminals. Others, such as insurance fraud, are much more complex and sophisticated. To succeed, complex crimes require a great deal of coordination among criminals, as well as infiltration of legitimate areas of the economy.

Motor Fuel Tax Fraud

The largest and most publicized frauds involving Russian émigrés have been motor fuel tax scams – frauds in which the perpetrators sell and resell gasoline and diesel fuel without paying required excise taxes.[35] These frauds have cost the government an estimated $1 billion annually in lost tax revenues during the last decade. Much of this money has been diverted to

La Cosa Nostra and its Russian-émigré partners.[36]

Prior to 1982, New York State required individual gas stations to be responsible for the collection of fuel taxes. Many of the stations, however, sold their fuel, failed to pay the required taxes, and then either went out of business or changed corporate ownership before revenue officials were able to collect the taxes due. To end this practice, New York shifted tax collection responsibility from retailer to wholesaler. Lost tax revenues continued, though, as unscrupulous criminals quickly identified a way to take advantage of the new law. The estimated national average of federal, state and sales tax for gasoline is 40.35 cents a gallon.[37]

Licensed fuel companies began to purchase bulk fuel and move it through bogus 'sales' to a series of dummy wholesale companies. This created what came to be known as a 'daisy chain.' The fuels never actually moved. The dummy companies simply filed invoices with the government, along with fraudulent tax exemption forms, stating that the company had bought and sold fuel. One of the dummy companies along the daisy chain was a 'burn company' which was ostensibly responsible for paying the taxes but which, instead, went out of business without doing so. Revenue collectors were left with a complex trail of paper that led to a dead end.

In New Jersey, the most significant motor fuel tax scams involve the purchase and sale of diesel fuel, which is used to power diesel engines in trucks and other vehicles. Diesel fuel is virtually identical in chemical composition to home heating oil.[38] At the refinery, both diesel fuel and heating oil are designated as number two fuel. When purchased for resale as home heating oil, the fuel is not taxable. When purchased as diesel fuel, however, it is subject to state and federal motor fuel excise taxes.

Russian-émigré criminals and other scam artists have found various ways to take advantage of this distinction. Typically, tax evaders buy number two fuel and sell it as diesel fuel to retailers, at a price that includes state and federal taxes, without remitting the taxes to the government. Sometimes, a daisy chain is used to commit the scam and the fuel is sold to several dummy companies, all or some of which file falsified invoices indicating the required taxes have been paid. Other times, scam operators simply purchase non-taxable heating oil and sell it as diesel fuel. Either way, the opportunity for illicit gain is great. In New Jersey, the total tax due on the sale of diesel fuel is 41.9 cents per gallon.[39]

Recently, the State of New Jersey recognized its motor fuel tax law needed revision. Prior to July 1, 1992, state law required that wholesalers collect motor fuel excise taxes. New Jersey's legislature changed this, however, in response to recommendations that resulted from a New Jersey State Commission of Investigation public hearing in the fall of 1991. State law now mandates that retail sellers of diesel fuel collect the required taxes.[40]

The daisy chain scam not only costs the government a great deal of money but has the added effect of forcing many legitimate fuel wholesalers and retailers out of business. This is because the unpaid federal and state taxes are not entirely pocketed by the perpetrators of this fraud. Rather, a percentage of these illicit profits, in the form of lower wholesale prices, is passed on to retailers who take part in the scam. Legitimate fuel retailers are unable to compete with the lower prices offered by the bootleggers.

The self-admitted originator of the daisy chain fraud was Lawrence Iorizzo, a Long Island businessman. In the early 1980s, Iorizzo began selling untaxed motor fuel through wholesale and retail companies he owned. In 1981, Iorizzo's businesses were threatened by a local gang of thugs and he contacted Colombo crime family member Michael Franzese for help. In return for protection from *La Cosa Nostra*, Iorizzo offered Franzese a partnership in the profitable business of selling untaxed gasoline.[41]

Contemporaneous with the development of the Iorizzo/Franzese partnership, Michael Markowitz, a Rumanian, was running his own daisy chain operation in Brooklyn. In addition, several Russian émigrés were also running fuel scams. When the Markowitz operation became the subject of scrutiny by authorities, Markowitz found it necessary to align his network with the Iorizzo/Franzese operation. Eventually, all the daisy chain operations in the New York area, many of which involved Russian émigrés, came under control of *La Cosa Nostra*, which regulated the operations as a cartel, mediated disputes between members, and appropriated a percentage of the profits.[42] The fuel tax scam gradually expanded beyond the New York–New Jersey market to Pennsylvania, Ohio, Texas, California, Georgia and Florida.[43]

During the past few years, a number of joint investigations by the Internal Revenue Service, Federal Bureau of Investigation and various state agencies have focused on motor fuel tax evasion. These investigations have led to the indictment and conviction of numerous Russian émigrés from the tri-state region. In April 1993, a federal grand jury indicted fifteen individuals and two businesses involved in a $15 million Pennsylvania tax fraud scam.[44] That same year, similar indictments were brought in New Jersey, where the federal government charged six Russian émigrés and several members of *La Cosa Nostra* in connection with a $60 million motor fuel tax scam,[45] and New York, where eighteen individuals, including five Russian émigrés, were charged in connection with a $34 million gas tax scam.[46] In 1995, twenty-five defendants, including fifteen Russian émigrés, were charged in a federal indictment filed in New Jersey with defrauding the government of more than $140 million in fuel tax.[47]

Insurance and Entitlement Fraud

Insurance fraud is another complex crime frequently committed by Russian-émigré criminals. One of the largest medical insurance frauds ever perpetrated in the United States was masterminded by a group of Russian émigrés in California during the middle to late 1980s. Led by Michael Smushkevich, the group set up phony medical clinics and mobile laboratories and solicited patients with promises of free physical examinations and diagnostic tests. The group then submitted fraudulent bills, supported by falsified medical reports and treatment forms, to insurance companies indicating that the clinics had provided medical services prescribed by doctors. Before being caught in 1991 by federal agents, the group had defrauded California insurance companies of over 50 million dollars.

The most impressive aspect of this insurance scam was the magnitude of the operation. The group set up more than 250 medical clinics and labs, employed dozens of doctors, technicians, clerical workers and administrative personnel, submitted thousands of claims totalling over $1 billion, and laundered illicit proceeds through 500 different shell companies and foreign banks. The group was so brazen that when claims were rejected, they were often re-billed under a different clinic name. In 1991, Smushkevich, his wife and brother, and ten others were indicted for racketeering, mail fraud and money laundering.[48]

Russian-émigré insurance fraud schemes have not been limited to medical coverage. In the early 1990s, a group of Russian émigrés in Pennsylvania perpetrated an insurance scam in which they staged auto accidents and submitted over $1 million in phony claims to various insurance companies. The scam was orchestrated by Alexander Zaverukha who, along with his business partner Victor Tsan, owned a medical clinic in Bucks County, Pa. Zaverukha recruited other Russian émigrés to take part in the scam, then set up eight different traffic accidents and brought the 'injured' parties to his clinic where they were treated for non-existent injuries. Zaverukha, Tsan and seven other persons, including a doctor who worked at the clinic, were indicted in 1995 by a federal grand jury.[49]

Government entitlement programs such as Medicare and Medicaid have also been the target of Russian-émigré criminals. These programs have reported numerous incidents of fraud involving the submission of bills for services or merchandise that were never provided. The submissions range from medical examinations to transportation in ambulettes to the purchase of medical equipment. In 1986, thirteen Russian émigrés fraudulently netted thousands of dollars by selling cheap shoes to Medicare recipients and then billing Medicare for the purchase of expensive orthopedic shoes.[50]

Similarly, a Russian-émigré in Pennsylvania tried to defraud the United States Food Stamp Program. Peter Cherepinsky, a resident of Philadelphia who owned a food store in Pennsauken, N.J., purchased $45,000 worth of fraudulently obtained food stamp coupons at a discount price and then deposited the coupons into his business checking account. Cherepinsky was indicted in connection with this scam in 1993.[51]

Confidence Schemes

There also have been many incidents in cities throughout the United States involving Russian-émigré criminals engaging in various types of confidence schemes. In many cases, the victims of the schemes have also been Russian. Most of the schemes are common scams such as jewelry switching, in which the perpetrator offers to inspect or appraise the victim's jewelry and then substitutes an inexpensive piece for the real one during the inspection. Philadelphia Police Department intelligence files indicate that, in 1981, the city's jewelry district suffered a rash of gem scams purportedly committed by a group of Russian émigrés. The most egregious scam involved the theft of $80,000 worth of diamonds in which the perpetrator allegedly substituted diamond 'look-alikes' for real gems. This case was never prosecuted as the victim subsequently withdrew the complaint.[52]

A recently uncovered scam underscores the ability of Russian-émigré criminals to identify and take advantage of weaknesses in workplace security systems. In September 1995, Bella Jakubovicz and Asya Drubich were indicted by a federal grand jury in Brooklyn for allegedly participating in the theft of over 35 million dollars worth of jewelry from their employer, NGI Precious Metals, a Manhattan jewelry manufacturer. The indictment alleges that the women, who emigrated to the United States from the Soviet Union in the early 1980s, would arrive at work before the company's metal detectors were activated, steal bracelets and other jewelry, hide them in the company locker room, and then return to work. The stolen goods were eventually sold to a fence for cash which was deposited in several Swiss bank accounts. Although NGI Precious Metals went out of business in 1990, authorities were unable to charge the two women until recently because of the difficulties involved in obtaining Swiss bank records.[53]

Many Russian-émigré confidence schemes have international aspects. Project staff members are currently participating in three separate investigations involving contractual agreements between parties in the United States and representatives of governments or private companies in various parts of the former Soviet Union. Each contract involves a multimillion dollar purchase of United States goods or technology. The purchases are either made from United States companies, or by United

States companies on behalf of the buyers. In either case, the United States companies, which are managed or influenced by Russian émigrés, require a sizable portion of the contract price prior to producing or delivering the product. Once paid, the companies subsequently default or disappear prior to fulfilling the contract, leaving the foreign entity without its purchase and with little recourse.

One of these investigations has recently resulted in the indictment of a group of Russian émigrés who allegedly stole more than $5.7 million from twenty-four Russian businesses and a charity set up to aid victims of the 1986 Chernobyl nuclear accident. In March 1996, Lev Breskin and Alexander Korogodsky of New Jersey, and Yakov Portnov and George Yosifian of New York City were charged in a federal indictment with conspiracy, wire fraud and money laundering.[54] The indictment charges that, in January 1992, the men set up a phony wholesale company in Manhattan and then attended a trade expo in Russia where they met customers seeking to purchase various United States products, such as computers, medicine and coffee, which are not readily available in that country. The men requested full payment in advance of the purchases but promised to deliver the products at very low prices. It is alleged that, after receiving the money, no goods were ever delivered to the victims.

Counterfeiting

Counterfeiting is another crime of deception in which Russian émigrés have been active. The Project has participated in several investigations of Russian émigrés involved in the production of counterfeit credit cards. In addition, Russian émigrés have been found to be expert counterfeiters of checks, passports, visas, and other types of identification documents. Research by Project staff has revealed there are well-established markets for these products within the local Russian communities and that Russian émigrés are now supplying other criminals with their products.

Counterfeiting of credit cards usually involves altering the magnetic strip on the back of a card. The counterfeiters first obtain account information from legitimate credit cards by stealing legitimate cards, obtaining credit card receipts from dishonest vendors, or copying account numbers while peeking over the shoulder of unsuspecting credit card users. The legitimate account information is then encoded onto the magnetic strip of another card. This may be a stolen card, a card which has exceeded its credit limit, or a bogus card produced by the counterfeiters.[55]

The card is then used to buy goods from an unsuspecting vendor or a vendor operating in collusion with the perpetrators. When the vendor slides the card through a magnetic reader, information from the legitimate account encoded on the magnetic strip is transmitted to the credit card issuer. Unaware that a bogus card is being used in the transaction, the issuer authorizes the purchase and the goods are charged to the account of the legitimate credit card holder. Although the issuer also transmits the number of the account which has been charged for the purchase, there is little chance that the counterfeiter will be caught even if the vendor is not part of the scam. Cashiers rarely match the account number transmitted by the issuer to the account number on the credit card. As long as the issuer authorizes the purchase, most vendors will only verify that the card and receipt signatures match.

Project staff encountered several cases of Russian-émigré counterfeiting. In August 1989, four Russian émigrés were indicted for, and later convicted of, manufacturing, possessing and selling 17 million doolars worth of counterfeit United States currency and 4 million dollars worth of bogus traveler's checks. A fifth conspirator, Roman Kolompar is presently a fugitive. The money and checks had been circulated in New York, Chicago, Los Angeles and Poland.[56]

Another case involved a group of Russian émigrés who sold counterfeit credit cards. The cards, which were printed in Israel and embossed in the United States, were sold to Russian émigrés in Brighton Beach. The operation, while successful for a time, did not produce high-quality cards. For example, Visa cards manufactured by the group displayed a hologram of a hawk rather than the 'Visa dove' and the cards contained obvious misspellings of the words printed on the reverse side. Members of this group were arrested by the United States Secret Service in 1992. The Project database was instrumental in identifying the group's printer in Israel who was arrested by Israeli Police in November 1992.

In the early 1990s, Alexander Semenov and several other Russian émigrés used re-encoded credit cards to purchase more than $120,000 worth of goods in New York, Pennsylvania, Massachusetts, Illinois and California. Upon arrest in 1993 by the United States Secret Service, Semenov tried to conceal his true identity by changing the spelling of his name and his biographical information. Using information from the Project's database, however, Project staff were able to connect him to other incidents of credit card fraud.

Violent Crimes

Like others who operate in the underworld, Russian-émigré criminals have employed violence in furtherance of their criminal pursuits or as a means of settling disputes. Russian-émigré criminals have been implicated in numerous murders, attempted murders, assaults and extortions. In most instances, police investigating the incidents have been unable to find any witnesses to the crimes. Witnesses who were located and interviewed, including victims, often refused to cooperate.

Homicide/Attempted Homicide

Project investigators and staff gathered information regarding more than seventy murders and attempted murders involving Russian émigrés committed since 1981.[57] All suggest that the victim, perpetrator or both were involved in ongoing criminal activity. Many of the victims were known criminals who had a prior criminal relationship with either the person who attacked them or the person who ordered the attack. In several cases, intelligence information obtained from confidential sources indicated that the victim was attacked as a result of a dispute between two individual criminals or gangs, or in retaliation for a prior violent act.

Many of the homicides appear to have been well planned and, in some instances, assassins or 'hitmen' were used to commit the crime. Those who carried out the attacks often used distractions, decoys, or other tricks to gain an advantage over victims. Fifty-three homicides involved the use of guns, including automatic, semi-automatic and silencer-equipped handguns. Victims were often shot either at close range, usually in the head or chest, or from a moving vehicle. One victim, who had been stabbed to death, was found floating in Sheepshead Bay, N.Y. Another was found frozen stiff in a snow bank at a Morris County, N.J. auto salvage yard, fully clothed in a suit and tie. He had been shot twice in the temple. During the autopsy, bullet wound scars were discovered on various parts of the deceased's body, indicating he had been the victim of prior shootings.

Extortion and Kidnapping

Extorting Russian émigrés who are successful in legitimate or illegitimate business endeavors is another practice among Russian criminals. The Project obtained information regarding several cases of extortion involving Russian émigrés. A reputed major figure in Russian-émigré crime in the United States, Vyacheslav Ivankov, was indicted by a federal grand jury in 1995 and charged with attempting to extort $3.5 million from two Russian-émigré businessmen in the United States The indictment alleges that the father of one of the extortion targets was beaten to death and left on a train platform in Moscow after the demands by Ivankov and his associates were not met. Ivankov was arrested after the two businessmen agreed to cooperate with United States law enforcement.[58]

In Brighton Beach, a Russian-émigré shoplifter was the extortion victim of Alexander Levichitz, also known as 'Sasha Pinya,' a particularly violent

Russian-émigré criminal. The basis for this extortion is notable. Pinya and his girlfriend became involved in an argument over Pinya's infidelity based upon information provided to Pinya's girlfriend by the shoplifter. Pinya demanded a monetary settlement from the shoplifter to atone for the problem he had caused. Eventually, a resolution was reached whereby the shoplifter provided Pinya with the names of other low-level criminals in Brighton Beach from whom Pinya could successfully extort money. In September 1993, Pinya was arrested by the Suffolk County District Attorney's Office with assistance from members of the Project staff.

In March 1995, four Russian émigrés from Brooklyn used threats and physical violence in an attempt to extort $25,000 from a Russian-émigré auto repair shop owner in Roselle, N.J.[59] The four pleaded guilty in May 1995. In 1992, a group of Russian émigrés in Philadelphia sponsored the arrival of women from the CIS to be employed as live-in domestics. The women were subsequently threatened with deportation if they did not turn over a portion of their weekly earnings to their sponsors.[60] In other cases, the extortion of Russian émigrés residing in the United States has been accomplished by kidnapping the victim and either demanding a ransom from the victim's family or forcing the victim to withdraw money from bank accounts or purchase money orders for their captors.[61]

Drug Trafficking

Since the demise of the Soviet Union, the FBI and Drug Enforcement Administration report that many of the new republics are being used as trans-shipment points for deliveries of Colombian cocaine into Western Europe.[62] In 1993, Russian authorities in St. Petersburg intercepted a one-ton shipment of cocaine, packaged in cans of corned beef, believed to be the product of a cooperative arrangement between crime groups in Russia and Colombian cartels.[63]

Russian émigrés are also involved with the Colombian cartels in United States drug activity. In the late 1980s and early 1990s, Russian-émigré Vladimir Beigelman, of Brooklyn, N.Y., was known to be involved in cocaine trafficking with the Cali cartel. On December 2, 1993, Beigelman was fatally shot in the face while exiting a van in Queens, N.Y. Witnesses described the assailants as two Hispanics. Evidence indicates Beigelman was murdered in a dispute over a large quantity of missing cocaine.[64]

In 1992, the United States Attorney for the Southern District of New York prosecuted sixteen individuals, including Russian émigrés David Podlog and Alexander Moysif, on charges of distributing heroin and cocaine.[65] The next year, twenty-four individuals led by four Russian émigrés were indicted for the manufacture of crack cocaine vials at factories in New Jersey and Pennsylvania. During the arrests, authorities seized more than $1 million in cash, along with several vehicles, stock portfolios and other property.[66] In 1994, another federal indictment was filed against Russian-émigré narcotics traffickers. In this indictment, Boris Nayfeld, Shalva Ukleba, Alexander Mikhailov, Simon Elishakov and Valery Krutiy were charged with participating in the smuggling, distribution and sale of heroin which originated in Southeast Asia and was smuggled into the United States via Poland.[67]

Money Laundering

The demise of the Soviet Union and its transformation to a market economy ignited a great deal of currency exchange activity with the United States and western Europe by Russia and other former Soviet republics. During the last few years, a massive influx of money originating as rubles has been exchanged for United States dollars, via financial institutions and front companies in this country and Europe, and then transported back to the CIS.[68] Fearful that the funds are being used to support criminal organizations, terrorist groups and drug cartels, law enforcement officials are trying to determine how much of this activity is legitimate.

There is some evidence that suggests the activity is linked to organized crime. The FBI reports that a substantial percentage of these funds is derived from fraud, theft and other criminal activities in the CIS.[69] In addition, many privately-owned banks which have surfaced throughout the former Soviet Union, and through which many of the transactions are being made, are alleged to be owned by Russian organized crime operatives. Also, during the past year, more than thirty people involved in the Russian banking system have been murdered. Russian authorities believe these events are the result of organized crime efforts to control the banking industry.[70]

Conversely, there is evidence that much of the increased activity is legitimate.[71] Many of the transactions involve Russian investment firms, financial institutions and other businesses engaged in international commerce which need convertible currencies, such as United States dollars and German marks, to transact business. In addition, Russian companies seeking to upgrade or expand facilities are forced to deal with the United States and other western nations due to the lack of modern technology in Russia. These businesses also exchange rubles for dollars and marks in order to purchase equipment.

Several factors make it difficult to determine which currency exchanges are legitimate business ventures and which constitute illegal money laundering schemes. First, based upon United States law, the transfer of money from one account to another is legal unless it is done for an illegitimate purpose.[72] Second, most of the currency exchanges are made through banks in other countries both before the funds enter and after they leave the United States This makes tracing the entire route of the funds nearly impossible. Finally, any crimes connected to the exchanges are usually committed in the country which initiated the transfer. Thus, even if United States law enforcement can show the funds are illicit and trace their path through the financial institutions involved in the exchanges, it may be impossible to establish jurisdiction over the crime.

During the past four years, Project staff members provided assistance to several agencies, including the FBI and United States Customs Service, conducting money laundering investigations. The Project assisted these agencies primarily by providing information from the Project's database. The Project also gathered information regarding various money laundering schemes which either occurred in or affected the tri-state region.

One case illustrated the high-tech sophistication of Russian criminals. In 1994, Vladimir Levin, operating in St. Petersburg, Russia, stole $10 million from Citibank via the bank's electronic money transfer system. Using only his computer hacking abilities and the assistance of several other persons, he was able to circumvent the bank's security system and wire transfer the misappropriated funds to accounts in Finland, Russia, Germany, the Netherlands, Israel, Switzerland and the United States.[73]

Other money laundering schemes examined by the Project are less sophisticated. Russian émigrés involved in fuel tax scams have used illicit proceeds to purchase vehicles in the United States which were then shipped to the CIS and resold at three to four times their United States retail prices.[74] On other occasions, Russians have simply smuggled money through international borders by secreting it in clothing or body cavities. In 1994, Yuri Anatoliyevich Desyatov pleaded guilty to smuggling $1.2 million into the United States.[75] Desyatov was also involved with extortion and weapons purchasing in addition to money smuggling.

Russian émigrés have also been conducting various types of money laundering schemes in hotels and casinos in Atlantic City, N.J.[76] Casino operators indicate that a significant number of Russian émigrés frequent casinos. Many of them are 'high-rollers' recognized as favored customers and, as such, have received such perks as limousine service, plush hotel suites, meal and alcohol allowances, and seating for prime events. One of the schemes observed by various law enforcement agencies, including the United States Secret Service and the New Jersey State Police, involves the use or attempted use of counterfeit currency and traveler's checks. Russian-émigré criminals use the bogus currency, in amounts below the federal

Currency Transaction Report threshold, to obtain cash and/or playing chips.[77]

In New York City and other financial centers around the country, the potential for Russian money laundering should not be underestimated. During a recent United States House of Representatives Banking Committee hearing, United States Federal Reserve Governor Edward W. Kelley, Jr., estimated that nearly $500 billion is laundered through United States banks annually.[78] As the use of electronic international banking grows, the vulnerability of these financial institutions to fraudulent transactions becomes a paramount concern to law enforcement everywhere. Manipulation of these institutions could seriously impact the economic stability of this country.

Vice Crimes

Project staff members have developed little data concerning Russian-émigré vice crimes. Although gambling and prostitution rings exist, they are predominantly small-scale operations in Brighton Beach and other Russian communities. The Project found no evidence that Russian-émigré criminal organizations are exercising wide-spread control over these types of criminal activities.

One recent case in New Jersey, however, reveals both the willingness and ability of Russian-émigré criminals to maximize profits by transporting criminal activities. Earlier this year, police in North Brunswick, N.J., investigating what they believed to be a prostitution ring, arrested several female dancers inside a local go-go bar. One of the females was a Russian juvenile who, police later learned, was an exotic dancer brought from Brooklyn, along with several other young Russian females, to dance in go-go bars and work in massage parlors in central and northern New Jersey. The dancers were being driven to and from New Jersey by a hired driver.[79]

AN ASSESSMENT OF THE PROBLEM

There is a tendency on the part of some in law enforcement and the media to readily adopt simplistic, stereotypical perceptions of organized crime. This has certainly been true in regard to Russian crime, where terms such as 'Russian Mafia' have been loosely applied. Superimposing descriptions which fit other known criminal groups upon Russian-émigré criminals impedes the ability of law enforcement to identify and address the real problem.

Project staff used *La Cosa Nostra*, solely for comparative purposes, to assist in analyzing and assessing Russian-émigré crime. *La Cosa Nostra* is the most familiar exemplar and best illustrates the harm potential of organized crime. This is not to imply that *La Cosa Nostra* is the only form of organized crime, nor does it suggest that any organized crime group which does not resemble *La Cosa Nostra* should not be viewed as a serious problem. Project staff also examined indigenous Russian organized crime to provide a frame of reference that might indicate potential organizational structures in the United States.

Russian Criminal Types

In Russia, criminals typically fall into three major types:

1. the *vory v zakone*;

2. the young entrepreneurs;

3. the 'thieves in authority.'[80]

Vory v Zakone

Reputed members of the *vory v zakone*, or 'thieves in law,' have been said to be the closest thing the ex-Soviets have to being a 'made guy' in *La Cosa Nostra*, and the top *vory* are portrayed as godfather-like figures.[81] The *vory* are the most sophisticated of the professional criminals. Their roots are generally traced to the Soviet prison system – more specifically, to the far-flung Gulag prison network established by Stalin in the 1930s. Most *vory* have spent the bulk of their lives in prison and profess a complete submission to the criminal life. They maintain their own laws and rules and reject any involvement with, or obligation to, the legitimate world. According to one Russian expert, the association of *vory* is a rather loose structure with little differentiation among its members, and with the elite being just the first among equals.[82] There are an estimated 600 *vory* in the former Soviet Union, with approximately 200 of them in Russia. The elite make up a Moscow-based politburo of 10–15 *vory* who govern the criminal world through their representatives.[83] Vyacheslav Ivankov is alleged to be one of the 200 *vory* in Russia, and perhaps even among the top leadership group.[84]

The *vory* share a number of characteristics with members of *La Cosa Nostra*: a set of rules, a code of behavior, nicknames, and their own vernacular.[85] They also have a system for mediating and resolving disputes. Whether there is any enforcement mechanism to back up the resolutions from these meditations is not clear. It should be reiterated, however, that the *vory*'s rules and code of conduct are practiced principally in the closed environment of the Soviet prison system, where they have lived most of their lives.

Of the three major types of Russian criminal, the *vory* most resemble the members of *La Cosa Nostra*. Thus, an argument can be made that they constitute the greatest criminal threat currently presented by Russians in the United States. The credibility of such a threat is conditioned, however, upon a number of factors such as the number of *vory* presently in the United States, how closely they are linked to the Moscow-based crime leaders, and how successfully they can organize and control the multitude of criminal ventures in which Russians are involved in the United States The FBI estimates that there have been as many as five *vory* in the United States at one time or another.[86] The real potential for harm from the *vory* will depend on how well internal discipline can be maintained outside the prisons walls where their roots lie. This control will be complicated by the fact that criminal activity is now taking place thousands of miles from Moscow.

Some experts challenge the primacy of the *vory*, both as a present and future threat.[87] It is alleged that the traditional initiation into the *vory* has been corrupted by the selling of this title. If so, this would affect whether and how well internal discipline can be maintained. The criminal expertise of the *vory* is also more likely to involve common crimes such as theft, robbery and extortion. More complex crimes such as international banking and commodities scams, money laundering, and dealing in strategic metals, may be beyond the scope of their criminal expertise. The *vory* are the most astute criminals at present, but may constitute less of a problem over the long term. Some experts believe that although the *vory* still dominate the traditional criminal world in Russia, especially in prison, the gangster bureaucrats, with their intertwined links to the government, will soon dominate the social, economic, and political structures of the former Soviet Union.[88] Russia is currently a very attractive venue for criminal pursuits. As those pursuits grow in size and sophistication, it is expected that these criminals will look to expand their interests internationally.

Young Entrepreneurs

The young entrepreneurs see crime as the easy route to riches. These are people in their late teens to mid-30s who were not criminals before the collapse of the Soviet Union, but who, out of necessity, had experience in the Soviet black market and shadow economy. Some are students or graduates of higher education, while others were in the military. Few, if any, have attractive job prospects in the legitimate sector. They constitute a pool for recruitment by criminal organizations in Russia or operate within their own small group. Unlike that of the professionals, their criminal behavior is not very well entrenched. They are first generation criminals, and their crimes are most often crimes of opportunity.[89]

Thieves in Authority

The 'thieves in authority' or *avtoritety*, arose during the last few decades of the Soviet Union, beginning during the Brezhnev era. Some were part of the Communist Party and/or were Soviet bureaucrats. They were part of what has been called the 'Soviet Mafia.' Some were deputy directors or former administrators of factories and other business enterprises. Others ran cooperatives during the Gorbachev era or were members of the national security and military establishments. Whatever their background, nearly all are well-educated persons who possess international connections. These 'gangster-bureaucrats' operate at the intersection of crime, capitalism, and government in the former Soviet Union. They have the knowledge, experience, sophistication, and contacts needed to run international banking schemes and major commodities deals. They are also the ones best suited to deal in black market nuclear materials. For these reasons, they have the greatest potential for future harm both within and outside the CIS.[90]

La Cosa Nostra and Russian-Emigré Criminals

In the view of some, Russian-émigré criminals are organized in a continuing structure to conduct a variety of criminal ventures.[91] There have been reports that between three and five Russian-émigré organized crime 'families' presently exist in the New York area.[92] Vyacheslav Ivankov's arrival in the United States was seen by many as proof that a centralized Russian criminal organization exists.[93] When he was arrested in 1995, Ivankov was labeled, in *La Cosa Nostra* terms, the *capo di tutti capi*, or 'boss of bosses,' of Russian crime in the United States.[94]

An opposing view is that Russian-émigré criminals have no defined organizational structure or hierarchy.[95] This view holds that Russian criminals are individuals who do not follow a rigid authoritarian structure. Instead, 'like liquid mercury on a countertop,'[96] they operate mainly as individual specialists or in fluid groups that occasionally unite to commit a crime.

Based upon its review and assessment of Russian-émigré crime, the Project believes that the reality lies somewhere between these two positions. With the exception of the *vory v zakone*, it is the Project's belief that Russian-émigré criminal organizations are not, by and large, like the families of *La Cosa Nostra*. There is no evidence of either a central 'commission' which oversees the various Russian-émigré criminal activities, or even a few hierarchical groups that engage in specialized criminal activities. Although Russian criminals have shown a propensity for extreme violence and possess the capacity to corrupt, they have yet to assert monopoly power in any of their United States criminal activities other than in the fuel frauds where they functioned as partners of *La Cosa Nostra*.

The professional criminals and opportunists who currently characterize Russian-émigré crime in the United States typically mistrust each other. There is generally little or no personal loyalty based upon common ethnic or cultural backgrounds, even though some of the criminals knew each other in the former USSR. The most prevalent network structure is usually an ad hoc team of specialists who are mustered for specific criminal ventures usually pertaining to crimes of deception. These specialists form opportunistic partnerships which are sometimes based on referrals by other Russian criminals. After the criminal objective is attained, the specialists may split up or may move together to other criminal ventures.

Networks of specialists, however, are not the only manner in which Russian-émigré criminals organize. Professional criminals who profess a propensity for violence have formed small criminal groups to commit extortions or engage in narcotics trafficking. These groups often center around one or more dominant individuals and the composition of the group is subject to frequent change.

One way to contrast *La Cosa Nostra* and Russian-émigré criminal organizations is to view the former as having a structure – a distinct, definable crime family – that is supported by criminal activities. The structure is continuous, and crime is used to carry out its objectives and maintain its strength and vitality. Russians, however, create floating structures on an as-needed basis to enable them to carry out particular crimes. The criminal opportunities come first, and the necessary structure to take advantage of those opportunities follows. Generally, *La Cosa Nostra* is structure-oriented; members use criminal activities to support the structure. Russian-émigré criminals are venture-oriented; they use structure to support their criminal activity.

Harm Capacity

The critical distinction between organized crime and all other crime lies in its capacity to cause harm. When the Project began its investigation in 1992, little was known about the structures of any Russian-émigré criminal networks. Likewise, little was known about their capacity to commit harm either in local communities, such as Brighton Beach and Northeast Philadelphia, or in the larger society. Assessing the harm potential of Russian-émigré criminals is, therefore, vital to understanding the Russian criminal threat.

Harm occurs in a variety of ways – economic, physical, psychological and societal. Economic harm includes monetary losses by victims, illicit gains by criminals, and detrimental effects to the marketplace. Physical harm is the violence used to attain and retain monopoly control over criminal ventures. Psychological harm involves the creation of a climate of fear and intimidation and a perception that criminal networks can avoid apprehension by law enforcement. Societal harm is the undermining of the system, the compromising of the political process, and the corruption of law enforcement and other institutions.

The motor fuel tax scams exhibit most of the harms caused by organized crime. First, economic harm is caused when conspirators keep the tax due and discount the fuel sold to motor fuel retailers. This allows those retailers who purchased their product from the conspirators to undersell their competitors, increase their profits and gain a greater market share. The price advantage enjoyed by these retailers destroys competition in the retail market over time. In this way, predatory pricing can upset the entire distribution system. Second, physical harm is caused. A cartel of motor fuel bootleggers enforces the rules of the cartel through the use of threats and violence. Third, psychological harm is caused when retailers are intimidated into purchasing non-taxed motor fuels from the cartel. Finally, societal harm may be caused if the cartels continue to grow in power and accumulate wealth. This could, eventually, permit them to entrench their position through corruption of the established political structure.

The capacity to cause harm is determined by the size, scope, sophistication and, especially, continuity of the criminal networks involved. The harm occurs when criminal organizations attempt to monopolize specific areas of the marketplace and employ violence and corruption to attain criminal objectives.

Monopoly Power

Just as a desire for market monopoly exists in the licit marketplace, so it exists in the illicit marketplace as well, and for the same reason – to optimize wealth and power. Monopoly power is attained by forcing out and discouraging competition. This is achieved through the threat and use of force and violence and by obtaining advantages over competitors, such as the ability to underprice, through other criminal activity. Market monopolies permit the accumulation of wealth and power which can then be used to corrupt the legal and political systems. This, in turn, further solidifies the criminal organization's position in the marketplace. This is the essence of organized crime. It is the most severe and insidious form of harm caused by organized crime.

La Cosa Nostra has monopolized many different areas of the marketplace. For the past several decades, law enforcement in this country has fought to eradicate *La Cosa Nostra*'s influence over these areas. Conversely, Russian-émigré criminals have not yet established monopoly control over any of their United States criminal activities. Although Russian-émigrés were among the first to take part in the motor fuel tax scams, monopoly control of this activity was not attained until members of *La Cosa Nostra* became involved.

Use of Violence

The demonstrated willingness to use force and violence to attain a monopoly, discourage competition, and intimidate witnesses is also one of the hallmarks of organized crime. It is systematic and functional in that it furthers the interests of the criminal organization. *La Cosa Nostra* uses violence as a calculated tool for business gain, to enforce mediated agreements, and to organize markets. On the other hand, Russian-émigré criminal violence appears to be a mix of the calculated and the ad hoc.

Russian émigrés have shown a willingness to use violent acts to achieve their criminal goals. There have been numerous murders and attempted murders involving Russian émigrés in the tri-state region, many of which remain unsolved. Generally, however, these crimes appear to be neither systematic nor designed to protect any particular criminal enterprise. Instead, they seem to have been motivated by greed or personal vendetta. For example, in 1995, Monya Elson and a group called 'Monya's Brigada' were indicted by a federal grand jury for, among other crimes, three murders and one attempted murder.[97] This violence reportedly resulted from Elson's desire for recognition and stature. Two of the victims were targeted by Elson because he was jealous of their status in the criminal community.

There have also been numerous extortions of Russian-émigrés in the region. Many of these were committed by enforcers, criminals who specialize in extorting Russian-owned businesses in Brighton Beach and elsewhere. The enforcers work for whomever pays them. Although, occasionally, there may be disputes between individuals or groups regarding certain extortion victims, most of the extortions appear to be opportunistic rather than a systematic approach to obtain power or control.

Russian violence is not random in the same sense as the drive-by shootings of street gangs. Russian-émigré criminals appear to exercise some care in choosing their victims and avoiding harm to innocent bystanders. Furthermore, several Russian-émigré murders and attempted murders resulted from attempts to assert hegemony over various market areas, such as the bootleg motor fuel business, or to settle scores between criminal groups. Nevertheless, there is a view among some in law enforcement that the Russians' reputation for violence exceeds the reality of its use, at least in the United States.[98] As has been true in United States drug markets, a great deal of Russian-émigré violence is attributable to the unregulated competition that exists in their criminal ventures.

Use of Corruption

The threat of Russian-émigré criminals using corruption as a means to further their criminal pursuits is more of a potential than an actual harm. *La Cosa Nostra* uses corruption to facilitate its criminal activities, eliminate competition, and entrench itself in the marketplace. At the present time, Russian-émigré criminals in the United States have not cultivated the appropriate political contacts to emulate *La Cosa Nostra*. Perhaps they presently see no need to maintain corrupt relationships to further criminal objectives. Should the situation change, however, Russian-émigrés do possess the capacity to corrupt. They are products of a system that is accustomed to bribing politicians and government officials, and in which corruption is a way of life.

In the meantime, the pervasive corruption that exists throughout the governments of the former Soviet republics creates problems for United States law enforcement agencies collaborating with their counterparts in those countries. For example, ascertaining whether a Russian-émigré suspect in the United States has a criminal history, or is currently under investigation in one of the former Soviet republics, is risky because the target may be informed about the inquiry. The United States Immigration and Naturalization Service indicates that it is often impossible to find out whether a United States visa applicant from one of the former Soviet republics has a criminal background.[99] In these and other ways, corruption in the former Soviet Union may facilitate Russian-émigré crime in the United States

CONCLUSION

Based upon its four-year investigation of Russian-émigré crime in the tri-state region, the Project concludes that Russian-émigré criminals constitute a serious and evolving crime threat in the United States. At present, Russian-émigré criminals do not possess either the organizational or harm capacity which would warrant considering this threat as critical as the threat posed by South America drug cartels or *La Costa Nostra*. Nevertheless, given the sophisticated nature of their criminal activities, as well as the extensive planning and coordination those activities require, it may be only a matter of time before the Russian-émigré crime threat reaches that level. Russian-émigré criminal groups in the United States do not resemble traditional organized crime, such as *La Cosa Nostra*. Russian-émigré groups lack the structure and permanence found in other crime groups. Instead, Russian-émigré criminals operate within an amorphous confederation in which roles are not as clearly defined and relationships among members not as continuous as those within other criminal organizations. Furthermore, the Project found little evidence, other than in connection with the motor fuel tax scams, that Russian-émigré criminals are employing or attempting to employ violence and corruption to attain monopoly power or organize the marketplaces in which they are functioning. Russian-émigré crimes have been, and are being, committed mainly by individual opportunists or ad hoc criminal groups.

Despite these differences, Russian-émigré criminals could very well prove to be more prolific and successful in this country than other, more structured crime groups. Although maintaining a permanent, continuous organization has, in the past, proven to be significantly advantageous in the criminal world, it has also led, in part, to the decline of many criminal groups. The very structure which enables criminal organizations, such as *La Cosa Nostra*, to survive continuously despite the loss of one or more of its members, also provides law enforcement with a window through which the organization can be attacked. Thus, although there is evidence that some Russian-émigré criminals are beginning to develop more structured, hierarchal organizations, the present lack of structure within Russian-émigré crime groups may prove to be even more troubling to law enforcement.

In any case, Russian-émigré criminals in the United States present a formidable problem for law enforcement. They are generally more intelligent and sophisticated than most criminals, and are imbued with a business acumen rarely seen in traditional organized crime groups. Having been 'trained' under the black market and shadow economy of the former Soviet Union, Russian-émigré criminals are adept at identifying weaknesses in legal, business and financial systems, and capitalizing on those weaknesses for their financial benefit. They survived under the strict, punitive control of the communists and are clearly willing to continue their criminal ways in this country.

History has shown that criminal networks often evolve into more harmful types of organized crime.[100] The evolution of Russian-émigré crime will be governed by the social context in which the criminal groups are operating. Consumer demand for its particular goods and services, its ability to expand, the amount of attention devoted to it by law enforcement, and competition from other crime groups will each influence the domestic growth of Russian-émigré crime. The task of American law enforcement is to shape the social context and create obstacles so as to keep Russian criminals from developing the capacity for greater harm.

The Project also recognizes a prospective Russian organized crime problem which may have no connection to Russian-émigré crime other than a common heritage. Yet, it is one that, potentially, may cause severe harm within the United States. Currently, within the CIS, there are numerous criminal organizations which are demonstrating an enormous capacity for harm.[101] They have acquired monopoly control of a broad array of illegal and legal enterprises, including some Russian banks, and have amassed considerable wealth and power within the CIS in a relatively short span of time. These organizations have used violence – against businessmen, journalists, and government and law enforcement personnel – to acquire and maintain their monopoly control and are also engaging in massive corruption to facilitate their criminal pursuits.

The geographic and political barriers which had impeded the Soviet Union from full participation in the global economy are gone. Ease of travel and enhanced global communications will continue the expansion of international business, both legal and illegal, in the CIS. As criminal organizations and gangster bureaucrats position themselves to further their political power and wealth, their business/criminal activities will continually extend internationally. The proliferation of money laundering between the CIS and the United States is evidence that this expansion is already underway.

The task for United States law enforcement is to counter both these Russian crime threats simultaneously. State and local agencies, with assistance and cooperation from federal agencies, must insure that more permanent and sophisticated criminal networks do not evolve within their jurisdictions. At the same time, federal law enforcement agencies must assume primary responsibility for countering the international organized crime threat. Together, these efforts can prevent the 'Russian Mafia' from becoming the twenty-first century's *La Cosa Nostra*.

CONTRIBUTING TO THIS REPORT:

THE NEW YORK STATE ORGANIZED CRIME TASK FORCE

GREGORY STASIUK
Special Investigator
ARTHUR SCHWARTZ
Special Investigator

DON SOBOCIENSKI
Strategic Analyst

THE NEW YORK STATE COMMISSION OF INVESTIGATION

HELENE B. GURIAN
Deputy Commissioner/Chief Counsel

WILLIAM F. FRIEDLIEB
Chief Investigator

ANTHONY CARTUSCIELLO
Assistant Counsel

ALFONSO CAMPAGNOLA
Special Agent

THE NEW JERSEY STATE COMMISSION OF INVESTIGATION

JAMES MORLEY
Executive Director

MARILYN CICHOWSKI
Special Agent

RUTGERS – THE STATE UNIVERSITY OF NEW JERSEY
SCHOOL OF CRIMINAL JUSTICE

JAMES O. FINCKENAUER
Professor of Criminal Justice

NOTES

1. Subsequent to the Project's inception, the Soviet Union collapsed. For purposes of simplicity, individuals from the former Soviet Union who might be classified as immigrants or émigrés will be referred to as Russian émigrés.

2. The project has continued beyond its original two-year term absent the Pennsylvania Crime Commission which was abolished as an independent agency by its state legislature in June 1994.

3. The officer returned to his country in 1994 after fulfilling his two-year commitment.

4. President's Commission on Organized Crime, 'The Impact: Organized Crime Today', Washington, DC (April 1986).

5. James O. Finckenauer, 'Russian Organized Crime in America', in Robert J. Kelly *et al.* (eds.), *Handbook of Organized Crime in the United States* (Westport, CT: Greenwood Press, 1994); Dennis J. Kenney, and James O. Finckenauer, *Organized Crime in America* (Belmont, CA: Wadsworth Publishing Co., 1995).

6. Ibid.

7. Ibid.

8. US v. Shae Presaizen, *et al.*, 95–CR263 (S.D.N.Y. 1995); US v. Monya Elson, 95–CR179 (S.D.N.Y. 1995); US v. Boris Nayfeld, 94–CR537 (S.D.N.Y. 1994); US v. Anthony Morelli, *et al.*, 93–CR210 (D.N.J. 1993); US v. Jacob Dobrer, *et al.*, 92–CR419 (E.D.Pa. 1993); N.J. v. Christopher Grungo, *et al.*, SGJ350 (1994).

9. Information provided by the US Immigration and Naturalization Service.

10. Information provided by the New York City Planning Commission.

11. Information developed by Project staff has revealed that Middlesex and Monmouth Counties in the central part of the state have become the bedroom communities of many former Brighton Beach Russian émigrés.

12. According to the Philadelphia Police Department, Russian populations in Camden and Burlington Counties, N.J., and Bucks County, Pa., have doubled during the last ten years while increasing seventy-five percent in Montgomery County, Pa., within the same period.

13. Pres. Comm. on Org. Crime; see also *New York Times*, Feb. 12, 1983, at B3, col.1.

14. Information provided by the Philadelphia Police Dept. See also *Philadelphia Inquirer*, April 24, 1983, at A1.

15. Philadelphia Police detectives noted a link between the two communities as early as 1981.

16. Lydia S. Rosner, *The Soviet Way of Crime: Beating the System in the Soviet Union and the USA* (South Hadley, MA: Bergin and Garvey Publishers, Inc., 1986).

17. Ibid. at 116.

18. Ibid.

19. Russian and Italian criminal associations allegedly began in the early to mid-1980s. See, US v. Morelli, supra; US v. Dobrer, supra; and US v. Joseph Reisch, 93–CR598 (E.D.N.Y. 1993). See also Nathan M. Adams, 'Menace of the Russian Mafia', *Readers's Digest* (Aug. 1992); Robert I. Friedman, 'Brighton Beach Goodfellas', *Vanity Fair* (Jan. 1993); M. Franzese. and D. Matera, *Quitting the Mob: How they Yuppie Don Left the Mafia and Lived to Tell His Story* (New York: HarperCollins, 1992).

20. Friedman.

21. Finckenauer, and Kenney and Finckenauer op. cit. See also, *New York Times*, Aug. 23, 1994, at A1, col. 5; *New York Law Journal*, Jan. 29, 1981, at 1, col. 2.

22. Adams, op. cit.; see also, *Philadelphia Inquirer*, April 24, 1983, at A1; *Los Angeles Times*, Jan. 28, 1982, at 1.

23. According to FBI Deputy Assistant Director James E. Moody, only a small fraction of Russian émigrés in this country are criminals (*New York Times*, Aug. 23, 1994, at A1, col. 5). See also, *New York Times*, Feb. 15, 1983, at B3, col. 1.

24. Peter Reuter, 'Research on American Organized Crime', in Kelly *et al.*, *Handbook of Organized Crime in the United States.*

25. Testimony of FBI Director Louis J. Freeh before the US Senate Permanent Subcommittee

on Investigations (May 25, 1994).

26. 1990 US Census Bureau estimate regarding *foreign-born* Soviet émigrés. The Census Bureau reported that, in 1990, more than two million people in the US claimed a Soviet ancestry.
27. Rosner; see also William Kleinknecht, *The New Ethnic Mobs* (New York: The Free Press, 1996).
28. *Los Angeles Times*, Oct. 10, 1994, at A8, col. 1.
29. Rosner.
30. Ibid., at 29.
31. Daniel Bell, 'Crime as an American Way of Life', *Antioch Review* 13, 131–154 (Sept. 1953).
32. James M. O'Kane, *The Crooked Ladder* (New Brunswick, NJ: Transaction Publishers, 1992).
33. Rita J. Simon, 'Families Adjustments and Aspirations: A Comparison of Soviet Jew and Vietnamese Immigrants', *Ethnic and Racial Studies* (Oct. 1983).
34. See Appendix C.
35. Fuel used to propel vehicles on highways is subject to federal and state excise taxes. See, 26 USC. §4041 (1995); N.Y. Tax Law §§282 et seq. (McKinney supp.1987–1995); N.J. Rev. Stat. §54:39–27 (West 1986 and supp.1995).
36. Franzese and Matera, op. cit.
37. *New York Times*, May 13, 1996, at A1, col.3.
38. Diesel fuel may contain additives which improve its burning quality in an engine.
39. Federal excise tax (24.4¢), plus NJ sales tax (13.5¢), plus NJ petroleum gross receipts excise tax (4¢). Information provided by the N.J. Department of Taxation.
40. N.J. Rev. Stat. §54:39–27.
41. Franzese and Matera.
42. Michael Markowitz was shot to death in 1989, allegedly on orders from *La Cosa Nostra*, to prevent his cooperation with the police (see Appendix E).
43. As evidenced by the numerous recent federal indictments filed in each of these states.
44. US v. Dobrer.
45. US v. Morelli.
46. US v. Reisch.
47. US v. Daniel Enright, 95–CR388 (D.N.J. 1995).
48. Smushkevich pleaded guilty in 1994 and was sentenced a year later to twenty-two years incarceration and ordered to pay restitution in the amount of 41 million. dollars US v. Smushkevich, 90–CR960D (C.D.Cal., 1990).
49. US v. Alexander Zaverukha, *et al.*, 94CR–515 (E.D.Pa. 1994). Zaverukha later pleaded guilty to racketeering. On Oct. 16, 1995, he was sentenced to forty-five months in prison, fined 25,000 dollars and ordered to forfeit 100,000 dollars and pay 100,000 dollars in restitution.
50. *Washington Post*, June 24, 1990, at C1.
51. US v. Peter Cherepinsky, 93–CR123 (E.D.Pa. 1993).
52. Information provided by the Philadelphia Police Department.
53. *New York Times*, Sept. 13, 1995, at B3, col. 1.
54. Breskin, Korogodsky and Yosifian have been arrested by the FBI Portnov is a fugitive believed to be in Russia. US v. Lev Breskin, *et al.*, 95–CR1091 (S.D.N.Y. 1996).
55. One method used by Russian-émigré criminals to produce bogus cards is to silk screen the logo of an issuing bank, color it onto a blank plastic card, and emboss the card with the account number of a legitimate credit card.
56. US v. Roman Kolompar, *et al.*, 89–CR429 (1989).
57. See Appendix E. The Project limited its information gathering efforts to those homicides and attempted homicides which were somehow related to the tri-state area.
58. US v. Vyacheslav Kirillovich Ivankov, Complaint No. 95–0899M (E.D.N.Y. 1995).
59. *The Star Ledger* (Newark), April 1, 1995, at 19.

60. Information regarding this matter was developed by the Pennsylvania Crime Commission.
61. Both New York City and Philadelphia Police Department records contain numerous complaints involving the kidnapping/extortion of Russian-émigrés.
62. FBI Dir. Freeh, Senate Perm. Subcomm. on Inv., supra.
63. Ibid.
64. Information provided by various N.Y.P.D., D.E.A., and US Customs Service agents.
65. US v. David Podlog, et al., 92–CR374 (S.D.N.Y. 1992).
66. US v. Henry Belkin, et al., 93–CR240 (E.D.Pa. 1993) and US v. Valery Sigal, et al., 93–CR241 (E.D.Pa. 1993.) All defendants have pleaded guilty. On March 15, 1996, Sigal was sentenced to forty-six months in prison and fined 25,000 dollars.
67. US v. Boris Nayfeld, et al., 93–CR965 (S.D.N.Y. 1994).
68. FBI Dir. Freeh, Senate Perm. Subcomm. on Inv., supra.
69. Ibid.
70. Ibid See also, Organized Crime Digest, Vol. 17:6, 1–3 (Mar. 13, 1996).
71. FBI Dir. Freeh, Senate Perm. Subcomm. on Inv., supra; see also, Friedman, Robert I., The Money Plane, New York Magazine (Jan. 22, 1996).
72. 18 USC. §1956.
73. Organized Crime Digest, Vol. 16:18 (Aug. 30, 1995).
74. Organized Crime Digest, Vol. 15:4 (Feb. 23, 1994); Wall Street Journal, Aug. 23, 1994, at A14.
75. Organized Crime Digest, Vol. 16:1 (Jan. 4, 1995).
76. A February 13, 1996, US General Accounting Office report indicated that casinos, especially those on riverboats and Indian lands, have the potential to become major money laundering conduits. Casino Crime Digest (March 1996).
77. Information provided by the N.J. State Police Intelligence Section.
78. Organized Crime Digest, Vol. 17:6, 1–3 (March 13, 1996).
79. Information provided by North Brunswick Police Director Thomas Maltese.
80. Stephen Handelman, Comrade Criminal (New Haven, CT: Yale Univ. Press, 1995).
81. B.I. Dep. Asst. Dir. Moody, Remarks before the Fifth Annual Economic Crime Investigation Institute Conference at Utica College of Syracuse University (Oct. 1994).
82. Vyacheslav Afanasyev, 'Organized Crime and Society', Demokratizatsiya, Vol. 2:3 (Summer 1994).
83. Ibid.
84. FBI Agent James Kallstrom, as quoted in The Times (Trenton), Aug. 14, 1995 at A1.
85. Handelman; Claire Sterling, Thieves' World (New York: Simon and Schuster, 1994).
86. See Remarks of FBI Dep. Asst. Dir. Moody.
87. Afanasyev, op. cit.
88. Ibid.
89. Handelman, op. cit.
90. Handelman; Sterling, op. cit.
91. The Times (Trenton), Aug. 14, 1995, at A1.
92. FBI Special Agent John Stafford, Remarks before the First International Law Enforcement Information Sharing Conference on Russian Organized Crime (Sept. 19–23, 1994).
93. Robert I. Friedman, 'The Organizatsiya', New York Magazine (Nov. 7, 1994); see also, Wall Street Journal, Dec. 22, 1994, at A10, col. 1; N.ew York Times, Aug. 23, 1994, at A1, col. 5.
94. The Times (Trenton), Aug. 14, 1995, at A1.
95. US Customs Agent Roy Surrett, Remarks before the First International Law Enforcement Info Sharing Conference on Russian Organized Crime (Sept. 19–23, 1994); Lydia S. Rosner, 'The Sexy Russian Mafia', Criminal Organizations Vol. 10:1 (Fall 1995).
96. New York Daily News, June 9, 1995, at 4.
97. US v. Elson.
98. Statement of former N.Y.P.D. Detective Peter Grinenko during interview by James O. Finckenauer (Oct. 9, 1993).

99. Statement of I.N.S. Special Agent Helene Berkholcs, during interview by James O. Finckenauer (June 14, 1995).
100. Mary McIntosh, *The Organization of Crime* (London: Macmillan, 1975).
101. Handelman, op. cit.; Louise Shelley, 'Post-Soviet Organized Crime: Implications for the Development of the Soviet Successor States and Foreign Countries', *Criminal Organizations*, Vol. 9:1, 15–22 (Summer 1994); Joseph Serio, 'Organized Crime in the Former Soviet Union: Only the Name is New', *Criminal Justice International*, Vol. 9:4, 11–17 (July–Aug. 1993). Officially is not listed as an international airport, but airplanes flying to and from Russia make a stopover here. Who boards them here, who deplanes, what they are carrying–nobody knows' (Yakov, 'Who Armed Dzhokar Dudayev?')

Appendix A
Tri-State Project Member Agencies

New Jersey State Commission of Investigation

The New Jersey State Commission of Investigation (SCI) was created in 1968 following extensive research and public hearings conducted by the Joint Legislative Committee to Study Crime and the System of Criminal Justice in New Jersey. That Committee, which was under direction from the Legislature to find ways to correct what was a serious and intensifying crime problem, attributed the expanding activities of organized crime to 'failure, to some considerable degree, in the system itself, official corruption, or both.' Sweeping recommendations for improving various areas of the criminal justice system were proposed.

Two of the Committee's most significant recommendations were for a new State criminal justice unit in the executive branch and an independent State Commission of Investigation. The Committee envisioned the criminal justice unit and SCI as complementary agencies in the fight against crime and corruption. The criminal justice unit was to be a large organization with extensive manpower and authority to coordinate and conduct criminal investigations and prosecutions throughout the state. The SCI was to be a relatively small, expert body which would conduct fact-finding investigations, bring the facts to the public's attention and make recommendations to the Governor and the Legislature for improvements in laws and the operations of government. The Committee's recommendations prompted immediate legislative and executive action and New Jersey now has a Criminal Justice Division in the Department of Law and Public Safety and an independent State Commission of Investigation.

To eliminate any appearance of political influence in the SCI's operations, no more than two of the four Commissioners may be of the same political party. Two Commissioners are appointed by the Governor and one each by the President of the Senate and the Speaker of the Assembly. It thus may be said the Commission is by law, bipartisan, and by concern and action, nonpartisan.

The SCI's enabling statute assigns to it a wide range of responsibilities and powers. The SCI may compel testimony and the production of other evidence by subpoena and has authority to grant immunity from prosecution to witnesses. Since the SCI does not have prosecutorial functions, it refers any findings of possible criminality to an appropriate prosecutorial authority.

The Commission emphasizes that indictments and convictions which result from referral of criminal matters to other agencies are not the only test of the efficacy of its public actions. More important are the corrective statutory and regulatory reforms spurred by arousing public and legislative interest. The Commission takes particular pride in all such actions which have resulted in improved laws and governmental operations.

New York State Commission of Investigation

With a broad statutory mandate to investigate 'any matter concerning the public peace, public safety and public justice,' the New York State Commission of Investigation undertakes investigations of corruption, fraud and mismanagement in New York State and local government. The Commission is also charged with conducting investigations into organized crime and labor racketeering and their relation to the enforcement of State law.

Established in 1958 as an independent, bi-partisan agency, with members appointed equally by the Governor, the President Pro Tem of the Senate and the Speaker of the Assembly, the Commission is uniquely qualified to investigate matters pertaining to the effective enforcement of State law. The Commission is authorized to conduct public and private hearings and issue public and private reports. Since its inception, the Commission has published over one hundred reports and has provided the impetus for Statewide change in many areas including the construction industry, municipal finance law, and eavesdropping and wiretapping statutes. The Commission is also mandated to work cooperatively with other State agencies and routinely responds to requests for assistance from out-of-state agencies and federal authorities as well.

The Commission's purely investigative character enables it to address problems – and suggest legislative and administrative remedies – beyond the jurisdiction of other State agencies. When evidence of criminal behavior is developed during an investigation, it is referred to an appropriate prosecutor. Of equal importance is the Commission's role as a 'sunshine agency' by which the Commission is able to focus public attention on particular problems of local or Statewide importance.

The Commission's investigative powers extend to more than 80 State agencies, divisions, boards and authorities as well as over 1,600 political subdivisions of the State – including the State's 62 counties and more than 500 villages, 900 towns and 60 cities. Its broad investigative jurisdiction also includes thousands of school, water and sewer districts throughout the State. In most circumstances, outside of the local district attorney, the Commission is the only independent investigative body in the State with the power to review and investigate allegations of fraud, waste, corruption and malfeasance. Unlike a local prosecutor's office, the Commission, through its 'sunshine' role, also has the authority to address these types of allegations outside the traditional criminal justice forum and highlight these governmental problems for the Governor, the legislature and the public.

New York State Organized Crime Task Force

The New York State Organized Crime Task Force ('OCTF') is a division of the New York State Department of Law that specializes in the investigation and prosecution of multicounty and multistate organized crime activities. Recognizing the complexity and diversity of organized crime and the need for a coordinated centralized approach to combat it, the New York State Legislature established OCTF in 1970 through the enactment of Section 70–a of New York's Executive Law. OCTF identifies emerging and existing organized crime enterprises and, through a broad array of civil and criminal enforcement techniques, seeks to undermine their structure, influence and presence within the State.

Section 70–a gives OCTF broad power to investigate and prosecute criminal activity throughout the State of New York. Its jurisdiction extends to all organized crime activity that crosses county or state boundaries. OCTF may conduct investigative hearings, compel the production of documents and other evidence, apply for search and eavesdropping warrants, and, upon the consent of the governor and the appropriate district attorney, appear before grand juries, conduct criminal and civil actions and exercise the same powers as the local district attorney.

OCTF has offices throughout the State of New York, with the largest concentration of its staff in While Plains and Albany. Most of its cases involve long-term investigations into such areas as narcotics trafficking, gambling, money laundering, grand larceny, official corruption and fraud. The attorneys, investigators and forensic accountants pool their expertise from the inception of an investigation through the resolution of any resulting criminal or civil case. Civil remedies, in particular, civil forfeiture, are used in conjunction with criminal sanctions to remove the economic capabilities of criminal enterprises and incentives for further criminal activity.

OCTF is also involved in analyses of particular organized crime problems to formulate enforcement strategies that may include legislative and administrative reforms in addition to case-specific criminal and civil remedies.

Pennsylvania Crime Commission

In response to a marked increase in crime during the 1960s, Pennsylvania Governor Raymond P. Shafer issued an executive order in March 1967, creating a temporary Crime Commission to look into the causes of crime, assess the adequacy of the State's enforcement efforts, and make recommendations to prevent, reduce and control crime. Eighteen months later, the Commission presented a report containing several recommendations for reform to the Governor and General Assembly. One recommendation proposed the creation of a permanent crime commission which would focus attention on the problem of organized crime.

Based upon that recommendation, the Pennsylvania Crime Commission was established in July 1968. Set up as an independent fact-finding agency, the Commission's primary responsibility was to investigate and expose the problems of organized crime and criminal justice along with all other types of systemic fraud or corruption. As stated by former Gov. Shafer, the Commission was 'empowered to investigate serious crime wherever it exists in Pennsylvania.'

The Commission's unique powers and duties distinguished it from other law enforcement and prosecutive agencies which focus on the development and prosecution of criminal cases. As a fact-finding body, the Commission was equipped to shed light upon the fundamental causes of problems in ways that traditional enforcement agencies could rarely accomplish. To perform its functions, the Commission was granted the power to hold hearings, subpoena witnesses and compel testimony regarding a broad array of issues.

For more than two decades, the Pennsylvania Crime Commission investigated all types of organized criminal activities and rooted out corruption throughout the state. Some of the Commission's more notable investigations focused on uncovering Italian organized crime involvement in the waste hauling industry, identifying the operations of Philadelphia's Junior Black Mafia, and targeting Philadelphia's Chinatown racketeers. Other investigative targets included Jamaican drug posses, Korean gambling organizations, and Vietnamese gangs, as well as numerous corrupt politicians, police officers and government employees. In addition, the Commission often served as a catalyst for positive change in the Pennsylvania criminal justice system. In 1970, the Commission drafted the Pennsylvania Corrupt Organizations Act, which was designed to curb racketeer infiltration into legitimate business. The Commission also continually proposed changes in State law to improve law enforcement's ability to combat organized crime. These proposed changes included improving the State's witness immunity statutes and reforming its electronic surveillance laws.

Following a highly publicized dispute with former State Attorney General Ernie Preate, the Pennsylvania Crime Commission was disbanded by the Pennsylvania Legislature in June 1994.

Rutgers – The State University of New Jersey, School of Criminal Justice

The Rutgers School of Criminal Justice, founded in 1973, is located in Newark, the largest city in the State of New Jersey. The School was authorized by an act of the New Jersey legislature in 1968, and was directed to develop a program of instruction, research and leadership. The School of Criminal Justice has programs of both undergraduate and graduate education, as well as research and public service. The goal of the School is to provide students with a basic understanding of delinquency and crime, of the criminal justice system, and of methods of assessing current problems and issues in these areas. The faculty of the School is interdisciplinary, being drawn principally from criminology, law, psychology, and sociology. This is necessary since no traditional academic discipline covers the wide spectrum of expertise required to accomplish the School's purposes.

The School of Criminal Justice is also a major national and international center for scholarly research on all aspects of delinquency, crime, and criminal justice administration. Among the School's recent research project's are studies of the sentencing of white-collar offenders, Chinese gangs, domestic violence, and Russian-émigré organized crime.

The Rutgers University research team, in collaboration with the Tri-State Project, conducted a nationwide mail survey of law enforcement agencies to determine the extent of Russian-émigré crime in the United States. A total of 750 questionnaires were mailed to law enforcement agencies across the country. In response, the team received 484 completed questionnaires from agencies in every state representing every level (federal, state, county and local) of government. The results of the survey are summarized below.

Survey Results

Participants in the survey were asked whether their agency had, within the previous five years, investigated, prosecuted or otherwise had contact with criminals or suspected criminals from the former Soviet Union. Of the 484 respondents, 167 (35 percent) replied 'yes.' Asked whether Russian-émigré crime was considered a major problem within their jurisdiction, 65 (13 percent) indicated it was. Of those agencies which have had contact with Russian-émigré crime, 47 (28 percent) have dealt with more than twenty Russian-émigré criminals, while 84 (50 percent) agencies have been able to obtain at least one criminal conviction against a Russian-émigré.

Since one of the Project's goals was to determine whether Russian-émigré crime in the United States is a form of organized crime, survey participants were asked, 'According to your agency's definition of organized crime, are any persons from the former Soviet Union considered part of organized crime?' One hundred and one agencies (64 percent) responded affirmatively. Participants were also asked about the types of crimes being committed within their area by Russian-émigrés. Fraud (53.3 percent) was the most common crime reported, followed by money laundering (31.7 percent), drugs (31.1 percent), violent crimes (31.1 percent), extortion (19.2 percent), forgery (18.6 percent), racketeering (16.8 percent), prostitution (12.0 percent) and loan sharking (4.8 percent).

Those respondents who indicated their agency has had contact with Russian-émigré criminals were asked several questions about their response to this problem. 40 respondents (24 percent) indicated they have attempted to obtain information from government agencies in the former Soviet Union. More than half of these attempts were successful and, in several instances, the agency's efforts were still in progress. 52 respondents (31 percent) indicated having staff members with Russian language skills, while 72 (43 percent) said that within their agencies, special efforts were being made to focus on Soviet-émigré crime. Finally, 79 respondents (47 percent) reported that there is a single person or group within their agency that handles most cases involving crime by Soviet-émigrés.

Appendix B

Russian-Emigré Populations in the Tri-State Area

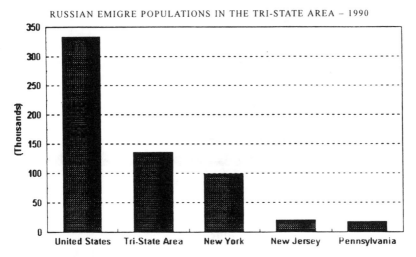

RUSSIAN EMIGRE POPULATIONS IN THE TRI-STATE AREA – 1990

Source: US Census Bureau

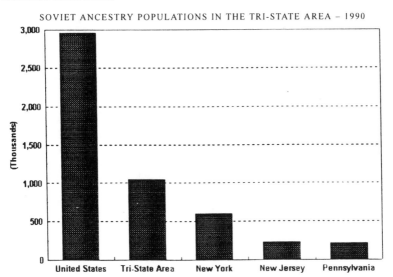

SOVIET ANCESTRY POPULATIONS IN THE TRI-STATE AREA – 1990

Source: US Census Bureau

Appendix C
Rutgers University/Tri-State Project Law Enforcement Survey

REPORTED RUSSIAN-EMIGRE CRIMINAL ACTIVITIES 1991–95

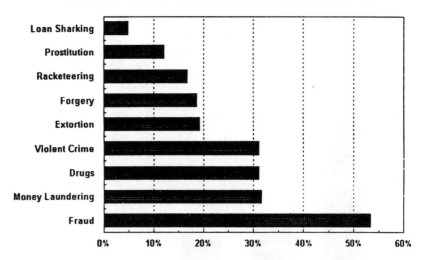

Appendix D
Russian-Emigré Crime Statistics for the Tr-State Area

NUMBER OF ARESTS OF RUSSIAN-EMIGRES IN NEW YORK STASTE
BETWEEN 1989 AND 1995

| | New York City | | | Non-New York City | | | |
Year	Felony	Misd	Total	Felony	Misd	Total	State Total
1989	268	326	594	30	178	208	802
1990	273	346	619	50	180	230	849
1991	306	388	694	64	214	278	972
1992	363	654	1017	53	246	299	1316
1993	334	618	952	48	278	326	1278
1994	434	799	1233	50	261	311	1544
1995	497	750	1247	64	278	342	1589

Source: NYS Dept. of Criminal Justice Services

RUSSIAN-EMIGRE CRIME STATISTICS
NEW YORK CITY

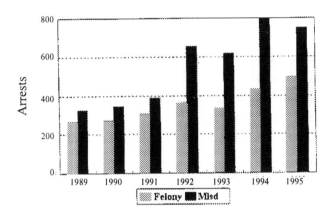

RUSSIAN-EMIGRE CRIME STATISTICS
NEW YORK CITY

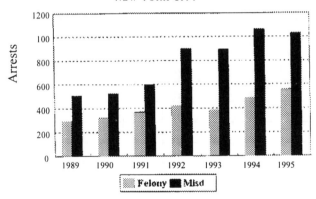

NEW JERSEY FINGERPRINT SUPPORTED ARRESTS:
RUSSIAN BORN SUBJECTS 1989–95

COUNTY	1989	1990	1991	1992	1993	1994	1995	TOTAL
Atlantic	10	8	4	12	24	32	22	112
Bergen	14	39	53	74	85	72	120	457
Burlington	4	3	2	10	6	10	14	49
Camden	1	8	13	9	10	17	17	75
Cape May	1	2	0	4	7	5	0	19
Cumberland	0	3	17	5	3	5	2	35
Essex	9	20	27	17	25	34	42	174
Gloucester	0	0	0	0	3	3	5	11
Hudson	11	21	17	19	21	17	11	117
Hunterdon	0	6	0	0	2	0	1	9
Mercer	5	2	12	11	18	11	18	77
Middlesex	29	34	83	58	66	72	71	413
Monmouth	18	28	76	36	15	63	29	265
Morris	6	7	13	13	10	16	19	84
Ocean	6	11	4	1	12	5	3	42
Passaic	5	7	10	11	13	25	23	94
Salem	0	0	0	0	3	2	0	5
Somerset	0	3	2	2	3	9	8	27
Sussex	0	0	0	2	1	3	0	6
Union	23	21	12	32	27	38	49	202
Warren	1	1	5	1	12	3	0	23
Unassigned	8	5	9	18	0	0	0	40
TOTAL	151	229	359	335	366	442	454	2336

Statistics supplied by New Jersey State Police.

NEW JERSEY FINGERPRINT SUPPORTED ARRESTS
RUSSIAN-BORN SUBJECTS 1989–95

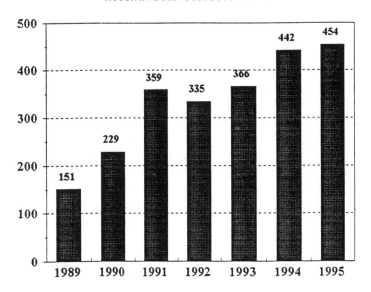

Statistics supplied by New Jersey State Police.

Appendix E

Russian-Emigré Homicides and Attempted Homicides 1981–95

1. **Rachmel Dementev**
   Shot to death on January 1, 1981, by Vladimir Reznikov. Dementev was allegedly killed after calling Reznikov an informant.

2. **Sheila and Slavi Shaknis**
   Mother and son shot to death on March 3, 1981, allegedly because their husband/ father failed to repay money owed to other criminals.

3. **Yuri Brokhin**
   Shot to death in his New York City apartment on December 5, 1982. Some time earlier, his wife had been found dead in their bathtub. Originally thought a suicide, she may have been murdered also.

4. **David Eligolashavili**
   Murdered in 1982. He was allegedly involved in loan-sharking and the sale of stolen Torah scrolls.

5. **Victor Malinsky**
   Found shot to death in Manhattan on February 6, 1983.

6. **Zurab Minakhi**
   Stabbed to death on August 21, 1983, in the Sadko Restaurant in Brighton Beach, Brooklyn, allegedly by Benjamin Nayfeld during a fight.

7. **Ilya Goldstein** (Attempt)
   Shot five times in Manhattan on December 15, 1983.

8. **Evsei Agron** (Attempt)
   Shot in the neck on January 24, 1984, as he exited an underground garage in the building in which he lived in Park Slope, Brooklyn. He survived the attack but was later killed on May 4, 1985 (see below). A self-proclaimed 'Russian Godfather,' Agron came to the United States in 1975 and, within a few years, built a criminal empire in Brighton Beach.

9. **Mikhail Tolstonog**
   Found shot to death in a boiler room on February 28, 1984.

10. **Evsei Agron**
    Shot to death on May 4, 1985, when an assassin fired two bullets into his head as he waited for an elevator in his building.

11. **Ilya Zeltzer**
    Shot to death on Feb. 3, 1986, during a shootout inside a gas distribution office ('Platenum Energy') in Brooklyn. He was allegedly shot by Vladimir Reznikov in a dispute over bootleg gas.

12. **Shaya Kalikman**
Shot to death on March 3, 1986, in a Brighton Beach social club, allegedly by Garik Verbitsky (see below).

13. **Oleg Vaksman**
Shot to death on April 26, 1986, inside a friend's Brighton Beach apartment. He was allegedly a mid-level cocaine dealer.

14. **Vladimir Reznikov**
Shot to death on June 13, 1986, while getting into his car in front of the Odessa Restaurant in Brighton Beach. He was allegedly killed by *La Cosa Nostra* at the request of Russian criminals involved in the bootleg gas scams.

15. **Anatoly Rubashkin**
Shot to death. His body was found in a lot in Sheepshead Bay, Brooklyn, on July 25, 1986.

16. **Garik Verbitsky**
Shot to death in a Brighton Beach social club on April 21, 1987. Also known as 'Jerry Razor,' he was suspected of murdering Shaya Kalikman (see above).

17. **Rosala Elyurina**
Stabbed to death on September 13, 1987.

18. **Boris Rubinov**
Shot to death in his car on November 18, 1987. He was believed to have been a low-level criminal killed over a drug debt.

19. **Lev Persits** (Attempt)
Paralyzed after being shot in the back on November 18, 1987. He was allegedly involved in the bootleg gas scams.

20. **Philip Moskowitz**
Found dead in North Brunswick, N.J., on December 5, 1987. His body exhibited signs that he had been tortured prior to his death. Moskowitz was a friend of Michael Markowitz (see below) and was also involved in the bootleg gas scams.

21. **Gregory Yampolsky**
Allegedly killed by Felix Furman (see below) on October 18, 1988.

22. **Felix Furman**
Shot to death in Brighton Beach on December 10, 1988, by Valery Zlotnikov from whom Furman was extorting money.

23. **Michael Markowitz**
Shot to death in a car on May 2, 1989. Arrested in connection with the bootleg gas scams, he was allegedly killed on orders from *La Cosa Nostra* to prevent his cooperation with police.

24. **Abram Khaskin**
Found shot to death inside a burning car on May 23, 1990.

25. **Nayfeld** (Attempt)
Unexploded bomb found under his car on January 14, 1991.

26. **Jerome Slobotkin**
Shot to death near his Philadelphia home by Antuan Bronshtein on February 19, 1991. In 1988, Slobotkin had testified against Nicodemo Scarfo and other Scarfo associates, claiming to be a victim of a Scarfo protection racket.

27. **Vladimir Vaynerchuk**
Bludgeoned to death in an elevator on February 28, 1991.

28. **Vyacheslav Lyubarsky** (Attempt)
Shot in the buttocks by an unknown assailant on March 3, 1991, in the hall outside his apartment. He was allegedly a member of a Soviet narcotics trafficking group that imported heroin into the United States through Bangkok, Poland and Brussels. He was later killed, along with his son, Vadim, in January 1992 (see below).

29. **David Shuster** (Attempt)
Shot on March 20, 1991. He was allegedly involved in the bootleg gas scams.

30. **Emil Puzyretsky**
Shot to death on May 11, 1991, inside the National Restaurant in Brighton Beach. A gunman shot him twice at close range with a silencer-equipped handgun and several additional times after he fell to the floor. Puzyretsky was a mob enforcer known for his use of knives. He was also involved in the bootleg gas scams.

31. **Monya Elson** (Attempt)
Shot in Brighton Beach on May 14, 1991. Reputed leader of a crime group involved in counterfeiting, drug trafficking and other criminal activities. He was allegedly involved in the murders of Elbrous Evdoev and the Lubarskys (see below). This attempt was suspected to have been in retaliation for the attempt on Vyacheslav Lyubarsky (see above). Other attempts on Elson's life are detailed below.

32. **Gintis Digry**
Shot to death in a car in Brooklyn on May 22, 1991. A second man, Richardas Vasiliavitchous, was wounded during the attack.

33. **Moisy Zusim and Leonid Khazanovich**
Zusim, the owner of a West Philadelphia jewelry store, and his employee, Khazanovich, were shot to death with semi-automatic weapons on June 11, 1991, during a robbery at the jewelry store.

34. **Fima Miller**
Murdered inside a Brooklyn jewelry store on July 27, 1991. He was alleged to be an associate of Namik Karafov and Fima Laskin (see below).

35. Namik Karafov
Shot to death inside his apartment on July 30, 1991. Several guns were found at the scene but not the murder weapon.

36. Yevgeni Michailov
Abducted in Brooklyn on July 8, 1991, his body was found in a lot near Kennedy Airport in New York City on August 27, 1991. He had been shot four times in the head. He was allegedly involved in jewelry theft and fraud.

37. Fima Laskin
Stabbed to death in Munich on September 27, 1991.

38. Roman Kegueles
Body found floating in Sheepshead Bay, Brooklyn, on November 6, 1991. He had been stabbed numerous times.

39. Robert Sason (Attempt)
Shot in the hand on December 15, 1991.

40. Vyacheslav and Vadim Lyubarsky
Vyacheslav ('Slava') and his son, Vadim, were shot to death on January 12, 1992, in the hallway outside their Brighton Beach apartment. After returning from dinner with Slava's wife, Nellie, they were ambushed by an assassin who emerged from the hallway shadows and shot both men, but not Nellie. In 1995, Monya Elson and others were charged in a federal indictment for these and other murders.

41. Efrim Ostrovsky
Shot to death on January 21, 1992, while exiting his stretch limousine in Queens, N.Y. The hit was allegedly arranged by Alexander Slepinin (see below) who was extorting money from Ostrovsky.

42. Said Amin Moussostov
Shot to death by two unknown gunmen on May 8, 1992, in the hallway of his home in Palisades Park, N.J. A former Soviet kick-boxer, he was reputed to be a member of a violent Chechen crime group. It is suspected that he was involved in the murder of Fima Laskin (see above).

43. Elbrous Evdoev (Attempt)
Shot in the jaw and back in New York City on June 5, 1992. Alleged to be involved in prostitution, Evdoev survived this attack but was later killed in early 1993 (see below).

44. Alexander Slepinin
Shot to death in his car on June 23, 1992. Allegedly responsible for the death of Efrim Ostrovsky (see above), Slepinin was shot numerous times in the head and back. In 1995, Monya Elson and others were charged in a federal indictment for this and other murders.

45. Elbrous Evdoev (Attempt)

Shot in the shoulder and hand on July 4, 1992, in New York City. Evdoev told police the shooting had been ordered by Monya Elson.

46. Boris Roitman
Shot to death on August 26, 1992.

47. Monya Elson (Attempt)
Shot in the forearm by an unknown assailant in Los Angeles on November 6, 1992. Elson was driven by Leonyard Kanterkantetes to a hospital where he was treated and released. Two days later, an Armenian attempting to plant a bomb under Kanterkantetes' car was critically injured when the bomb detonated prematurely.

48. Vladimir Zilbersteyn (Attempt)
Shot in the face and upper body by shotgun pellets fired from another vehicle while driving in Manhattan on November 20, 1992. The shooting was allegedly caused by a dispute with Italian mobsters involved in the bootleg motor fuel tax scams.

49. Vanya Sargsyan
Body was found early in the morning on January 1, 1993, in an industrial area in Lynbrook, Long Island. A Brighton Beach resident, he had been shot three times in the head, chest and shoulder with an automatic weapon. He was allegedly shot over a dispute regarding the trade of colored metals.

50. Elbrous Evdoev
Body was found fully dressed, frozen solid in a snow bank at an auto salvage yard in Pine Brook, N.J., on March 6, 1993. He had been shot three times in the head. Evdoev had been the target of two previous shootings (see above).

51. Lev Gendler
Found dead in his apartment on March 23, 1993. He had been shot numerous times in the head and body. Gendler's criminal history included arrests in the United States and Israel for counterfeiting, extortion, kidnapping and bank fraud.

52. Michael Libkin (Attempt)
On June 10, 1993, Michael Libkin was shot inside his antique store in Manhattan by Peter Gripaldi, a California 'hitman' who had arrived in New York a few days earlier. Gripaldi entered the store, spoke briefly with Libkin, removed a silencer-equipped, automatic handgun from his briefcase and shot Libkin in the groin. After a struggle, Libkin took out his own gun, followed Gripaldi out of the store and shot him in the chest. Both men were taken to Bellevue Hospital and released a few days later. Gripaldi was later convicted for this shooting on the basis of an indictment filed by the Manhattan District Attorney.

53. Monya Elson (Attempt)
Elson, his wife and bodyguard, Oleg Zapinakmine, were shot in front of Elson's Brooklyn home by Boris Grigoriev on July 26, 1993. All three were treated and released after a brief stay at a local hospital. The attempts on Elson's life resulted

from a dispute between Elson and other criminal factions within the Brighton Beach community.

54. Oleg Zapinakmine
On September 24, 1993, two months after the failed attempt on Monya Elson, bodyguard Oleg Zapinakmine was shot once in the back and killed by an unknown assailant. At the time he was shot, Zapinakmine was checking a flat tire on his car in front of his Brooklyn home.

55. Georgiy Sidropulo (Attempt)
Shot three times in the jaw, chest and shoulder while sitting in front of a Brighton Beach cafe on October 20, 1993. The shots were fired from a van. Sidropulo was believed to be part of a Russian and Hispanic narcotics group known as 'T.F.' (Together Forever).

56. Vladimir Beigelman
Shot to death by two unknown males who fired four shots into his head, neck and back as he exited a van in Queens, N.Y., on December 2, 1993. Witnesses told police the shooters appeared to be Hispanic. Reputed to be a major cocaine trafficker with ties to both the Cali Cartel and *La Cosa Nostra*, Beigelman may have been blamed for losing a large shipment of cocaine.

57. Alexander Gutman
Shot to death execution-style by Northeast Philadelphia resident and Soviet émigré Antuan Bronshtein (see above) on January 11, 1994, at the victim's Philadelphia jewelry store.

58. Oleg Korataev
Shot to death on January 12, 1994, near the Arbat Restaurant in Brighton Beach. A former Soviet boxer known to be a brutal mob enforcer, he was attending a party at the restaurant and was shot in the back of the head as he stepped outside to get some air.

59. Alexander Levichitz ('Sasha Pinya') (Attempt)
Shot three times in the head near the Arbat Restaurant in Brighton Beach on the evening of January 17, 1994. He was allegedly a close friend of Monya Elson.

60. Vladimir Karak
Shot to death on January 21, 1994.

61. Yanik Megasaev
Body was found on March 23, 1994, in a pile of garbage in a wooded area near Shore Parkway in Brooklyn. Megasaev had been shot four times in the face and chest.

62. Alexander Graber
Was shot along with two other men in Moscow on June 16, 1994, by unknown assailants in a car. Graber had lived in Brighton Beach for over a year and allegedly had ties to local organized crime.

63. **Naum and Simeon Raichel** (Attempt)

On July 11, 1994, Naum Raichel was shot three times in the chest and stomach near the Winter Garden Restaurant in Brighton Beach. That same day, his brother Simeon was severely beaten in Berlin, Germany. Both men survived the attacks.

64. **Arkady Shvartsman**

Shot and killed by two gunmen on January 18, 1995, as he sat in his vehicle during the evening rush hour, just a few blocks away from the Philadelphia Police Department headquarters. Shvartsman's briefcase, which contained over 10,000 dollars, was left untouched by the gunmen on the seat next to Shvartsman.

65. **Heinrich Barel** (Attempt)

Shot in the face on April 20, 1995.

RECENT DEVELOPMENTS

The American Bar Association's Central and East European Law Initiative (CEELI) has provided the following information on criminal law developments as reported by the press from Central and Eastern Europe and the former Soviet Union. CEELI is currently involved in a partnership with the US Department of Justice to provide criminal law assistance to the countries of Central and Eastern Europe and the former Soviet Union. The DOJ/CEELI program uses American and European lawyers to participate in their programs on a pro bono basis. Interested parties should contact John Brandolino at CEELI. (FAX number: (202) 662-1597.)

Legal Issues

On December 6, 1995 Russian President Boris Yeltsin rejected a new Criminal Code and a law that would enact it. Both had been approved by the State Duma on November 24, 1995. In a statement released by the presidential press service, the Code was rejected in order to ward off a danger of legislative gridlock that would be practically impossible to institute criminal proceedings. 'In his letter to the State Duma', reported *ITAR–TASS*, 'Yeltsin expressed surprise at the absence of a number of crimes from the Criminal Code, including acts hindering journalists from the fulfillment of their legal professional duties. Speaking at a democratic press forum on October 1, the president described the absence of an article dealing with such crimes as "either the lawmakers" negligence or their aversion to a free press'. Yeltsin suggested setting up a reconciliation committee to work out a compromise version of the Criminal Code'. (*ITAR–TASS*, December 6, 1995, in *FBIS–SOV*, December 7, 1995, p. 28.)

On December 9, the Federation Council approved the laws 'On the Battle Against Corruption' and 'On the Battle Against Organized Crime'. The laws were accepted by the State Duma after being finalized by a bilateral conciliatory commission. 'The law on the battle against organized crime is needed to settle an important area of legal relations – the creation of a legal framework to step up the battle against new forms of crime, which pose a major threat to not only the rights and interests of citizens, but also the security of society and the state as a whole', *ITAR–TASS* reported. 'This was said by the committees of the Federation Council for security, defense, constitutional legislation and judicial issues. The new version of the law contains additional measures for supervision by the procurator and the courts and the means of putting this into effect. It also contains measures to protect witnesses. The number of bodies, given the right to combat organized crime has been substantially reduced. Rules on how long someone can be detained and when they have to be cleared are laid down in accordance with the criminal process code. The new law is important because there are no differing interpretations and applications of legal norms in it, according to deputies'. (*ITAR–TASS*, December 9, 1995, in *FBIS–SOV*, December 11, 1995, p. 44.)

On January 16, 1996 Vladimir Klimov wrote in *Rossiyskaya Gazeta* about the laws 'On the War Against Organized Crime' and 'On the War Against Corruption', both of which were vetoed on December 22 by Russian President Boris Yeltsin. The Law 'On the War Against Organized Crime' was first vetoed by Yeltsin in August 1993. According to Klimov, Azaliya Dolgova, the head of the division of general problems of criminology and the war against crime at the Scientific Research Institute of Problems of Strengthening Legality and Law and Order, 'is convinced that it is manifestly mafia forces that are standing in the way of the laws' passing. Those standing at the helm of the shadow economy who have been able to get their own people into both the legislative and executive organs of power'. Mikhail Krasnov, an aid to the president on legal issues, related to Klimov his support for both laws on the whole, but the stated that the unwise application of certain statutes could give rise to relapses back to 1937, the highpoint of Stalin's purges.

Klimov also stated that the laws contain articles that contradict democratic principles. Part three of Article 15 of the Law 'On the War Against Organized Crime', for example, contains a clause that obligates individuals to reveal the financial and real estate operation of their clients to law enforcement. In addition, he stated that parts one and two of Article 13 of the same law, which cover the seizure of financial means and property, violate the Constitution because a person whose money or property are confiscated must prove that he or she obtained them legally – a violation of the presumption of innocence. With regard to the Law 'On the War Against Corruption', Klimov wrote that 'the draft law included in its list of potential corruptees aids of elected officials'. That draft law also stated that the requirement of financial control be extended to the spouses of those applying for state service or employed in it, which Klimov also viewed as violating 'the constitutional right to the sanctity of private life, personal and family privacy'. Furthermore, Klimov also commented that the law contradicted the Civil Process Code with regard to the seizure of property, financial funds and other valuables from those who violate the law.

Finally, Klimov emphasized the need for new laws. 'I have had occasion to speak with practicians', he wrote. 'Their opinion is unambiguous: we need these laws now like we need air. With their help, employees of specialized law enforcement organs feel that within a year or two we would be able to liquidate the leaders of organized crime and the shadow economy, cleanse government service of bribe-takers. That is, do that which we struggle with from day to day, but, alas, the cart stays in the same place'. (Vladimir Klimov, *Rossiyskaya Gazeta* (Moscow), January 16, 1996, in *FBIS–SOV*, Supplement Issue, February 1, 1996, p. 44.)

On February 14, the Russian State Duma passed a bill reducing the period in which suspects can be held in custody without indictment to ten days. Currently, according to a June 1994 presidential decree on measures to combat organized crime, suspects can be held for a period up to thirty days without an indictment being initiated. (*OMRI Daily Report*, Part I, February 16, 1996.)

On March 7, President Boris Yeltsin issued a decree on measures to combat terrorism, which included the creation of an antiterrorism coordinating body. The decree instructed several ministries to draft amendments to antiterrorism laws within the next two months. The Foreign Intelligence Service was tasked with uncovering the international links of 'illegal armed formations' operating in Russia and with cutting off such organizations' funding and supply of weapons. The decree recommended that the Prosecutor General's Office tighten its supervision over the observance of Russian legislation in the media coverage of terrorist acts. The Federal Security Service (FSB) also was ordered to create in 1995 a nationwide database on terrorists and terrorist acts. (*Interfax*, March 8, 1996, in *FBIS–SOV*, March 8, 1996, p. 11.)

On March 16, Russian Prime Minister Viktor Chernomyrdin signed the RF Government Decree No. 291 'On the Ratification of the Statute on the Procedure for Exports From and Imports to the Russian Federation of Radioactive Materials and Products Based on Them'. (*Rossiyskaya Gazeta* (Moscow), March 27, 1996, in *FBIS–SOV*, March 28, 1996, p. 31.)

On April 23, Moscow's *Nezavisimaya Gazeta* published an interview with Boris Maksimov, deputy director of the Russian Federation State Duma

Health Care Committee apparat, regarding the draft law 'On Narcotic Substances and Psychotropic Substances', which was scheduled to be submitted in the first reading at the plenary session of the State Duma on April 24. 'I must say that legislation on narcotics as a rule includes three components: regulation of legal trade in narcotics substances; without fail a law which is devoted to countering illegal trade; and a law establishing the norms of responsibility', state Maksimov. 'In our Russian reality, they are the Criminal Code, the Code of Criminal Procedure, and the Code on Administrative Offenses. So we [in this draft law] did not have a very large section related to the legal narcotics trade and countering their trade at all. There were merely a few articles in the Criminal Code'.

Maksimov also quoted from an appraisal of Russian legislation with regards to this sphere by the executive director of the United Nations Drug Control Program (UNDCP), Mr. Giacomelli, written on December 8, 1995. 'The legal instruments in the area of the legal narcotics trade now in effect in Russia do not conform to the new development of the situation and thus have proven themselves ineffective', Giacomelli wrote. 'Similarly, the situation in the area of stopping contraband narcotics does not take account of new methods used by the smugglers. Money laundering, which represents a serious threat to the normal operation of the state's economy, is not covered by legislation at all'. (Boris Maksimov, *Nezavisimaya Gazeta* (Moscow), April 23, 1996, in *FBIS–SOV*, Supplement Issue, May 13, 1996, p. 39.)

On May 8, Russian Prime Minister Viktor Chernomyrdin signed Government Decree No. 574 'On Approving the Statute on the Procedure Governing the Export and Import of Nuclear Materials, Equipment, Special Nonnuclear Materials, and Corresponding Technologies'. (*Rossiyskaya Gazeta* (Moscow), May 23, 1996, in *FBIS–SOV*, June 4, 1996, p. 33.)

On May 22, the Russian Federation State Duma approved on first reading a long-delayed bill that would tighten legal penalties for bribe taking. (*OMRI Daily Report*, Part I, May 23, 1996.)

On May 24, during a second debate, the Duma passed a revised version of the Russian Criminal Code that included amendments suggested by President Yeltsin. The Code has been under discussion in the parliament for three years. Parliament members discussed around 2,000 amendments in the process of three readings of the draft bill and preparations for the final debates. On December 6, 1995, after a criminal code had passed both houses of parliament, President Yeltsin vetoed the previous version upon the recommendation of law enforcement agencies. Presidential representative Alexander Kotyonkov stated that one of the reasons for the president's criticism of the earlier code was 'the absence of a number of articles suggested to be introduced by judicial bodies'. In its final form, the Criminal Code 'can be used as a basis for fighting all kinds of organized crime', Kotyonkov quoted law enforcement representatives as stating. If the Federal Assembly passes the latest version, the Code will be effective as of January 1, 1997. The Code would retain capital punishment for five rather than for eighteen crimes. Russia's recent entry into the Council of Europe required that the death penalty be abolished by early 1999. (*OMRI Daily Report*, Part I, May 27, 1996; Ivan Novikov, *ITAR–TASS*, May 24, 1996;

On May 27, the Constitutional Court began to review the legality of one of the articles of President Yeltsin's June 1994 decree on organized crime. The plaintiff, Valerii Shchelukhin, through his lawyer, has argued that the provisions on 'collecting evidence against those suspected of belonging to a criminal group without the institution of criminal proceedings' and permitting suspects to be held for up to thirty days without charges are unconstitutional and violate human rights. Shchelukhin, who is being held in a pre-trial detention center, is also contesting the constitutionality of the clause in the Criminal Procedure Code, which excludes the period of time the accused spends studying the case against him from the total time he or she spends in detention. Hence, the plaintiff argued, preliminary detention can be extended at the whim of the investigators. A member of the Russian Constitutional Court told *ITAR–TASS* that this case is the third one of late which lacked the presence of representatives of the state bodies. Hence, in the view of this, the Court would not be able to establish all the viewpoints on all sides of the issue. (*OMRI Daily Report*, Part I, May 28, 1996; and Igor Belsky, *ITAR–TASS* (Moscow), May 27, 1996.)

On May 30, Moscow's *Moskovskiy Komsomolets* reported that the Main Protection Directorate will be renamed in the near future as the Russian Federation Federal Protection Service (FSO). Under a federal law 'On State Protection', signed by President Yeltsin recently, eight top state positions are subject to state protection – the president, the prime minister, the speakers of both houses of the Russian parliament, the general prosecutor and the chairmen of the Constitutional Court, Supreme Court and Higher Court of Arbitration. The federal protection bodies are to be controlled by the president. (*Moskovskiy Komsomolets* (Moscow), May 30, 1996, in *FBIS–SOV*, May 31, 1996, p. 25.)

Crime Statistics

On November 23, 1995 *Moscow News* published rates for contract killings – a growth industry in the former Soviet Union. To fix up an average contract killing in Russia would set one back $7,000, providing the victim did not have a bodyguard, while the price for killing someone with a bodyguard currently costs $12,000 with half paid up front with a photograph, address and a description of the victim's car. The remainder would have to be paid within two days of the 'hit' being carried out. 'Rubbing out' President Boris Yeltsin would cost $180,000. Police in Russia's organized crime-fighting unit calculated the cost of killing the president. 'This sum embraces a 96 percent guarantee of success in the attempt, its technical preparation, expenditure for covering and organizing the escape of the killer from the crime scene and even, if necessary, the elimination of the killer himself', the newspaper wrote. (*Reuters World Service*, November 23, 1995.)

On November 25, *Rossiyskiye Vesti* published statistics on crime in Russia, suggesting that the situation has not improved in the current year. In 1995, '[t]here were 2,317,700 registered crimes, half of them grave, committed in its first ten months, which is 5.5 percent more than in the same period last year', the *Russian Press Digest* stated in its summary of the *Rossiyskiye Vesti* article. 'Moreover, a plurality of them were marked by thorough organization. There were also 123,000 economic crimes (14 percent up on the previous year). In this connection, the paper singles out as the most destructive factor, one affecting the state of society as a whole and the crime situation, the high rate of concentration of capital and production means in the hands of private individuals. The process has helped to exacerbate the fight for the spheres of influence among the New Russians, many of whom have either a criminal past record or ties inside the criminal world, says the paper. According to its information, there are 6,500 organized criminal groups active in Russia. The most dangerous of these are 46 inter-regional groups, manned by over 6,000 fighters. Yet another danger is represented by 870 criminal groups formed on the ethnic principle, which engage in money-laundering with a turnover worth 30 billion US dollars per year. Regrettably, says the paper, the Government's opposition to crime is inconsistent and runs athwart many factors .... Another national-scale problem is the level of official corruption. According to data available to the Interior Ministry, one in every ten organized criminal groups is under protection of a corrupt official'. (*Rossiyskiye Vesti*, November 25, 1995, in *Russian Press Digest*, November 25, 1995.)

On November 28, *ITAR–TASS* reported that a total of 1.5 trillion rubles in revenues were appropriated by Russia's criminal groups in 1994 as a result of shadow deals, according to Aleksander Kartashev, the first deputy chief of the Russian Interior department for fighting organized crime. In 1994, the Interior crime fighting department detected over 400 criminal groups on Russia's territory. Armed clashes among the different crime groups resulted in the deaths of 156 active members and in the wounding of 200 other crime gangsters. (Larisa Kislinskaya, *ITAR–TASS*, November 28, 1995.)

On November 28, *Nezavisimaya Gazeta* published an article on the rate of crimes by ethnic groups in Moscow. 'According to Moscow GUVD [Main Administration of Internal Affairs] RUOP [Regional Anti-Organized Crime Administration] information', the article stated, 'the range of crimes committed by members of ethnic groups is very broad – from apartment burglaries and extortion to controlling farmers market trade and foreign currency and financial operations. According to Mikhail Suntsov, a Moscow GUVD RUOP department chief, this situation is due to a considerable degree to the influx of criminal elements in Moscow caused by a sharp change in the political and economic situation in the Transcaucasus and North Caucasus. The region has suffered economic degradation, and in connection with this local criminal groups, under the protection of high-ranking officials, have divided spheres of influence. While those who were 'left out' had to look for other sources of income – and this is how some criminals ended up in Moscow'.

'There are currently seven ethnic communities in the capital, within which 116 organized crime groups have been identified (103 as of nine months of 1994)', the article detailed. 'Total number of active participants – about 2,000. At the top of the list are natives of Azerbaijan – 32 organized crime groups. Next on the list is Dagestan – 20 organized crime groups, Chechnya – 20 organized crime groups, Armenia – 17 organized crime groups, North Ossetia – nine organized crime groups, and Ingushetia – four organized crime groups. The sum result of their activities over nine months of this year is this: 2,484 crimes, which is 743 more than the analogous period of last year. The record was set by the citizens of sovereign Georgia – they committed 977 crimes. The Azerbaijanis are not far behind – 881 crimes. Armenians account for 278 crimes, Dagestanis – 145, Chechens – 121, North Ossetians – 66, and Ingush – 27 crimes. According to RUOP data, criminal charges were filed against 2,355 persons, which is 688 more than over nine months of 1994. Compared to last year, there was an increase in the incidence of such crimes as murder, theft, illegal drug trafficking, grave bodily harm, and illegal foreign currency operations committed by "ethnic" criminal groups. There was practically no change in the number of robberies and muggings. Inhabitants of Georgia, Azerbaijan, and Armenia continue to exert a substantial influence on the state of the operational situation in Moscow. The number of crimes committed by them has increased by 320, 299, and 113, respectively. Over nine months of this year, RUOP personnel liquidated 101 criminal groups, with 335 active members. The positions of the "Chechen group" have been substantially weakened – not a single prominent Chechen leader is currently in the city. According to Mikhail Suntsov, the city currently is experiencing an influx of what is in police jargon called "persons who have descended from the mountains". They engage in unsystematic robberies and extortion. In the opinion of the police, however, these groups are rather weak'. (Dmitriy Maslennikov, *Nezavisimaya Gazeta*, November 28, 1995, in *FBIS–SOV*, Supplement Issue, December 18, 1995, p. 90.)

On December 8, Russian Interior Minister Anatoliy Kulikov stated that a total of 1.6 million crimes and offenses, including 700,000 grave ones, were committed in Russian in the first eleven months of 1995. 65 percent of the crimes were exposed. Over 100 criminal groups operating outside Moscow were eradicated. (*ITAR–TASS*, December 8, 1995.)

On December 20, in a briefing by Moscow Police Department Deputy Chief Vladislav Selivanov, who stated that the criminal situation in Moscow is out of police control, statistics were given on the number of organized gang leaders in the capital city. 'There are about 80 gang leaders, mostly Georgians, in Moscow', Larisa Kislinskaya reported on the briefing for *ITAR–TASS*. '27 of them are residing in the capital. For the whole CIS [Commonwealth of Independent States], the number of gang leaders known to police amounts to 780, with 380 of them residing in Russia. 25 band leaders were arrested in Moscow over the past 11 months. The absence of specific laws on organized crime and corruption in the country makes it difficult to fight the crime. The arrested mobsmen were charged only with illegal possession of drugs and arms. After the arrest, they are as a rule let out on bail and escape from trial. Sometimes, criminals manage to buy judges. For example, it took 800,000 US dollars to free one of the eldest mobsmen nicknamed Tsirul, Selivanov said. According to the official, the law enforcement forces will continue to suffer defeat in the fight against organized crime until it is swept out of the economic, political and business spheres and locked within traditional spheres – drugs, prostitution and so on'. (Larisa Kislinskaya, *ITAR–TASS*, December 20, 1995.)

On December 27, the Moscow police announced that there were 106 criminal explosions in the first eleven months of 1995. Fifteen people were killed and 56 wounded in the explosions, but arrests were made in only six cases. (*OMRI Daily Report*, Part I, December 28, 1995.)

On January 17, 1996 an article in *Literaturnaya Gazeta* observed that Internal Affairs Minister Anatoliy Kulikov recently stated that over eleven months of 1995 more than 570 million rubles and $4.4 million worth of money and valuables were seized from criminal organizations. (Igor Gamayunov, *Literaturnaya Gazeta* (Moscow), January 17, 1996, in *FBIS–SOV*, Supplement Issue, February 1, 1996, p. 50.)

On January 30, *ITAR–TASS* reported that a total of 60 contract murders have been in Moscow's crime statistics for 1995. Only seven of these cases has been unraveled. 'The Russia-wide detection rate of detection of such murders is ten percent', the article stated. The crime statistic were cited at the Russian Security Council's Crime and Corruption Commission meeting on January 30, which was chaired by Justice Minister Valentin Kovalyov. (Olga Solodova, *ITAR–TASS*, January 30, 1996.)

In the February 4–11 issue of *Moskovskiye Novosti,* an interview with Mikhail Slinko was published regarding the rising professionalism of killers in Russia. Slinko is a former Moscow City Procuracy employee who earlier worked as a deputy head of the division for the investigation of banditism and murders. Currently, Slinko is working on a dissertation in Moscow State University's legal department on organized crime and, specifically, on contract murders. 'The distinguishing features of the modern contract murder are, first, that the motive is economic, more rarely political; second, that the level of professionalism in execution has increased sharply; third, that, as a rule, military firearms, and less frequently – explosive devises are used in their commission', stated Slinko.

He stated that nearly a third of the contract murders in Moscow occur in the central district. 'In 1991, in Moscow, 19 contract murders or murders during the course of criminal disputes were committed', he said. 'In 1992, that indicator grew to 54 murders. In 1993, 148 were registered, which, incidentally, accounted for every tenth murder, while accumulated practice has now allowed us to count 24 of them as purely contract murders. Eight of the victims were part of the so-called authorities of the criminal world. In 1994, the total number of murder victims during disputes and at the hands of hirelings was 181, with 60 of them – contract murders, 19 of the victims – "authorities" and "outlaws". In the first half of 1995, a certain drop in the number of contract murders has occurred, but it was compensated for in the second half. The experience of 1991–92 has allowed us to draw the practical conclusion that we are dealing with a qualitatively new form of crime, which requires not only a special criminal-legal approach, but also specific investigative methods. We have gradually begun to separate more distinctly within the general mass murders those that can be counted as contract or dispute. With the lack of clear circumstances that usually accompanies an investigation, that distinction is not always easy to make, but often the signs of a contract murder are fairly obvious'.

Slinko stated that entire companies are appearing whose specialty is contract murders. In April 1995, for example, one such crime group comprised of eleven members was arrested for having committed 41 contract murders in Moscow, Moscow Oblast and Novkuznetsk from 1993 to 1995. Slinko distinguished between contract murders and dispute murders, which are committed by rank-and-file members of competing criminal groups. 97 percent of all contract murders in Moscow were committed with firearms or explosive devices as opposed to knives, strangulation or poison. 'While in 1993, the share of solved contract and dispute murders solved was 8.3 percent, in 1994 – it was 11.7 percent, and for the first half of 1995 – 14.3 percent', Slinko continued. 'For the first nine months of last year, solvability for contract murders rose to 18.6 percent, and for "disputes" – to almost 19. These figures are comparable with analogous indicators in such countries as the US, Italy, Japan. The tendency towards greater solvability for this type of crime will continue to grow, although it is highly unlikely that it will ever become high enough, due to the peculiarities of this type of crime'. (Leonid Nikitinskiy, *Moskovskiye Novosti* (Moscow), February 4–11, 1996, in *FBIS–SOV*, Supplement Issue, March 5, 1996, p. 43.)

On February 16, Russian Interior Minister Anatoliy Kulikov presented crime figures for 1995 at a press conference. Last year, 2,755,000 – 60 percent of which were termed 'heinous' – were committed in Russia. Also, in 1995, over 10,000 criminal cases were instituted against organized crime. Approximately 24,000 crimes definable as 'organized' were discovered, including 239 cases of banditism, 1,695 cases of extortion and 370 first-degree murders. Some 6,400 pieces of arms were seized from criminal organizations last year. Repetitive crimes numbered 459,600, as opposed to 343,000 repetitive crimes in 1994. 140,000 economic crimes were revealed in 1995, of which 53,000 were grave. (*ITAR–TASS*, February 16, 1996.)

On February 28, following a recent mob hit at the Nevsky Palace hotel in

St. Petersburg in which a British lawyer was killed, the *Times* of London reported on the violent crimes that have taken place in Western hotels and restaurants frequented by Westerners over the past year. 'In December, guests having coffee in the cafe of Moscow's most expensive hotel, the Baltschug – Kempinski (245 [British pounds] a night for a double room) were forced to lie on the floor for half an hour as riot police burst in on the track of an armed gang', the article stated. 'The same day the German-run Angara beer restaurant in central Moscow installed metal detectors after a shootout in which a Chechen was killed and a British businessman, Peter Somerhill, was wounded in the arm. Russia's annual murder rate "stabilized" last year at 31,700, most the victims of organized crime. In Moscow there are estimated to be about 20 gangland murders a week. Although most murder victims are gang members themselves, hitmen homing in on their target rarely worry about who is in the vicinity. During a gun-battle at the Sadko Arcade, an expensive shopping mall in central Moscow in November, an innocent driver of a Volga was killed as he turned into the car park. The intended victim, in a Lincoln, escaped. The unluckiest Westerners in Russia are Finns and Britons, the Russian Interior Ministry said yesterday. Last year about 550 crimes were recorded against Britons and about 900 against Finns. Muggings, burglary and car theft are the biggest problems and the detection rate is poorer than in the West'. (Thomas de Waal, *Times* (London), February 28, 1996.)

On March 15, Moscow's *Pravda-5* reported that in Leningrad Oblast, the oblast in which St. Petersburg is located, nearly 70 percent of the participants in organized criminal groups whose activities were stopped in 1995 were between 18 and 25 years old. 'Over the last five years, a firm tendency has been towards a rise in crimes committed by minors (for Leningrad Oblast, of nearly three times)', the article reported. 'The highest peak was registered in 1993 – over 3.5 thousand crimes. The greater part of these were of the violent, mercenary kind. In 1995, their share accounted for close to 90 percent of the total number. Robberies increased by 8.5 percent, muggings and thefts became more frequent. Premeditated murders rose by over two times (from 8 to 18 cases). Motive – gaining possession of another's property'. (Aleksey Tarabrin, *Pravda – 5* (Moscow), March 15 – 22, 1996, in *FBIS–SOV*, Supplement Issue, April 10, 1996, p. 102.)

On May 6, Prosecutor General Yuri Skuratov stated that the number of crimes in Russia will rise by 2.5 times by the year 2000. Crime already has doubled since 1991. In 1995, 2.7 million crimes were brought to the police, but Skuratov stated that the actual number of crimes was three times higher.

(In 1994, the FBI reported that nearly 14 million major crimes were committed in the US) (*New York Times*, May 7, 1996, p. A8.)

On May 18, Moscow's *Trud* reported that the number of murders in Russia has risen from 15,500 in 1990 to 32,000 in 1995. In 1995, there were 500 contract murders, of which 61 were solved. While 73 percent of murders in Russia are solved – a figure slightly higher than that in the US, only forty percent are solved in Moscow. (*OMRI Daily Report*, Part I, May 22, 1996.)

On May 21, 1996 while attending the Third International Symposium on Russian Organized Crime in London, Valery Serebryakov, a senior official of the chief directorate for organized crime, told a news conference that over 5,000 crime rings involving a total of 32,000 members are active in Russia today. About 100 Russian organized crime groups comprising about 2,000 members are in contact with foreign crime rings. Of these groups, some 400 members are on international wanted lists. While listing racketeering, blackmail and money extraction as the most dangerous crimes in Russian currently, Serebryakov stated that finance-related crimes deserve the most concern. (Viktor Solomin, *ITAR–TASS* (Moscow), May 21, 1996.)

International Agreements/Issues

On November 14 and 15, 1995 Hungarian police chief Sandor Pinter held talks with Russian Interior Minister Anatoliy Kulikov and other top officials in Moscow. In speaking to reporters, Pinter stressed that cooperation with the Russian police is especially important as organized crime and drug trafficking is expected to increase over the next two years. He stated that Hungary could become a transit route for drugs supplied from the east. Pinter hoped that cooperation could help prevent organized crime money being invested in Hungary. (*MTI Hungarian News Agency*, November 16, 1995.)

On November 17, the Costa Rica Embassy in Russia announced that Russian citizen Sergei Mikhailov, who was Costa Rica's Honorary Consul in Moscow, had been fired. The Costa Rica Embassy stated that the decision was made after reports in the Moscow press, which unmasked Mikhailov as a 'godfather' of one of the Solntsevo-based criminal gangs that is also one of Moscow's most notorious mafia clans. *Izvestiya* reported that the gang has close ties to the Colombian cocaine cartel and is making efforts to corner the lucrative drug market in Russia. Costa Rican Ambassador Jorge Alfredo stated that Mikhailov's appointment *International Agreements/Issues* On December 5, Moscow's *Krasnaya Zvezda* reported that Russian Federal

Security Service (FSB) Director Mikhail Barsukov and his Belarusian counterpart, Uladzimir Yahorau, signed a cooperation agreement the previous week. In addition to working out an agreement for the Belarusians to safeguard Russian troops temporarily stationed in their country, the two directors also appealed to their respective governments to develop bilateral cooperation in combating terrorism, drug trafficking and arms smuggling. (*OMRI Daily Report*, Part I, December 5, 1995.)

On December 7, Moscow's *Kommersant–Daily* published an in-depth profile of Sergei Mikhailov, the Solntsevo mafia kingpin who was fired on November 17 from the Costa Rica Embassy, where he served as Costa Rica's Honorary Consul in Moscow. (Yekaterina Zapodinskaya, *Kommersant–Daily*, December 7, 1995, in *FBIS–SOV*, Supplement Issue, December 21, 1995, p. 40.)

On December 27, 1995 the *Jerusalem Post* reported that a police liaison officer and his family were forced to flee Russia and return to Israel after receiving death threats from the Russian mafia. The police officer was stationed in Moscow in order to crack down on international Russian mafia activities. 'Police sources said the officer, deputy commander Aharon Tal, has since gone back to his post in Moscow', the newspaper stated. 'The sources, as well as the police spokesman, declined to comment further on the case. According to a report in *Yediot Aharanot*, the threats began after police here opened an investigation into allegations by a Russian banker that he was cheated out of $60,000 by a member of the Russian mafia in this country. The banker did not know he was dealing with a Russian mafia member when he employed him to set up a branch of his bank in Cyprus, according to *Yediot*. Tal, his wife and his daughter received death threats from the Russian mafia, and Tal was warned by the mafia not to try to have their man in Israel arrested. The Tals left Moscow and returned to Israel for several weeks. They eventually returned to Moscow, after the banker was slain by the Russian mafia. Police believed that with the banker's murder there was no longer a threat to the Tal family, according to the report'. (Bill Hutman, *Jerusalem Post*, December 27, 1995, p. 3.)

On January 29, 1996 a meeting was held between delegations of Ukrainian and Russian border and customs institutions. The delegations' leaders were Commander-in-Chief of Ukrainian Border Guards, Gen. Col. Viktor Bannykh, and the Federal Border Service of the Russian Federation, Gen. Andrey Nikolayev. At the meeting, it was revealed that, since January 1993, over ten thousand various types of arms and over two million of different types of ammunition have been confiscated at the Ukrainian – Russian border. This amount represented 96 percent of the total amount of arms confiscated along Ukrainian borders. Both sides approved a plan between the Southern Division of the Ukrainian Border Guards and the Caucasian Special Russian Border Division, which would provide for joint control over the Azov Sea and the Kerch Channel regions. (*Infobank* (Lvov), January 31, 1996, in *FBIS–SOV*, January 31, 1996, p. 53.)

On February 3, Interpol President Bjern Erikson was quoted as stating at a recent news conference that the problem of a 'Russian Mafia' has been exaggerated. The Interpol chief did admit that Russian criminals were active in the United States, Great Britain, Germany and Scandinavia. He suggested that two big problems for Interpol in Russia are money laundering and drug trafficking. (Yelena Shesternina, *Russian Press Digest*, February 3, 1996.)

On February 26, agreements between the Russian and Latvian border guard services were worked out in St. Petersburg. According to one agreement, in the future, illegal refugees stopped at the Latvian – Russian border will be sent back to the country from which they came. Authorized representatives from the Russian and Latvian border guards will make a decision on a case-by-case basis regarding the expulsion and taking back of refugees. Also, on February 26, the two border guard services signed an agreement providing for cooperation in fighting organized crime and in preventing the smuggling of contraband, narcotics and weapons. (*Radio Riga Network*, February 28, 1996, in *FBIS–SOV*, February 29, 1996, p. 72.)

On March 7, Swiss police handed over former Kontinent Bank Chairman Igor Kosarev to Russian authorities at Moscow's Sheremetyevo airport. According to *Izvestiya* on March 12, this was the first such extradition of a criminal suspect from Western Europe to Russia. Kosarev has been investigated in relation to the April 1995 killing of Maj. Vladimir Markov, a Russian Tax Police inspector. Before his death, Markov had conducted an audit of Kosarev's, which resulted in the bank paying a $360,000 fine. (*OMRI Daily Report*, Part I, March 12, 1996.)

On March 27, a seminar on transborder cooperation of the countries of the Baltic region opened in the Swedish town of Karlskrona. The seminar was attended by representatives of the Northwestern regions of Russia, Poland, Germany, Baltic and Nordic countries and focused on the role of local authorities in fostering international cooperation. Swedish Minister for International Cooperation and Development Pierre Schori spoke at the meeting, emphasizing the importance of integrating Central and East European countries and Russia into European democratic structures. 'We can facilitate the attainment of this objective in conjunction with neighboring countries by strengthening confidence-building measures and supporting efforts aimed at consolidating the police corps and customs services, coast guards and border checkpoints, as well as by undertaking new steps in the struggle against organized crime and trafficking in drugs and radioactive elements', he said. The seminar was regarded as a stage in the preparations for a meeting of the heads of the governments of the member countries of the Council of Baltic Sea States which is scheduled to take place in May in Visby, Gotland Island. (Nikolai Vukolov, *ITAR–TASS* (Moscow), March 27, 1996.)

On March 28, during a visit to Moscow, Poland's Minister of Internal Affairs Zbigniew Siemiatkowski met with Russia's Interior Minister Anatoliy Kulikov to discuss combatting criminal groups formed by Russian nationals. The Russian interior minister was reported to be particularly interested in the activities of the Chechen Information Center in Cracow, which has been established as a social initiative and enjoys the support of local authorities. Meanwhile, with regards to combatting Russian organized crime in Poland, Siemiatkowski proposed holding a conference with the interior ministers of Belarus, Poland, Russia and Ukraine to discuss the matter. Kulikov suggested that the ministers from the Baltic States attend as well and suggested that cooperation between the Kaliningrad District and Poland's northern voivodships would be useful. In 1995, Russian nationals committed about 697 various crimes on Poland's territory. Lithuanian citizens committed about the same amount of offenses; Ukrainian citizens committed about three times more offenses; and Belarussians committed about twice as many offenses. Polish citizens violated Russian law in only seventeen cases in 1995. In addition, during the meeting of the interior ministers, a joint Polish–Russian commission was agreed to be established to deal with the legal offenses committed by Russian nationals in Poland as well as to protect Russian transit cargo freights in Poland and Polish cargo freights in Russia. (*Rzeczpospolita* (Warsaw), March 28, 1996, in *Polish News Bulletin* (Warsaw), March 28, 1996.)

On March 29, Moscow's *Segodnya* reported that a delegation of representatives of Russian investors defrauded of their money was received the day before a the US Embassy in Moscow. Four diplomats received the group, who complained about corruption in the upper tiers of Russian political power, organized crime and the Chechen crisis as affecting their investments. (Igor Dvinskiy, *Segodnya* (Moscow), March 29, 1996, in *FBIS–SOV*, March 29, 1996, p. 43.)

On April 2, Russian Interior Minister Anatoliy Kulikov signed a police cooperation agreement with Slovak Interior Minister Ludovit Hudek in Bratislava. Hudek emphasized that criminal activities among Russian citizens have not increased since visa-free relations were established last August. Kulikov noted that Russian citizens account for less than one percent of the crime in Slovakia while Ukrainians account for 7 percent. On April 3, Slovak Prime Minister Vladimir Meciar and Russian Interior Minister Anatoliy Kulikov met to discuss Russian – Slovak cooperation in the fight against organized crime and the smuggling of strategic materials and drugs. Slovak Interior Minister Ludovit Hudek stated that, in the meetings, Slovakia had shown interest in Russian-made arms designed for police purposes. 'The rate of crime committed by foreigners, or Russian citizens, has not increased, but conditions for trade and tourism have improved', Hudek stated. (*CTK National News Wire* (Prague), April 3, 1996; and *OMRI Daily Report*, Part II, April 3, 1996.)

On April 3, *Reuters* reported that the European Union and the US are planning to assist in the training of Russian experts in Western methods of accounting for nuclear material. Later this year, in Obninsk, near Moscow, the Russian Methodological and Training Center will be established to train hundreds of Russian experts in order, according to the European Commission, 'to help develop a true safety culture that will be a key element in the program to tighten monitoring and control of nuclear materials in the former Soviet Union'. (*OMRI Daily Report*, Part I, April 4, 1996.)

On April 26, a bilateral agreement on cooperation in combatting organized crime was signed by Latvian Interior Minister Dainis Turlais and Russian Interior Minister Anatoliy Kulikov. The countries committed themselves to providing each other assistance in preventing, detecting, investigating and eliminating criminal organizations. An exchange on information and suspects was also agreed. Another accord on the handover and delivery of arrested suspects was postponed until details could be worked out. Commenting on crimes committed on the Russian–Latvian border, Kulikov stated that most of the crimes regard illegal arms shipments to Russia via Latvian territory. In 1995, Russian border guards detained about 500 pieces of foreign-made firearms that entered Russia from Latvia. 'Money laundering by joint ventures and banks opened by the mob' also has been a common problem in Russia and Latvia, Kulikov stated. (*Baltic News Service* (Tallinn), April 26, 1996, in *FBIS–SOV*, April 30, 1996, p. 91; and *Interfax* (Moscow), April 26, 1996, in *FBIS–SOV*, April 30, 1996, p. 91.)

On May 12, Moscow's *ITAR–TASS* reported that the chiefs of the Russian Federal Service for Currency and Export Control and of the Belarusian Presidential Control Service are planning to sign a protocol on cooperation and mutual assistance in the area of currency and export control. The protocol would make possible the cooperation in combatting currency and export-import violations as well as to fight the legalization of criminal incomes. (Irina Bolshova, *ITAR–TASS* (Moscow), May 12, 1996.)

On May 22, in Havana, Russian Foreign Minister Yevgeny Primakov and Cuban counterpart Roberto Robaina signed several cooperation accords as well as agreed to fight organized crime. In a declaration of principles, the two sides agreed to combat international terrorism, drug trafficking and the smuggling of weapons and items of historical and artistic value. (*Deutsche Presse–Agentur*, May 22, 1996; Viktor Khrekov and Konstantin Zhukovsky, *ITAR–TASS* (Moscow), May 23, 1996.)

On May 23, Moscow's *Komsomolskaya Pravda* issued an apology to a firm for an article published in its newspaper on May 14, entitled 'The Estonian Connection in Ulster and Chechnya: The FSB Presents Evidence'. 'We cited a source when publishing this information and, since we were unable to verify the said information because of its secrecy, at the end of the article we expressed the hope that if our special services take this step "they have at their disposal irrefutable evidence and not just words, which even counterintelligence agents have been generous with of late",' the explanation read. 'After the article, the editorial office was contacted by representatives of the Nordex firm, against which extremely serious charges had been leveled, in particular of illegal arms dealings and links with the Chechen mafia. They flatly deny everything that the counterintelligence officers said about Nordex'. (*Komsomolskaya Pravda* (Moscow), May 23, 1996, in *FBIS–SOV*, May 28, 1996, p. 24.)

Other Criminal Issues

Generally

On November 20, 1995 a gangster shootout occurred in Saratov, in which 11 people were killed and two severely wounded. One of the victims, Igor

Chikunov, was a large crime boss. The police stated that the rest of the victims were members of his crime group. On the night of November 20, following the discovery of the murders, a large-scale operation involving more than 1,000 people and 89 motorized police patrols was conducted by the Internal Affairs Directorate. 'According to information of law enforcement agencies, there are several large criminal associations operating in Saratov Oblast', *Kommersant–Daily* reported. 'After the publication of the president's edict on gangsterism, 177 crime groups were discovered (which included 1,217 people). The criminals have large financial funds, up to half of which are used to bribe officials. In the time since the adoption of the edict, during the course of solving crimes law enforcement agencies have confiscated money and valuables worth a total of more than 578 million rubles and more than $57,500. The most spectacular incident of recent months was the suicide of the chief of the Saratov RUOP [Regional Organized Crime Administration], Vladimir Yeremkin. The policeman shot himself after the Ministry of Internal Affairs of Russia undertook an investigation of his department. At that time two workers of the directorate were in a preliminary detention facility – they had been accused of corruption'. (Aleksandr Raskin, Yelena Komarova, and Maksim Shashkov, *Kommersant–Daily*, November 23, 1995, in *FBIS–SOV*, Supplement Issue, December 11, 1995, p. 45.)

On December 21, *Sovetskaya Rossiya* reported that a scientific and practical conference on problems of countering organized crime had been held recently in Tver. The article summarized information presented at the conference with regards to different sectors of organized crime in Russia. 'According to the MVD [Ministry of Internal Affairs] research institute, the entire territory of Russia is controlled by over 6,000 criminal groupings', the article stated. 'They differ in size. The major ones have a "staff" of 100 or more. In Moscow, Yekaterinburg, St. Petersburg and other big cities organized crime has a key position in the economy. Last year, according to specialists' estimates, the capital of "shady operators" was more than one-fourth of GNP. Groupings are formed on various bases. Territorial groupings are the most common: There are over 30 in Moscow alone. They include one whose "staff" consists of former professional sportsmen and Spetsnaz servicemen. The St. Petersburg community is big: It has 2,000 soldiers [boyeviki] alone .... Or take the Far Eastern "Politburo", which controls salmon fishing (the caviar business), timber procurement and port deals. There are ethnic groupings: Chechen, Armenian, Azerbaijani, Georgian .... There are also so-called professional groupings. Practice shows that it is precisely criminal elements that have been most receptive to the market economy. It is primarily they who have taken advantage of the fruits of privatization and the destatization of property, and on every territory, in the territory's key sectors'.

The article continued to comment on the extent of economics-related crimes currently being committed in Russia. 'According to the MVD Main Administration for Combating Economic Crime, the credit and financial system is in second place in terms of embezzlement in the economic sphere and in first place in terms of the acquisition of money by means of fraud', the article reported. 'Crimes in this sector are subdivided into two main groups: those perpetrated against banks and those that are perpetrated by banks themselves or by using them. Here are just the facts that have been uncovered. Staffers of the credit and financial system have themselves committed over 3,000 swindles. This is twice as many as in trade and industry. Of course, bankers themselves are also victims. In the past year alone around 100 of them have been killed .... And the bullets, poison, or bombs usually get officials of commercial banks. As a rule, these crimes are still not cleared up at all, despite all the endeavors of operations officers, investigators and the prosecutor's office. One of the reasons is that there is no help from witnesses – vice presidents, accountants, cashiers, secretaries, bodyguards. Citing commercial secrecy, they all refuse to give the investigation any information. They even conceal the source of the bank's original capital'.

The article commented on the support given to criminal groups. 'The organized criminal community today is a complex hierarchical formation', *Sovetskaya Rossiya* reported. 'It includes direct perpetrators and superstructure components that carry out control, protection and ideological management functions. As a rule, the top brass in these communities are beyond the reach of the law. In other words, a criminal bureaucracy has emerged. It is the belief among operations officers that many criminal groupings have their own high-ranking officials or deputies at various levels. In a number of cases deputies are actually preferable, since they can lobby against decisions that are dangerous for their "employers".'

Finally, the conference reported some encouraging trends in the fight against crime. 'For instance, it was noted that over the last 18 months around 18,000 criminal groups have come to the notice of internal affairs organs, and the activity of over 12,000 of them has been stopped', the article continued. 'Thousands of firearms and a great deal of ammunition and explosives have been removed from circulation. The infrastructure for the fight against organized crime is improving, albeit more slowly than we would like. Specialized structures are gaining experience and their level of training and ability to "outsmart" even the most sophisticated criminals are improving'. (Yuri Burov, *Sovetskaya Rossiya* (Moscow), December 21, 1995, in *FBIS–SOV*, December 22, 1995, p. 23.)

On January 14, 1996 *Deutsche Presse–Agentur* reported on the interaction between sport and crime in the former Soviet Union that has resulted in some recent murders. 'Crime is casting a shadow over sport in the former Soviet Union', the report began. 'The once sporting superpower has since its breakup become a hotbed of criminal activity ranging from break-ins to murder – and sportsmen and women are often caught in the violence. Russia was shocked by the recent death of diving star Yelena Miroshina in circumstances that remain unclear. The 21-year-old Olympic high diving silver medalist in Barcelona was found dead outside her apartment in Moscow shortly before Christmas. Miroshina, who was pregnant, had plunged from a window nine stories up. Police, having first suspected crime, now believe Miroshina took her own life, but teammate Svetlana Timoshina thinks she was murdered ....In another incident, Igor Kuperman, captain of the Russian national rugby team, was shot dead at Krasnoyarsk in Siberia. Meanwhile the former high jump world record holder, Igor Paklin from Kyrgyzstan, is alleged to have committed a murder. Paklin, indoor world champion in 1987 and European champion in Stuttgart in 1986, is accused with a friend of killing a business partner. Paklin, vice-president of the Kyrgyzstan athletic association, is alleged to have beaten the victim so badly that he died of his injuries'. (Peter Juny, *Deutsche Presse–Agentur*, January 14, 1996.)

On February 16, Moscow's *Nezavisimaya Gazeta* published an in-depth profile of the mafia groups that divide up the capital city. 'If statistics can be trusted, the police break up at least two organized crime gangs each day, but the same sources prove that "nature abhors a vacuum",' the article began. 'Each vanquished 'combatant' is immediately replaced by a new one. The crime mobs began dividing Moscow into "spheres of influence" in the middle of the 1980s – just at the time when the first rumors about the mafia were making the rounds. The cutthroats from the Lyubertsy and "Caucasian" gangs were the first to strike fear into the hearts of citizens, using exclusively criminal methods. Now there are more than 200 such groups of note in the capital, and their "overlords" are much more "civilized". Each of the criminal leaders has his own firm to "handle" the contributions from the territory under his control. Nevertheless, bloody "altercations" between gangs are still an almost daily occurrence'.

The article stated that the Solntsevo gang and the 'Chechen community' criminal association were thought to be the most powerful in Moscow. The

Solntsevo gang, which controls the south of Moscow, was reported to control almost all of the gas stations, the largest stores, and the vehicle dealerships in South Port. Sergey Timofeyev, also known as the 'Silvestr' or 'Novgorod Serezha', was said to be the most famous 'overlord'. The article stated that there are rumors that the September 1994 murder of Timofeyev was staged and that he is still alive. The Chechen gang was said to have 'no strictly defined zones of influence', but that 'no expert, however, could name a single location in Moscow without a Chechen mafia patron'. In the center of the city, the group was said to control many hotels as well as hundreds of stores, restaurants, coffee shops and commercial firms. The center of Moscow was also said to be controlled by the Georgian community and the so-called Mazutkinskiy group, which includes the Bauman, Tagan and Sokolniki gangs and other small organizations. The eastern part of the city was reported to be under the control of the related Izmaylovo and Lyubertsy gangs, which are headed by Anton Malevskiy ('Anton'), who lives in Israel, and Vyacheslav Shestakov ('Sliva'), who is in a prison camp. The main 'base' of the Izmaylovo gang was reported to be the 'Izmaylovo' tourist center. The Odintsovo mob, headed by an overlord known as the 'Coin', was said to rule the western district of the city. The northern part of Moscow was reported to be run by the Koptevo–Dologoprudnyy gang, which is a union of several Moscow city and oblast criminals. This group was said to have been dealt serious blows recently by the police and to have been torn apart by internal struggles. The article also described tricks used to fool law enforcement. 'The locations for meetings at 16:30, for example, are announced at 16:00', the article stated. 'Half an hour does not give the authorities enough time to send their "eyes and ears" to the right place'. (Oleg Kutasov and Stanislav Romanov, *Nezavisimaya Gazeta* (Moscow), February 16, 1996, in *FBIS–SOV*, Supplement Issue, March 5, 1996, p. 40.)

On February 24, Moscow's *Kommersant–Daily* reported on crime and corruption at Sheremetyevo-2, Moscow's international airport. According to police officers working at the airport, the only incidents of crime appearing at the airport have been thefts of passengers' baggage and narcotics trafficking. According to the newspaper, however, Chechen, Koptevo, Khimiki and Lonya gangsters have firms at the airport that they control. 'They do not commit serious crimes – they collect tribute from the taxi drivers and engage in intimidation at the currency exchange outlets', the newspaper stated. 'The Chechens pay the local police officers R250,000 [rubles] each on the last Thursday of every month. The leadership of the Lobnya Internal Affairs Administration knows nothing about this'.

According to Col. Gennadiy Gubanov, chief of the local police, the baggage handlers that steal directly from baggage being loaded and unloaded from aircraft are being tackled. 'We are sacking whole teams', said Gubanov. 'They are now being watched not only by my officers but various security services also. True, it is not doing much good – things are going missing, all the same'. (Maksim Varyvdin, *Kommersant–Daily* (Moscow), February 24, 1996, in *FBIS–SOV*, March 14, 1996, p. 35.)

On March 6, a Moscow court ruled that the left-wing *Sovetskaya Rossiya* newspaper should compensate popular singer Iosif Kobzon for printing that he had ties with organized crime. In 1993, an article by Larisa Kislinskaya (who incidentally now writes for *ITAR–TASS* on matters concerning crime and corruption) stated that Kobzon had personal ties to crime kingpins. The paper and the journalist were ordered to pay Kobzon a total of 15 million rubles ($3,100). (*OMRI Daily Report*, Part I, March 6, 1996.)

On April 3, Moscow's *Segodnya* published excerpts from Nikolay Modestov's book *Moskva Banditskaya*, which will be published by the 'Tsentropoligraf' Commercial Publishing Association. The book was described as a study of the history and current situation of Moscow's criminal world, discussing individual criminal groupings such as the 'Chechen commune' and various crime kingpins such as Vyacheslav Ivankov, known as the 'Yaponchik' ('Little Japanese' in Russian), and the killer Aleksandr Salonikm, known as 'Sasha Makedonskiy' ('Sasha the Macedonian' in Russian). 'The Chechens were the first, with a perfect mastery of the art of making a "roof" for businessmen and putting a tax on trade, to switch over to the manufacture of counterfeit letters of advice – a type of crime that for a long time had been ignored by the law-enforcement agencies and that cost the state, even according to the most modest estimates, tens of trillions of rubles', Modestov wrote. The excerpts elaborated on the gang wars in the city, analyzing why the Chechen grouping became the leader of organized crime in the capital city. (Nikolay Modestov, *Segodnya* (Moscow), April 3, 1996, in *FBIS–SOV*, Supplement Issue, April 25, 1996, p. 58.

Drug-Related Crime

On December 5, 1995 Moscow's *Delovoy Mir* published an interview with Lt. Gen. of Militia Mikhail Nikiforov, chief of the Internal Affairs Administration of Irkutsk Oblast. 'Illegal drug dealing in the region is clearly "going uphill",' Nikiforov stated. 'Over the past five years, the number of crimes associated with the manufacture, acquisition, storage, transportation and sale of substances containing drugs has more than quadrupled. Today more than 6,000 persons are on the books in internal affairs organs for using drugs and extremely strong substances. Drugs are coming to Irkutsk, Angarsk, Bratsk and other cities and raions in the oblast in large quantities from Central Asia, Ukraine, the central region of Russia and the Far East. Strong and well-concealed criminal groups of manufacturers, shippers and sellers of drugs with interregional and international ties have been formed in the oblast. The theft of drugs and strong medicinal preparations from medical and pharmaceutical institutions has become one of the critical problems. During the course of the "Doping – 95" operation, we found dozens of violations of the regulations for the recording, storage and sale of drugs and strong substances, for which 43 criminal proceedings were instituted, an illegal attempt to obtain medical substances valued at 400 million rubles through the Red Cross was stooped and teofedrin [possibly: theophedrin] was put on the record'. (Anatoliy Malyshev, *Delovoy Mir*, December 5, 1995, in *FBIS–SOV*, Supplement Issue, December 19, 1995, p. 33.)

On January 25, 1996 *ITAR–TASS* reported that the Khanka district, located in the south of the Maritime Territory in Russia's Far East, has become a center for mass production and marketing of marijuana, which grows abundantly in the area. Over 35 kilograms of 'pot' were seized in the district this January by the drug control division on the Maritime Territory police department. (Eduard Popov, *ITAR–TASS* (Moscow), January 25, 1996, in *FBIS–SOV*, January 25, 1996, p. 28.)

On January 28, the *New York Times* reported on a banking scandal by which 'a few Kremlin-favored banks lent the [Russian] government money last year in return for a chance to buy shares in some of the state's most valuable assets at dirt-cheap prices'. The scandal, known as 'loans-for-shares', posed a threat to the future of privatization in Russia as Anatoly B. Chubais, the last free-market reformer in President Yeltsin's cabinet, lost his job as first deputy prime minister for the favoritism that accompanied privatization in Russia. (Alessandra Stanley, *New York Times*, January 28, 1995, p. A1.)

In January, in the Moscow journal *Ekonomika i Zhizn,* the Russian Federation State Customs Committee provided detailed statistics on the confiscation of narcotics by the customs organs. In 1995, the Russian Federations customs organs apprehended 6,457.3 kilograms of narcotics and 200 kilograms of chemicals that serve as the basic raw ingredients for illegal production of narcotics in 767 separate incidents. By contrast, in 1994, 3,126.74 kilograms of narcotics were seized in 418 separate incidents. Among many factors, the journal article remarked that 1995 saw 'the discovery of a new channel for smuggling large batches of cannabis group narcotics in container shipments from Nigeria through Europe to Russia'; a rise in smuggling of synthetic narcotics; a rise in cocaine shipments; and continued importation of poppy stems through Ukraine into Russia. In addition, the article noted popular contraband channels as well as provided tables delineating amounts of narcotics seized by type of transport and by type of concealment. (*Ekonomika i Zhizn* (Moscow), January 1996, No. 3, in *FBIS–SOV*, Supplement Issue, February 9, 1996, p. 66.)

On February 7, Russian police in the Maritime region in the Russian Far East seized the largest opium haul this year from two individuals each of whom was selling 160 and 200 grams of the drug, respectively. The drug usually sells for 50,000 rubles a gram. (Eduard Popov, *ITAR–TASS*, February 7, 1996.)

On March 1, Vladimir Yegorov, director of the Russian Center for the Study of Drug Addiction, stated that at least half a million Russians are dependent on illegal drugs and that the number of drug users could be as many as 1.5 million. (*OMRI Daily Report*, Part I, March 4, 1996.)

On March 2, a report in Moscow's *Rossiyskaya Gazeta* highlighted the problems posed by Chinese ephedrine smuggling in Khabarovsk. While it is possible to stop isolated shipments of smuggled opium, the article observed that combatting the importation of ephedrine from China has become more difficult since the drug is not considered a narcotic in China's northern provinces. (*Rossiyskaya Gazeta* (Moscow), March 2, 1996, in *FBIS–SOV*, March 5, 1996, p. 42.)

On March 13, Moscow's *Pravda* reported that the actual illegal drug trade in Russia totaled more than 3.5 trillion rubles in 1995, according to specialists' estimates. 'Over ten years, the number of persons abusing drugs has more than doubled', the article stated. 'Around 2 million Russian citizens are engaging in the nonmedicinal use of drugs (on a regular basis!). The number of crimes uncovered annually, which are associated with drugs, has increased by a factor of 4.5 (in comparison with 1985) and reached 80,000 last year. Over the decade, the volume of narcotic substances removed from the illegal trade increased by a factor of 20 .... In comparison with last year: in all, the number of registered addicts stood at 90,000, while, this year, after several months, it stands at 130,000. There are 11,500 minors among them .... Over the last year, more than 4,500 crimes committed in drug-related groups have been exposed. Ten times more drugs have begun to be seized in large amounts. But all this is just a drop in the sea flooding in from abroad of cocaine, heroin, opium and designer drugs being manufactured in underground laboratories. The rising prices for drugs are stimulating their illegal supply. Alcoholics have a lesser degree of loss of control over their consciousness than drug addicts: annually, "druggies" commit 50,000 bold crimes, murders and rapes. The proportion of brutal crimes among drug addicts is higher than among other groups at risk. The drug trade is spurring overall crime. In some regions, up to 60 percent of the property crimes are being committed because of drug addiction'. The article also stated that in 1995, the Illegal Drug Trade Administration arrested more than 11,000 criminals for drug dealing, most of whom were given minimum term sentences and only ten of whom were given eight years imprisonment. (Liliya Seredina and Aleksandr Sergeyev, *Pravda* (Moscow), March 13, 1996, in *FBIS–SOV*, Supplement Issue, March 29, 1996, p. 49.)

On March 16, Moscow's *Rabochaya Tribuna* reported that one out of every ten drug producers in the Transcarpathian Region is a pensioner. Since the beginning of 1996, some 100 kilograms of lethal poison has been confiscated by law enforcement organs from 'narcogrannies' and 'narcograndads' in the oblast. (*Rabochaya Tribuna* (Moscow), March 16, 1996, in *FBIS–SOV*, March 19, 1996, p. 34.)

On March 19, Vitaliy Strugovets viewed the growth of drug trafficking in a commentary for Moscow's *Krasnaya Zvezda*. In 1992, approximately 50 kilograms of narcotic substances were seized on Russia's borders. In 1993, the number was 500 kilograms; in 1994, 3.5 tons; and in 1995, 6.5 tons. Drug smuggling, according to Strugovets, has increased over 130 fold in four years. Strugovets also quoted data from the Ministry of Internal Affairs which stated that about 1 percent of Russia's population (1.5 million people) were drug addicts in 1993. According to the International Narcotics Committee, there were 6 million drug addicts in 1995, of whom 1 million were teenagers. About 20 million more Russians (including 5 million schoolchildren) have tried drugs at least once. Strugovets attributed the laundering of criminal money and the possibility of making 'superprofits in the sphere of the drugs business' as providing favorable conditions for Russia's drug problem. 'In the opinion of specialists, every ruble invested in the Russian drugs business yields a net income of R1,100 – considerably higher than the overall world level', said Strugovets. 'At the same time,

Interpol President Bjorn Eriksson pointed out at a meeting with journalists in Moscow that "the risk of arrest in Russia is not as great as in other states".

In addition, Interpol specialists ascribe the attention that international drug cartels pay to Russia to the intensified fight against the drug business in West European and American countries, which is forcing criminals to look for new drug transportation routes and sales markets'. (Vitaliy Strugovets, *Krasnaya Zvezda* (Moscow), March 19, 1996, in *FBIS–SOV*, March 27, 1996, p. 29.)

On April 13, Moscow's *Rossiyskaya Gazeta* reported on why the Duma has not adopted a law on the narcotics trade. The roots to proposals for a law on narcotics goes back to 1991. Since then, the Ministry of Health and the Ministry of Internal Affairs became involved in the law-making process, but the Ministry of Health regarded its continued participation in the work on the State Duma drafts useless as its proposals were not considered. A draft by Bela Denisenko, the chairwoman of the State Duma Committee on Health Care, was rejected by the Duma in 1995 on both the first and second readings. Eight ministries and departments subsequently proposed a variant of the law 'On Narcotic and Strong-Acting Substances'. The Duma council decided to combine the drafts of the Committee on Health Care and the ministries, which furthered the conflict between the Ministry of Health and Denisenko. The draft has not been introduced to the Duma yet.

Meanwhile, the number of drug addicts among young Russians was said to be increasing by 70 to 80 percent a year. An estimated 200,000 professionals were reported to be in the narcotics business in Russia. They received an estimated $7 billion in 1995 from the drug trade. In some regions of Russia, drug addicts were said to commit up to 60 percent of property crimes. (Natalya Kuzina, *Rossiyskaya Gazeta* (Moscow), April 13, 1996, in *FBIS–SOV*, Supplement Issue, April 25, 1996, p. 53.)

On April 23, Moscow's *Nezavisimaya Gazeta* published an interview with Boris Maksimov, deputy director of the Russian Federation State Duma Health Care Committee apparat, who provided statistics on the use of narcotics in Russia. 'Today the number of narcotics users in our country comes to about 1.5 million people, contrasted with tens of thousands a few years ago; the illegal narcotics trade, according to some estimates, is over $600 million; the number of confiscated narcotics in the early 1990s was on the order of hundreds of kilograms, and now it is in dozens of tons', he stated. Accompanying the interview was a table providing the following data:

CRIMES INVOLVING NARCOTICS IN THE RUSSIAN FEDERATION

Year	Number of Crimes	Number of Kilograms of Narcotics Confiscated
1980	6,599	643
1985	16,665	3,805
1990	16,255	16,260
199	119,321	20,832
1992	29,805	21,886
1993	53,162	53,726
1994	74,708	81,960

(Boris Maksimov, *Nezavisimaya Gazeta* (Moscow), April 23, 1996, in *FBIS–SOV*, Supplement Issue, May 13, 1996, p. 39.)

On May 20, 1996 Moscow's *NTV* reported that Boris Fedorov, the president of the National Sports Foundation and the Natsionalnyi Kredit Bank, was arrested after drugs were found in his home. Fedorov was said to be an associate of Shamil Tarpishchev, President Yeltsin's tennis coach and a co-founder of the National Sports Foundation. (*OMRI Daily Report*, Part I, May 22, 1996.)

Economics and Business-Related Crime

In November 1995 Moscow's *Biznes I Banki* published an article by Y. N. Myslovskiy, the president of the 'Antimafia' Fund for Combatting Organized Crime and Corruption, regarding the current banking crisis and criminal aspects of banking relations in Russia. 'The misfortune of today's law enforcement agencies lies in the fact that they are completely removed from the economy as such, especially from the activity of the monetary-finance system', Myslovskiy wrote. 'They have no elementary understanding of how money is made, and what a bank is in its essence. Entire generations of workers of the law enforcement agencies have been brought up under conditions when there was only one Gosbank [State Bank] in the country, which could not even theoretically go bankrupt. They have no concept of the conditions of operation of commercial banks, or of the character of legal violations which are committed every day and every hour within this system. Therefore, up until recently, it never even occurred to the heads of the prosecutor's office to perform an analysis of the operation of a commercial bank-not a specific one, but a bank as a new financial institution'.

Myslovskiy clearly blamed the Central Bank for failing to control the activity of commercial banks. 'There are laws defining the functions of commercial banks and the functions of control over their operation', he continued. 'The Law on the Central Bank places the functions of control over the activity of commercial banks on the Central Bank, on its specialized Administration for Oversight of Activity of Commercial Banks. The law clearly states what activities it should engage in and what measures it must take (up to revocation of licenses for violation of the rules of operation of commercial banks or for abuses). The Central Bank is fulfilling these functions poorly, which is evidenced, specifically, by the developing crisis. In this case, we may speak of criminal negligence. The workers of the Central Bank are public officials, and therefore Article 172 of the Criminal Code of Russia is applicable to them. It states: "Failure to fulfill or improper fulfillment by an official of his responsibilities due to careless or negligent attitude toward them, and resulting in infliction of significant harm upon the state or public interests, or upon the lawfully protected rights and interests of citizens...." If I were the Prosecutor General, I would bring to responsibility certain officials of the Central Bank for criminal negligence, leading to a mass crisis of the commercial banks and significant material loss for the Russian economy and for millions of citizens. This would force all the officials involved in this case to work more diligently and to give early warning about the catastrophe threatening the banks, and to strive to prevent it altogether. In this way, it would be possible to achieve normalization of activity of the entire banking system to a significant degree'. (Y. N. Myslovskiy, *Biznes I Banki*, November 1995, No. 48, in *FBIS–SOV*, Supplement Issue, January 5, 1995, p. 10.)

On November 21, International Federation of the Phonographic Industry (IFPI) General Director Nicholas Garnet stated that Russia is currently the world's second largest producer of illegal recordings after China. Foreign producers of recordings lost nearly $300 million Russian pirates, according to IFPI estimates. (*Reuter Textline Novecon,* November 21, 1995.)

On November 24–30, Moscow's *Trud-7* newspaper published an interview with Lt. Gen. Vladimir Tsekhanov, chief of the Federal Security Service (FSB) Economic Counterintelligence Administration. Tsekhanov stated that of the regions in Russia bogus financial documents most often have been issued in the Kabardino–Balkar Republic, where some 323 such attempts were made last year totalling 151 billion rubles. Tsekhanov was also asked about the extent of corruption in the entire country. 'The situation here is fairly alarming', he stated. 'Criminal economic activities continue to be accompanied by widespread corruption. More or less one in every two or three state or municipal officials who are responsible for the issue of this or that permit in the business sphere, are caught in its web. In the period between January and June 1995 alone, more than 1,000 corruption-related cases were being "processed". On average we begin hearing five to six new cases every day. This is twice as many as last year. Bear in mind that we do not deal with 'trifles', but only with officials within the organs of power and administration, including those in the law enforcement departments'. Tsekhanov, in conclusion, presented some figures showing how economic crime has increased. 'In the last year and the first nine months of this year alone', he said, 'the FSB, together with other law enforcement agencies, has halted the illegal export from Russia of raw and other materials and valuables worth 1 trillion rubles and of precious metals and precious stones worth $50 million; more than three tons of narcotics have been confiscated; and hundreds of icons, pictures, works of art, and treasures which are Russia's national heritage have been returned to museums, state depositories and the church'. (Vitaliy Golovachev, *Trud-7*, November 24–30, 1995, in *FBIS-SOV*, November 28, 1995, p. 29.)

On November 28, Chief of the Central Directorate of Economic Crimes Alexander Dementeyev held a briefing on criminal groups specializing in illegal hard currency transactions. 'If 1,200 "foreign currency" crimes were recorded in the Soviet Union over the entire [year of] 1989, in Russia 12,000 such cases have been registered in the past 10 months', wrote *ITAR-TASS* correspondent Larisa Kislinskaya. 'The police major-general noted that a kind of industry of crimes has gained roots in the sphere of oil-production, refining and selling gold, as well as diamonds. An aggravation of the criminal situation in gold-producing regions has to a great extent contributed to a disintegration into a specific separate independent enterprises'. Dementeyev also revealed that stolen valuables are also supporting extremist nationalist and separatist movements, are even sold to invest in the arms business, and help finance military activities in 'hot spots'. 'Customs authorities of Russia have confiscated foreign currency equivalent to almost 47 billion rubles during the past nine months', Kislinskaya reported. 'Against a background of rampant growth of crimes in this sphere, what surprises is almost no attention paid to "foreign currency" problems in the new Criminal Code of Russia, since such a clause does not figure in it at all'. (Larisa Kislinskaya, *ITAR-TASS*, November 28, 1995.)

On November 29, *Literaturnaya Gazeta* published an interview with Andrey Nechayev, co-chairman of the Russian Business Roundtable and president of Russian Finance Corporation, and Aleksandr Orlov, executive director of the Russian Business Roundtable, under the headline 'Officials Are Driving Businessmen to Crime'. 'The criminalization of society is my greatest concern today', stated Nechayev. 'The state has effectively given up its main function as the protector of property and the property owner. To whom? To criminal gangs. They are already performing the functions of arbitrators, marshals of the court, tax collectors, bodyguards, etc. There are so many law enforcement and regulatory bodies in the country, but the courts are on the very bottom rung of the hierarchy of state agencies. Even when a court rules in your favor, this does not necessarily mean that the ruling will be enforced'.

Nechayev blamed officials for the fact that many law-abiding businessmen are turning to gangsters rather than the courts. 'Criminal elements will disappear when we have a normal system of laws and law enforcement with the judicial system playing the first violin', he stated. 'Law-abiding businessmen would much rather take their grievances to the courts (as they do in the rest of the world) than to gangsters. Regrettably, in our present situation a person can either petition a court, wait months for a decision, pay bribes (let us call a spade a spade), and still have no guarantee that his interests will be protected, or be can go to gangsters, pay them a certain fee, and then have the highest expectations that his wishes will be fulfilled. This, however, gives rise to a colossal danger: As soon as you appeal to the crime world for help, you automatically become its hostage. Unfortunately, officials often drive businessmen to crime with their unsystematic economic policy. The best-known example is the tax system. If we compare it to the German system, or even the Swedish one, it appears quite acceptable on the surface. We must not forget, however, that the present tax burden, in our unique situation as a transition economy, is not simply excessive, but completely intolerable. This is the reason for the constant efforts to evade tax inspectors. There might be hundreds of billions – or perhaps even trillions by now – in unreported income roaming the countryside. All of this "illegal cash" has to be transferred, protected, and distributed. This is another case in which business inadvertently comes into contact with the crime world'.

Nechayev also acknowledged the fact that many members of the business community order the crimes. 'For them, a bullet is a simple way of solving a protracted economic dispute or of collecting an unpaid debt', he said. 'It is here that the business community can make a difference. Even before the [Ivan] Kivelidi [the former chairman of the Russian Business Roundtable who was poisoned to death in August] matter, the Russian Business Roundtable (KSBR) initiated the drafting of a Charter of Business

Integrity (or Charter of Business Ethics), advising businessmen to voluntarily and consciously reject violence as a way of doing business. Some feel that this is a romantic notion. I think that the business stratum has been close enough to the limit to realize the danger: The only choices now are physical annihilation, expatriation, or vigorous and decisive action. If this kind of action is taken, it will be important to unite our efforts, and this will necessitate the exclusion of people who violate business ethics from our community. The charter will be ready for endorsement soon'. (*Literaturnaya Gazeta*, November 29, 1995, in *FBIS–SOV*, Supplement Issue, December 26, 1995, p. 34.)

On December 4, Aleksandr Khandruyev, first deputy chairman of the Central Bank of the Russian Federation, held a news conference in which he announced that four cases involving the manufacture of forged one hundred US dollar bills of the new design already have been uncovered in Russia even before the US Federal Reserve System has begun printing the new model. The Central Bank representative acknowledged that the introduction of the new bills will be accompanied by an increase of counterfeit bills. According to the Central Bank's preliminary estimates, as many as several billion fake US dollars could surface in Russia in early 1996. In addition, the new hundred dollar bill design is causing some concern in Russia as the old hundred dollar bill will not be withdrawn from circulation and still should be accepted at its full value. Nevertheless, banks are expected to charge substantial commission fees for exchanging old hundred dollar bills for the new version. Khandruyev attempted to relay fears by stating that financial institutions will be forbidden from charging more than 2 percent commissions for exchanging the old bills. (*Komsomolskaya Pravda*, December 6, 1995, in *FBIS–SOV*, December 7, 1995, p. 50; Yelena Bazhenova, *Kommersant–Daily*, December 5, 1995, in *FBIS–SOV*, December 7, 1995, p. 50; and *OMRI Daily Report*, Part I, December 5, 1995.)

On December 7, *Nezavisimaya Gazeta* published an interview with an unidentified Regional Organized Crime Administration officer who stated that there are ties linking criminals and top officials. 'Such an analysis, according to our data, has never been conducted by anyone', he stated. 'But the fact that the leaders and kingpins in the criminal world have a great influence not only on the economic, but also on the political situation, that they play no small role in these structures, is clear even to a blind man'. When questioned on why known criminal leaders are not simply arrested, the officer answered, 'We could detain them tomorrow. We would have the grounds. I can walk around Moscow and in a day exchange greetings with a dozen crime bosses and kingpins. We know practically all of them by sight and we know a lot about their inside information. A certain "Zakhar", for example, has been convicted five times, but that does not mean that he has to be picked up again then and there. For the jurists, evidence and facts are important. Yes, we know that this or that crime boss is behind this or that murder. But he plays the role of the organizer, for which there is not yet justice in any one of our laws. No one ever points a finger at a crime boss, saying that he committed or ordered a crime'. The officer also stated that approximately 30 to 50 crime bosses and 'about four times as many kingpins' live permanently in Moscow. (Oleg Rubnikovich, *Nezavisimaya Gazeta*, December 7, 1995, in *FBIS–SOV*, Supplement Issue, December 21, 1995, p. 45.)

On December 30, 1995 *Rossiyskaya Gazeta* published an article on the counterfeiting of US dollar bills. The newspapers asked analytical specialists in the Economic Crimes Administration of the Ministry of Internal Affairs of Russia regarding the counterfeiting expected with the introduction of the new US $100 bill. 'This is some kind of non-science fiction', the unidentified analysts stated. 'There are currently two centers in the world for the production of fake dollars. One is the Near East where they make the so-called "superdollars". Judging from everything, their manufacture in one of the countries there has been put at the state level. The second center is Eastern Europe, Poland most of all, where they also make a high-quality product' and are not limited just to dollars; they make European currency as well. Both centers have proven distribution channels, and Russia is not part of their network. Who would get the idea of bringing fakes here through a host of customs, exchanging them for rubles that nobody needs, and then buying dollars with them again? Absurd. That leaves only our own craftsmen. But you have to take one specific feature into account – the counterfeiter does not work "for private consumption". He makes a batch that can be sold, and immediately tries to get rid of it; otherwise he would be caught before he can earn anything. So to speak of the appearance of a sea of mythical 'sacks' is, to put it mildly, incompetent'. The analysts also dismissed a possible increase in fake Russian rubles. 'The Presidential Edict on the mandatory registration of copying and reproducing equipment and went into effect, and helped us a great deal', they stated. 'It is very difficult to sneak an inkjet printer into the country today. We thus are not expecting any particular outburst of activity from that angle'. (*Rossiyskaya Gazeta*, December 30, 1995, in *FBIS–SOV*, Supplement Issue, January 30, 1996, p. 27.)

On January 9, 1996 statistics on the number of tax crimes in 1995 were reported. Russia's Federal Tax Police detected 27,147 tax crimes during the year, of which 9,013 were considered to be on a large scale. The trade sector registered the greatest number of tax violations. (*Economic News Agency* (Moscow), January 9, 1996, in *BBC Summary of World Broadcasts*, January 10, 1996.)

On January 13, Moscow's *Komsomolskaya Pravda* reported that of the $20 billion circulating in Russia, $4 billion are counterfeit $100 bills. 'Viktor Melnikov, chief of the department for monitoring exchange transactions at the Central Bank of Russia, requested the US State Department to mount a widescale operation to uncover the superbills', the newspaper stated. 'In his words, of the $20 billion circulating in Russia, $4 billion are superbills. In all there are $20 billion in counterfeit dollar bills in circulation in the world. This has brought Washington around to thinking that a certain "state hostile to the United States" is behind the production of the American money. So far the finger has been pointed at Iran. The only solution is to cancel the old C-notes and introduce new ones. In 60 years, $350 billion have been issued in the $100 denomination, and their exchange and withdrawal from circulation will take seven years'. (Maksim Chikin, *Komsomolskaya Pravda,* January 13, 1996, in *FBIS–SOV*, January 16, 1996, p. 14.)

On January 25, *Rossiyskaya Gazeta* published an interview with Aleksandr Dementyev, chief of the Ministry of Internal Affairs (MVD) Administration for Combating Economic Crime (GUEP). 'It is wrong to say that "everything has been sold off",' Dementyev stated. 'Yes, in our analytical center's estimate, about 80 percent of commercial banks are controlled by criminal groups or conduct operations with their money. Yes, by some estimates, 40 percent of all cash in the country circulates in the shadow economy. From the standpoint of our service, this country can be brought to order and even within a quite finite time frame, but ... on only one condition. First of all, it is necessary to pass a number of legislative acts regulating general economic relations in Russia.... Speaking of the absolutely necessary, though, what should have been adopted yesterday – it is a package of economic laws and the new criminal, criminal process and administrative codes'. Dementyev spoke of the need to pass laws that are still in the discussion stage – the laws 'On Entrepreneurship', 'On Corruption', and 'On Penalties for Legislation of Criminal Income'. Dementyev also listed three concrete groups of 'untouchables' – people's deputies at all levels, which includes hundreds of thousands of people; procurators; and judges. 'The law explicitly prohibits us from conducting search and surveillance actions against these categories of citizens', Dementyev said. Finally, Dementyev defined the first task of his department as getting a legal basis on the books in order to fight economic crime and the second task as combatting corruption and bribe-taking. (Sergey Goncharov, *Rossiyskaya Gazeta* (Moscow), January 25, 1996, in *FBIS–SOV*, Supplement Issue, February 6, 1996, p. 1.)

On January 27, *Rossiyskaya Gazeta* published an article on state and private security services. The article noted that, according to sociological surveys, more than half of Russia's businessmen are victims of criminal groups each year and that in 90 percent of the cases in which businessmen seek out gangsters' 'protection', the 'defenders' take over the management of the business. According to Viktor Kiryushin, deputy chief of the Moscow Regional Administration for Combating Organized Crime (RUOP), the RUOP has signed cooperation agreements with 20 private security enterprises, including agreements on sharing information. (Maksim Zarezin, *Rossiyskaya Gazeta* (Moscow), January 27, 1996, in *FBIS–SOV*, Supplement Issue, February 6, 1996, p. 5.)

On February 6, the 'Segodnya' newscast on *NTV* broadcast a report on an unprecedented operation carried out by the service for illegal armed formations and banditism of the Moscow Federal Security Service directorate and by the Moscow Region department for fighting organized crime that succeeded in the arrest of six counterfeiters. The six men utilized legal materials and equipment available in Moscow stores to forge $100 and $50 US banknotes. The report indicated that over the $50 billion in circulation in Russia, about 10 percent are forged banknotes. The *NTV* report also indicated that the US responded in an apathetic manner to the arrests. 'The US state bodies have displayed no interest whatsoever in the work of the Russian counterintelligence workers, who are doing in their own country everything possible to avert any collapse of the US economy', *NTV* reporter Nikolay Nikolayev stated on the air. (Tatyana Mitkova and Nikolay Nikolayev, *NTV* (Moscow), February 6, 1996, in *FBIS–SOV*, February 7, 1996, p. 35.)

On February 12, Viktor Ilyukhin, head of the Duma Security Committee and member of the Russian Communist Party faction, relayed at a news conference that about $200 billion worth of Russian capital is located abroad. Those who send capital abroad would face penalties according to a new article in the Criminal Code. Ilyukhin also stated that the Security Committee had drawn up a draft law on amnesty for those who exported their capital but informed the authorities about this within 100 to 150 days and ensured the possibility of returning the capital. (*Interfax*, February 12, 1996, in *FBIS–SOV*, February 13, 1996, p. 41.)

On February 27, Moscow's *Rabochaya Tribuna* published an interview with Maj. Gen. Aleksandr Dementyev, chief of the Internal Affairs Ministry Economic Crimes Administration. 'Our service sets itself precisely the goal of undermining the mafia's financial strength', Dementyev stated. 'Today, according to our estimates, over 40 percent of monetary assets are circulating in the shadow economy. It is perfectly obvious that this money is not being invested in industry, agriculture or the social sphere. This money reproduces crime'. Dementyev stated that in 1995, criminal proceedings were instituted against 40 bank employees. He also explained that his department was working with the Duma on the laws 'On the Legalization of Criminal Incomes', 'On the Declaration of Income' and 'On Accounting'. He stated that commercial structures do not keep accounting records. (Gennadiy Lyulkin, *Rabochaya Tribuna* (Moscow), February 27, 1996, in *FBIS–SOV*, March 4, 1996, p. 27.)

On February 28, Gen. Alexander Dementev, head of the Interior Ministry's directorate on economic crime, stated that the Interior Ministry is completing investigations into corruption cases involving state losses worth hundreds of millions of dollars. 'These cases will stun Russia', he told *Interfax* news agency. He explained that his directorate aimed to 'undermine the financial might of the mafia, which is profiting from up to 40 percent of the country's total assets, and combat corruption which is sapping the machinery of state'. (*Agence France Presse* (Paris), February 28, 1996.)

On March 2, Moscow's *Trud* published an article on economic crimes committed by a 'Nigerian mafia' by Aleksandr Goloviznin, a senior detective officer in the Russian Internal Affairs Ministry Main Administration for Economic Crimes. 'The world has long known of the existence of the so-called "Nigerian mafia", which specializes in swindles', wrote Goloviznin. 'The credit-financial system is a sphere to which it pays close attention, particularly in the field of noncash transactions. In our country 11 cases of embezzlement involving the use of plastic [credit] cards were brought to light in Moscow in 1994, but the number increased to 25 in 1995. Since this market is undergoing rapid growth in Russia, while legislation, as always, is lagging behind the realities of life, specialists of the Russian Federation Ministry of Internal Affairs Main Administration for Economic Crimes are forecasting geometric growth in crimes of this kind over the next few years, and there is every reason to believe that representatives of Africa will make a substantial contribution to these statistics, particularly as the social preconditions for this have already been created. According to the migration services, the number of illegal [immigrants] in Russia is estimated at 100,000, and Africans account for the lion's share of them'. (Aleksandr Goloviznin, *Trud* (Moscow), March 2, 1996, in *FBIS–SOV*, March 5, 1996, p. 16.)

On March 8, an article on the Russian feudal-style protection system known as the 'krysha', or 'roof', by Vladimir Shlapentokh, a sociology professor at Michigan State University, was published in the *Christian Science Monitor*. 'According to Mark Galeotti, a British researcher of the Russian criminal world, about 80 percent of all enterprises in Russia "buy a roof" from the mafia', wrote Shlapentokh. 'This "roof" typically costs 20 to 30 percent of their profits. As an alternative, businesspeople could choose corrupt policemen, who for the same amount of money deliver similar protection against criminal gangs. Usually police and criminal structures observe the division of an area among themselves, and follow the rule of "first come, first serve" in regards to who provides a particular client with a "roof".' (Vladimir Shlapentokh, *Christian Science Monitor* (Boston), March 8, 1996, p. 19.)

On March 26, a conference on corruption was held at the Interior Ministry Institute. 'About 20,000 crimes connected with corruption are recorded in Russia every year now, but experts are sure this figure is insignificant and is less than one percent of the real scale of corruption', *Russian Television* correspondent I. Gritsenko stated. 'Last year, over 4,000 crimes were recorded in Moscow last year which involved bribery of officials. Only half of these cases came to the courts. A poll of businessmen in the capital showed that several thousand bribes are given and taken in Moscow alone – in one day'. At the conference, it was observed that one-fifth of oil was exported last year in the form of contraband. Specialists estimated that $300 billion worth of capital of Russian origin is in foreign banks.

'In today's legal language, the concept of corruption does not exist', Ye. Gracheva, head of a department of the Interior Ministry Institute, was recorded as stating. 'This concept has not been defined, and we lawyers favor very clear concepts of categories and definition, and if we don't know and cannot define what corruption is in the law, then it becomes pretty much a problem and difficult to fight this thing'. (*Russian Television Network* (Moscow), March 26, 1996, in *FBIS–SOV*, March 27, 1996, p. 23.)

On March 26, Aleksandr Dementiev, head of the Russian Interior Ministry's Economic Crime Department, stated at the Interior Ministry Institute in Moscow that the Russian Interior Ministry (MVD) has materials 'on rather high-ranking officials, and we will work on these cases until the end'. The cases are currently being investigated by the Prosecutor General's Office while the MVD is providing operative assistance. What matters now is 'not just how many incidents of bribe-taking were uncovered, but who was implicated and how good the proof is', Dementiev added. He said that the MVD has materials on an official who received a bribe estimated at $2 million. 'However, this is by far not the limit, there are bigger bribes but they require a more large-scale approach, serious operative and investigative work', he commented. (*Interfax* (Moscow), March 26, 1996, in *FBIS–SOV*, March 27, 1996, p. 23.)

On March 26, *Interfax* reported that the Russian Interior Ministry is claiming that organized crime in Russia has stashed away fund amounting to between to between 60,000 to 70,000 billion rubles (12 to 14 billion dollars.) Kuzma Shalenkov of the Interior Ministry's anti-organized crime unit stated that the Russian mafia had accumulated this sum of money after stealing 4,000 billion rubles in 1992 and 1993 by exploiting weaknesses in the banking transfer system. 'Key measures during the first phase of transition, such as the lifting of most restrictions on currency exchange and of government price controls and the accelerated privatization program, had negative consequences which fed crime and corruption in Russia', he stated. Shalenkov viewed the numerous murders of bankers in Russia as a visible sign of a war now being fought among the mafia organizations for control over these illegally accumulated funds. 'This war will continue until cash and banking and business funds are cleansed of the dirty money in circulation', he said. (*Agence France Presse* (Paris), March 26, 1996.)

On April 17, Moscow's *Izvestiya* reported that Russians do not trust the new $100 bills and are reluctant to exchange the old bills for the new ones. Russian experts claim that the new bills look like a black and white photocopy while forged currency detectors used in Russian banks and currency exchange booths and often unable to detect the magnetic strips on the new bills. (*OMRI Daily Report*, Part I, April 18, 1996.)

On April 25, Vladimir Brokhin, the head of the Perm Oblast Employment Center, was reported to have been arrested on corruption charges. Brokhin was accused of possessing a number of bank accounts in the US and several apartments and of making money by distributing about 6 billion rubles ($6.4

.million) in government credits to commercial enterprises. Allegedly, he received a share of the money in bribes while the rest of the money was left unaccounted. Recently, the heads of the Perm Mandatory Health Insurance Fund and the Housing and Communal Services Center were arrested as well. (*OMRI Daily Report*, Part I, April 26, 1996.)

Law Enforcement

On November 16, 1995 Interior Minister Anatoliy Kulikov stated that some 2,000 police officers nationwide are awaiting trial on charges of corruption or abusing their office. 'In one of the boldest examples of corruption', wrote the *Moscow Times*, 'an entire Moscow precinct near the Kremlin was suspended last spring after it was discovered that officers were running a prostitution ring, even driving prostitutes to jobs in patrol cars'. In October, Deputy Police Chief Boris Kondrashov stated that in Moscow alone, some 960 officers were dismissed this year for misconduct. (*Moscow Times*, Weekly Edition, November 19, 1995, p. 19; and *New York Times*, November 17, 1995, p. A4.)

On November 18, Igor Korolkov in *Izvestiya* wrote about Interior Minister Gen. Anatoliy Kulikov's recently declared war on corruption, code-named 'Clean Hands'. 'In issuing the order to punish high-level ministry officials, he has put his finger into an anthill, and at this point, only God knows how it will end', he wrote. 'Does the minister have the strength to cleanse the militia of workers who have joined ranks with the criminal world, or will the criminal world, through bribery, blackmail or scare tactics kick out the most persistent of his allies, and in so doing strengthen even more their positions in the MVD [Ministry of Internal Affairs]? Dismissed generals are rushing to the mass media so they can appear before the public as victims of the latest in a long line of personnel shakeups, "a new sweep".' The article details several cases of corruption gleaned from materials from the judicial investigation into the MVD on which Kulikov's order was based. (Igor Korolkov, *Izvestiya,* November 18, 1995, in *FBIS–SOV*, Supplement Issue, December 18, 1995, p. 46.)

On December 1, Interior Minister Anatoliy Kulikov called for the creation of a special bureau to investigate the large number of contract killings in Russia. (*OMRI Daily Report*, Part I, December 5, 1995.)

On December 4–10, Moscow's *Interfaks–AIF* published a long interview with Maj. Gen. of Justice Leonid Titarov, chief of the investigative unit of the Investigative Committee of the Ministry of Internal Affairs (MVD), regarding the investigation of a criminal cases concerning bribery among officials of the Central Bank of Russia. According to investigators, Ravil Sitdikov, chief of the Central Operational Administration of the Central Bank, and three of his deputies are accused of allocating favorable credits in the sum of 5 billion rubles to a number of commercial enterprises and banks at a profit to themselves in 1992. In addition, 550 million rubles were issued by the Central Bank employees in the form of cash. 'The Central Bank lost 554 million rubles from payments that were made at credit rates that were lower than required, and 600 million rubles because of unpaid credits', Titarov said. (Yuri Shcherban, *Interfaks–AIF*, December 4–10, 1995, in *FBIS–SOV*, Supplement Issue, December 15, 1995, p. 39.)

On December 6, *Komsomolskaya Pravda* reported that the Ministry of Internal Affairs (MVD) 'clean hands' operation, authorized by Interior Minister Anatoliy Kulikov to combat corruption in the MVD, has prompted other law enforcement agencies to consider similar operations in their own ranks. 'According to testimony of Vladimir Kirakozov, representative of the Russian Federation General Prosecutor's Office, at a routine press briefing, the retributive sword of the law is raised today even over those who were considered untouchable for a long time', the article stated. 'Two priests of the goddess of Justice, two staffers of the FSB [Federal Security Service], and even two staffers of the supreme oversight body itself (the General Prosecutor's Office) are now facing investigation and trial for various crimes of office. As usual, the police has outdone everyone when it comes to corruption. This year alone, nearly 800 staffers of the MVD system have been 'brought to book' for abuses of power, and more than 400 cases are already being examined by the courts. Approximately 30 percent of them involve gross violations for the benefit of third parties. To put it more simply, the guardians of law and order shared the department's secrets with mafia organizations; turned a blind eye to "escapades" on the part of subordinates who had, as the professionals say, "bought them off"; and falsified criminal cases'. (Ilya Goritsvet, *Komsomolskaya Pravda*, December 6, 1995, in *FBIS–SOV*, December 6, 1995, p. 39.)

On December 20, 1995 *Moskovskii Komsomolets* reported that a special service of procurators and detectives will be set up to investigate contract killings in Moscow. Only two of the 45 contract killing in the capital city this year have been solved. Half of the victims were businessmen and half were members of criminal organizations. On December 1, Interior Minister Anatoliy Kulikov had called for the creation of a special bureau to investigate such killings in Russia. (*OMRI Daily Report*, Part I, December 21, 1995.)

On December 26, Moscow's *Izvestiya* published an article by Boris Reznik on stolen service firearms in Russia's Far East. 'Buying any weapons on the Far East black market does not present a problem', he wrote. 'Theft of huge quantities of arms from military arsenals has become a routine matter in the Army, Navy and Air Force and no longer surprises anyone. As a rule, these arms surface in the criminal world, crippling and killing people'. Reznik provided colorful examples of large-scale theft of handguns. 'Amazingly, investigative and judiciary agencies pay no attention to the original causes of such tragedies', Reznik concluded. 'Complete anarchy still reigns in the system of records and safekeeping of arms in all departmental arsenals. Arms are stolen from some, while others do not learn the appropriate lessons from such incidents and create the same conditions facilitating thefts. Many questions should be addressed to the Blagoveshchensk police. Just think: Two hundred and fifty handguns are distributed on the local market, almost the entire criminal world is armed, and the police do not know anything about it, despite maintaining an agent network and operative services'. (Boris Reznik, *Izvestiya*, December 26, 1995, in *FBIS–SOV*, Supplement Issue, January 12, 1996, p. 23.)

On December 31, the Russian Border Guard Service told *Interfax* that Russian border guards detained over 2,800 persons trying to illegally cross the border in 1995. 'Border guards also seized about 2.5 tons of drugs and 535 items of firearms', *Interfax* reported. 'Border guards helped Russian customs officers seize contraband and transferred to the federal budget 27 billion rubles worth of contraband in 1995. The Federal Border Guard Service said the 120 billion to 130 billion rubles of targeted state expense on border guards in 1996 "are not just budget expenditures but a promising investment in the country's security which will help prevent more significant economic losses".' Meanwhile, *ITAR–TASS* reported also on December 31 that the border guards of the Caucasian Special Border District apprehended 3,931 border trespassers in the Russian state border section along the Caucasus, from the Caspian to the Black Sea, alone in 1995. During the year, border guards in the district reported to have confiscated contraband merchandise worth 1,821,000 million rubles. (*Interfax*, December 31, 1995, in *FBIS–SOV*, January 2, 1996, p. 22; and Nikolay Styazhkin, *ITAR–TASS*, December 31, 1995, in *FBIS–SOV*, January 2, 1996, p. 27.)

In January, 1996 *Ogonëk* magazine stated that in 1995 criminal proceedings were instituted against 2000 employees of the Russian Ministry of Internal Affairs. 755 police officers were prosecuted. 40 of them were convicted of taking bribes. The others were punished for 'creation of the conditions for crimes to be committed'. The Minister of Internal Affairs Anatoliy Kulikov considered the 'main priority' not to be the cleaning of ranks but the 'guarantee of safety of the population in the streets'. (*Ogonëk*, No. 1, January 1996, p. 10.)

In January, Vladimir Shepovalnikov wrote in *Ogonëk* magazine about the 'Clean Hands' operation in the Ministry of Internal Affairs (MVD) initiated by Interior Minister Anatoliy Kulikov. Already Kulikov 'with the stroke of the pen' has expelled four generals from the department, given strict penalties to three of his assistants and nine big chiefs. (Vladimir Shepovalnikov, *Ogonëk*, No. 1, January 1996, p. 36.)

On January 4, *Izvestiya* reported on the latest stage of Operation Foreigner, the latest stage of which was launched several days before the New Year in Maritime Kray to counter illegal migration and smuggling. 'The kray police and the Pacific border district reasoned, entirely justly, that thousands of illegals from the PRC [People's Republic of China] who have lived for months and years in Maritime Kray would want during the holidays to warm themselves at their native family hearths, and would undertake all possible steps toward this end', *Izvestiya* reported. 'In connection with this, the document 'Plan on Measures Regarding the Concentrated Use of Force and Weaponry Within the Framework of Operation Foreigner' was worked out. Whoever has had the occasion to read it must certainly have thought that on the territory of Maritime Kray, war had been declared either on opponents who were armed to the teeth or on a frightful epidemic'. (Natalya Ostrovskaya, *Izvestiya* (Moscow), January 4, 1996, in *FBIS–SOV*, Supplement Issue, February 1, 1996, p. 5.)

On January 17, *Literaturnaya Gazeta* published an article on conflicts in law enforcement that began when the Ministry of Internal Affairs (MVD) Regional Administration for Combating Organized Crime (RUOP) initiated a criminal case on bribes among the police, prompting the local police to 'retaliate'.

After the RUOP exposed some arms traffickers, among whom were several policemen, in Saratov, the local police 'retaliated' by arresting some 15 RUOP staff over the next several months. Almost all were later released as two are still detained. (Igor Gamayunov, *Literaturnaya Gazeta* (Moscow), January 17, 1996, in *FBIS–SOV*, Supplement Issue, February 1, 1996, p. 50.)

On February 21, 1996 *Izvestiya* reported on an effort by the Ministry of

Internal Affairs to intensify their efforts against computer crime. Internal Affairs Minister Anatoliy Kulikov has ordered economic crime departments within the ministry and regional police departments in major industrial and financial centers to form organizations aimed at fighting embezzlements involving the unauthorized access to computer networks. In December, an agreement regarding computer crime was signed by the Ministry of Internal Affairs and the Association of Russian banks. (*Izvestiya* (Moscow), No. 34, p. 12, in *RusData DiaLine–BizEkon News*, February 21, 1996.)

On February 24, a senior Interior Ministry official stated that senior officials of the State Committee for Precious Metals and Stones (Komdragmet) had cheated the state out of $171.6 million. Earlier in the week, President Yeltsin had dismissed Yevgeny Bychkov, the head of Komdragmet, who is now under criminal investigation for embezzlement. (*Agence France Presse* (Paris), February 28, 1996.)

On February 20, Moscow's *Nezavisimaya Gazeta* reported on a recent report by the Ministry of Internal Affairs (MVD) on the internal affairs organs' activities in 1995. According to the report, of the number of exposed criminals, 45 percent did not have a source of permanent income. The main seats of activity of the largest criminal organizations remained to be the central region, first and most prevalent in Moscow and Moscow Oblast, as well as the republic, kray and oblast centers. According to Interior Minister Anatoliy Kulikov, the presidential edict 'On Urgent Measures for Protection of the Population from Gangsterism and Other Manifestations of Organized Crime', is the only normative document that allows the police to at least maintain parity in the fight against the mafia. Kulikov did recognize that soon this edict would be inadequate for the fight against organized crime. The interior minister regretted that the adoption of the federal laws 'On the Fight Against Organized Crime', 'On the Fight Against Corruption', and 'On Responsibility for the Legalization of Criminal Incomes' has been delayed. With regards to organized criminal groups, about 24,000 crimes were solved in 1995, including 60 contract murders. Criminal proceedings were initiated against nearly 15,000 leaders and active members of gangster groups. 'Last year, the number of solved crimes increased by 4.9 percent and totaled 64.5 percent', the article stated. 'Guilty parties were ascertained in the commission of 837 grave criminal offenses. Valuables in the sum of R715.3 billion were confiscated from criminals. In suppressing [organized criminal group] activity, the police confiscated 11,000 individual weapons, including 6,400 individual firearms'. The Ministry entered 1996 with a debt of 3.4 trillion rubles. (Irina Skarnikova and Oleg Rubnikovich, *Nezavisimaya*

Gazeta (Moscow), February 20, 1996, in *FBIS–SOV*, March 4, 1996, p. 26.)

On March 5, Yekaterinburg's *Oblastnaya Gazeta* published an article on a press conference given the week before at the Yekaterinburg Administration For the Fight Against Organized Crime (UOP), under the Sverdlovsk Oblast Administration of Internal Affairs (UVD). The article stated that once a year UOP chief Militia Col. V. Barabanshchikov 'makes himself available to the mass media'. Since the leaders of organized crime are moving their capital into legal channels, the newspaper reported that the criminal situation has calmed down somewhat since six months ago, when the UOP focused on trying to identify legalized economic structures belonging to mafia organizations and was involved in the fight against extortion and kidnapping. 'Today it can be said that the criminal community in the center has ceased to exist as a single whole', stated Barabanshchikov. 'A schism on the basis of the repartitioning of the spheres of influence occurred among the so-called "blues", who control the north of the oblast. With respect to members of that criminal community, 94 cases are being investigated. A total of 167 individuals have been brought to responsibility'.

'By the present time UOP subdivisions have discovered a total of 46 organized groupings', *Oblastnaya Gazeta* reported. 'A total of 521 persons have been brought to criminal responsibility, including 42 leaders and "authorities" in the criminal environment. Last year, the following items were confiscated from criminals: 71 firearms; 4698 units of ammunition, including 73 grenades; more than 19 kilograms of explosives; and 15 kilograms of narcotics. The value of the confiscated valuable gem (emeralds) exceeded 15 billion rubles. The UOP directs its basic forces at eliminating gangster formations. In 1995, four criminal cases were initiated on the basis of Article 77 of the RF Criminal Code–gangsterism'. (Tatyana Kirova, *Oblastnaya Gazeta* (Yekaterinburg), March 5, 1996, in *FBIS–SOV*, Supplement Issue, May 13, 1996, p. 56.)

On March 5, Prosecutor General Yuri Skuratov stated at a meeting of the National Congress for Legal Reform that the level of crime in Russia is a threat to national security. 'Today we lack basic legal norms in social life and there is a gap between constitutional norms and real life', he said. (*Interfax News Agency* (Moscow), March 5, 1996, in BBC Summary of World Broadcasts, March 5, 1996.)

On March 6, Moscow's *Kommersant–Daily* reported that the Regional Administration for Organized Crime (RUOP) carried out several operations on March 4. During one of them, more than 400 cut and uncut diamonds worth an estimated $1 million were confiscated from Armenian jewelers. Nine Chinese were arrested after trying to fly out of Russia on forged Vietnamese passports. On March 5, during the arrest of active members of the Lenkoran gang, which is said to control half of Moscow's drug market, an intern with Moscow's Southern District Regional Department for Organized Crime was fatally wounded. (Dmitry Kuybyshev and Fedor Maksimov, *Kommersant–Daily* (Moscow), March 6, 1996, in *FBIS–SOV*, Supplement Issue, April 10, 1996, p. 63.)

On March 25, Moscow's *Ekspert* reported that representatives of Russian businesses and the chief of the Federal Tax Police Service Sergey Almazov agreed to fight organized crime together at a meeting of the Russian Business Roundtable on March 15. (Maksim Rubchenko, *Ekspert* (Moscow), March 25, 1996, in *FBIS–SOV*, Supplement Issue, April 25, 1996, p. 55.)

On May 21, Moscow's *Finansovye Izvestiya* was reported to have presented the latest figures from the Council for the security of entrepreneurship in Russia, which indicated that organized crime controls in varying degree over 40,000 businesses with diverse ownership patterns. 'Among them are around 1,500 big government-run enterprises, over 500 joint ventures, 550 banks, and all but the entire commercial fairs and agricultural produce markets', the report stated. 'Experts estimate the mafia's illicit gain in 1995 amounting to USD 2 billion. Nearly seventy percent of commercial firms have to regularly stump up kickbacks to racketeers, and increasingly the latter are finding those fixed percentages inadequate and pushing for their own shares of profits. Common crooks are on the loose as well, setting businesses nationwide USD twenty-three million back in 1995. Close on sixty-five percent of domestic criminal gangs have links to countries elsewhere in the Commonwealth of Independent States and to the Baltic nations. They are reaching farther afield as well, according to Russia's interior ministry, keeping in touch with their like in twenty-nine countries worldwide. They routinely transfer their ill-gotten hard currency into foreign bank accounts or invest in real estate outside Russia. Anywhere between USD sixty billion and 120 billion were taken out of Russia between 1990 and 1993, and another USD thirty billion fled in 1994 and 1995. This escalating capital with criminal origins accumulates from the fleecing of individual businesses, tax evasion, and all shades of illegal business undertakings'. (Yelena Krivyakina and Stanislav Pavlov, *Finansovye Izvestiya* (Moscow), No. 52, p. 1, in *RusData DiaLine – BizEkon News* (Moscow), May 21, 1996.)